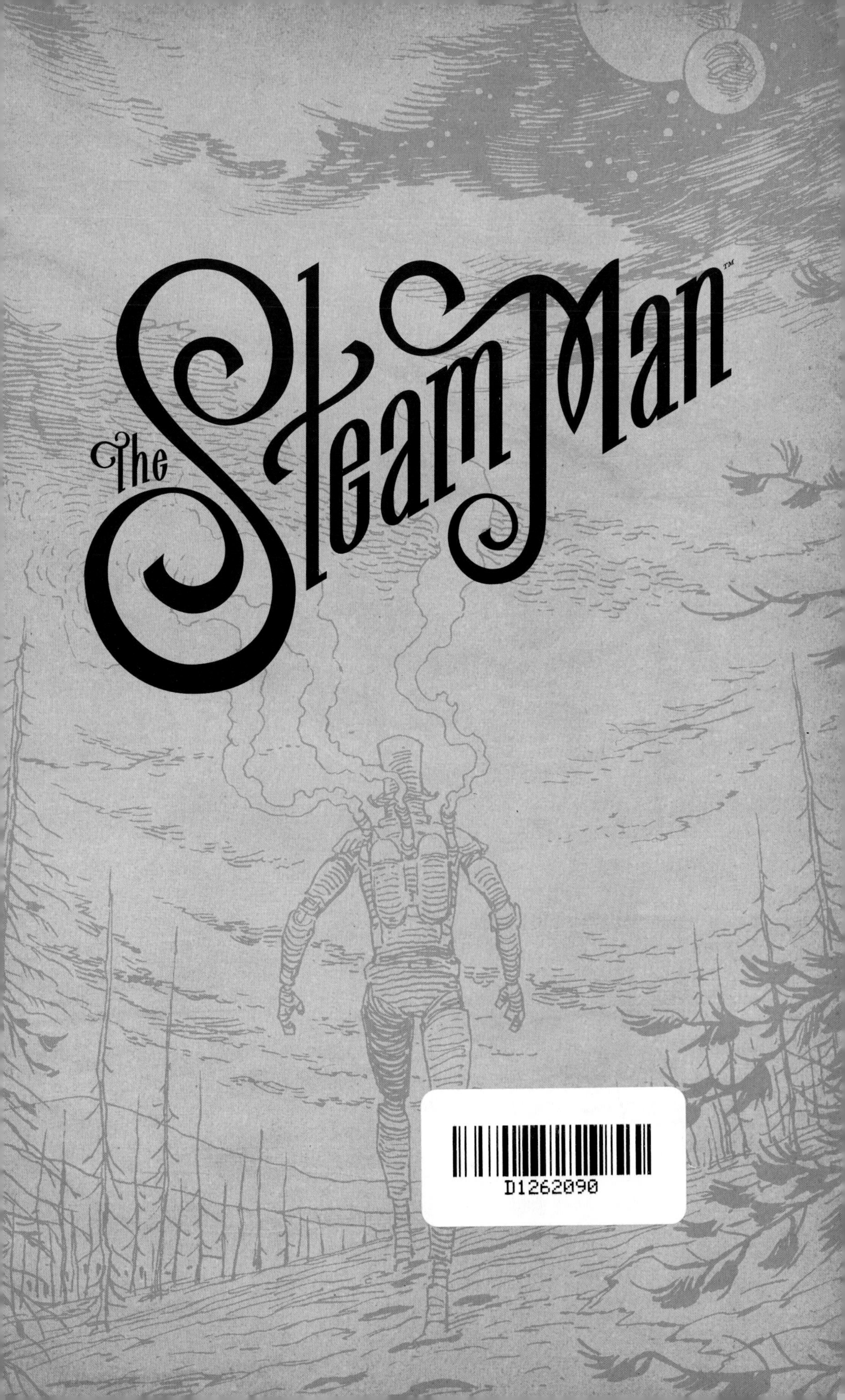
The Steam Man™

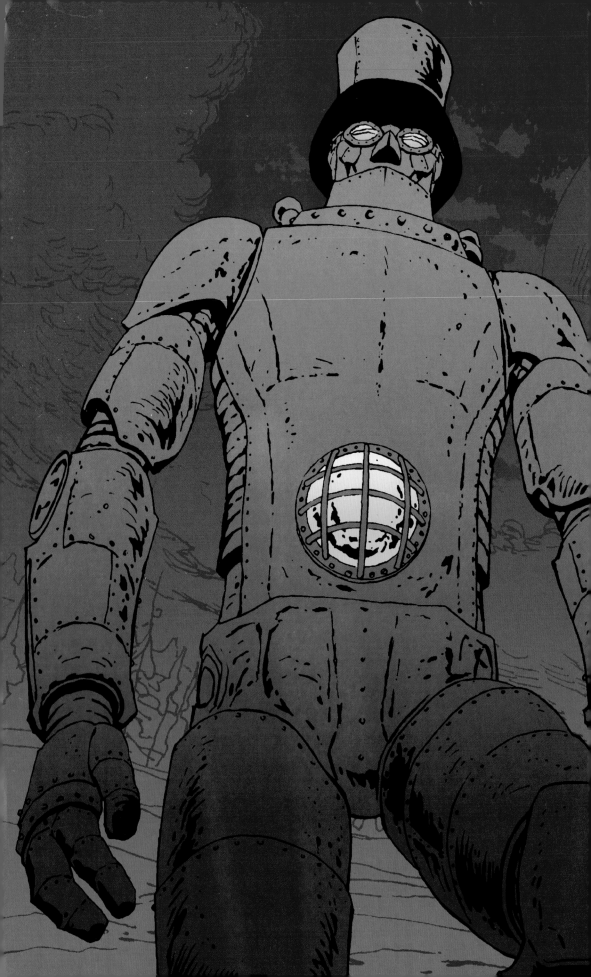

The Steam Man of the Prairie AND THE DARK RIDER GET DOWN

STORY BY
JOE R. LANSDALE

SCRIPT BY
MARK ALAN MILLER

ART BY
PIOTR KOWALSKI

COLORS BY
KELLY FITZPATRICK

LETTERS BY
NATE PIEKOS OF BLAMBOT®

COVER ART AND CHAPTER BREAKS BY
PIOTR KOWALSKI WITH AURORE FOLNY

DARK HORSE BOOKS

PRESIDENT & PUBLISHER
MIKE RICHARDSON

EDITOR
DANIEL CHABON

ASSISTANT EDITORS
IAN TUCKER & CARDNER CLARK

DESIGNER
JIMMY PRESLER

DIGITAL ART TECHNICIAN
CHRISTINA McKENZIE

THIS VOLUME COLLECTS ISSUES #1–#5 OF THE DARK HORSE COMICS SERIES *THE STEAM MAN*.

LIBRARY OF CONGRESS CATALOGING-IN-PUBLICATION DATA

NAMES: LANSDALE, JOE R., 1951- AUTHOR. | MILLER, MARK ALAN, AUTHOR. |
KOWALSKI, PIOTR, 1973- ILLUSTRATOR. | FITZPATRICK, KELLY, 1988-
ILLUSTRATOR. | PIEKOS, NATE, ILLUSTRATOR. | FOLNY, AURORE, ILLUSTRATOR.
TITLE: THE STEAM MAN OF THE PRAIRIE AND THE DARK RIDER GET DOWN / STORY BY
JOE R. LANSDALE ; SCRIPT BY MARK ALAN MILLER ; ART BY PIOTR KOWALSKI ;
COLORS BY KELLY FITZPATRICK ; LETTERS BY NATE PIEKOS OF BLAMBOT ; COVER
ART AND CHAPTER BREAKS BY PIOTR KOWALSKI WITH AURORE FOLNY.
DESCRIPTION: FIRST EDITION. | MILWAUKIE, OR : DARK HORSE BOOKS, 2016. "THIS
VOLUME COLLECTS ISSUES #1–#5 OF THE DARK HORSE COMICS SERIES THE STEAM
MAN."
IDENTIFIERS: LCCN 2016000457 | ISBN 9781616559625
SUBJECTS: LCSH: GRAPHIC NOVELS. | COMIC BOOKS, STRIPS, ETC.
CLASSIFICATION: LCC PN6728.L25 S74 2016 | DDC 741.5/973-DC23
LC RECORD AVAILABLE AT HTTP://LCCN.LOC.GOV/2016000457

PUBLISHED BY DARK HORSE BOOKS
A DIVISION OF DARK HORSE COMICS, INC.
10956 SE MAIN STREET | MILWAUKIE, OR 97222

DARKHORSE.COM

TO FIND A COMICS SHOP IN YOUR AREA, CALL THE COMIC SHOP LOCATOR SERVICE TOLL-
FREE AT 1-888-266-4226.
INTERNATIONAL LICENSING: (503) 905-2377

FIRST EDITION: JULY 2016
ISBN 978-1-61655-962-5

10 9 8 7 6 5 4 3 2 1
PRINTED IN CHINA

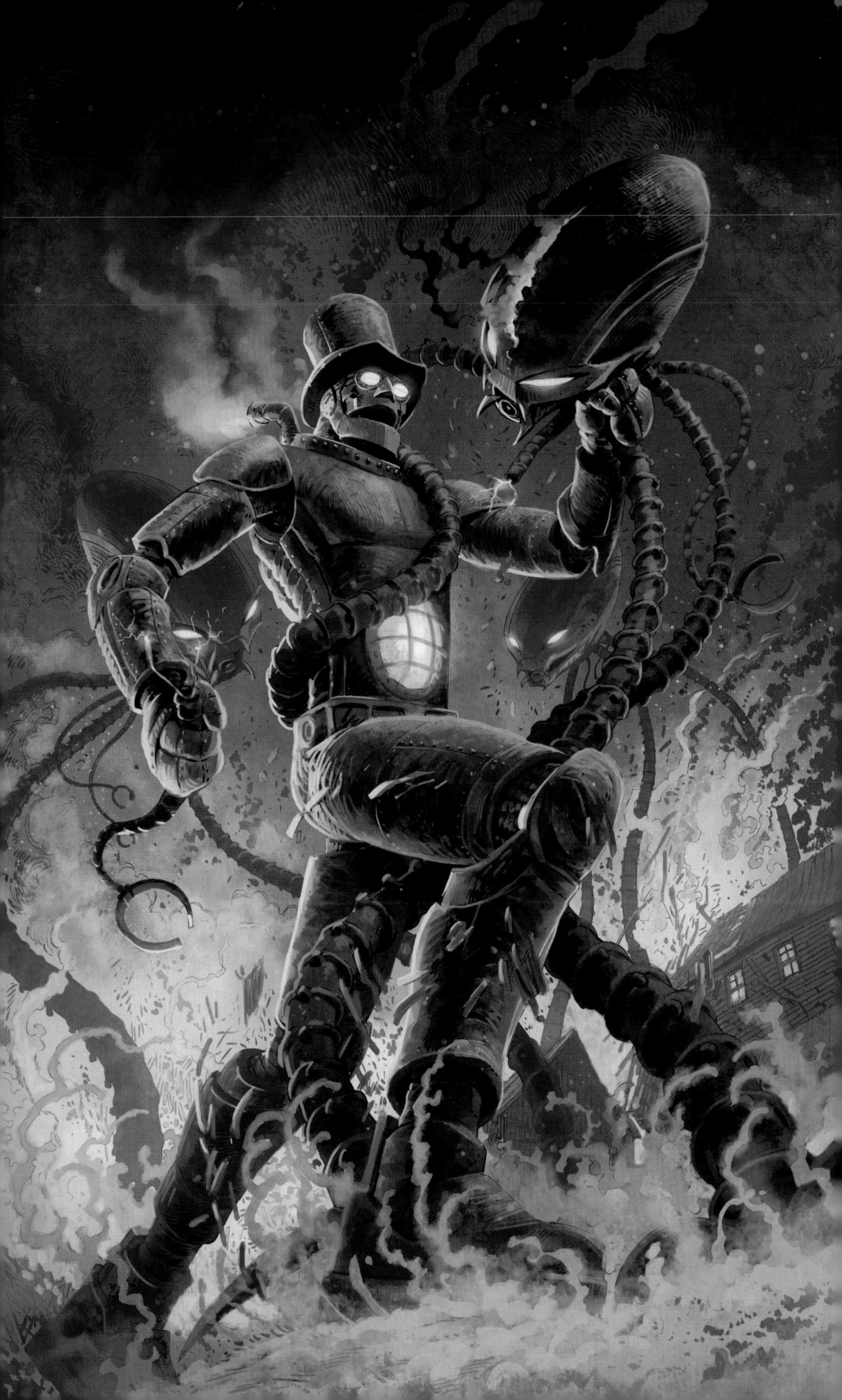

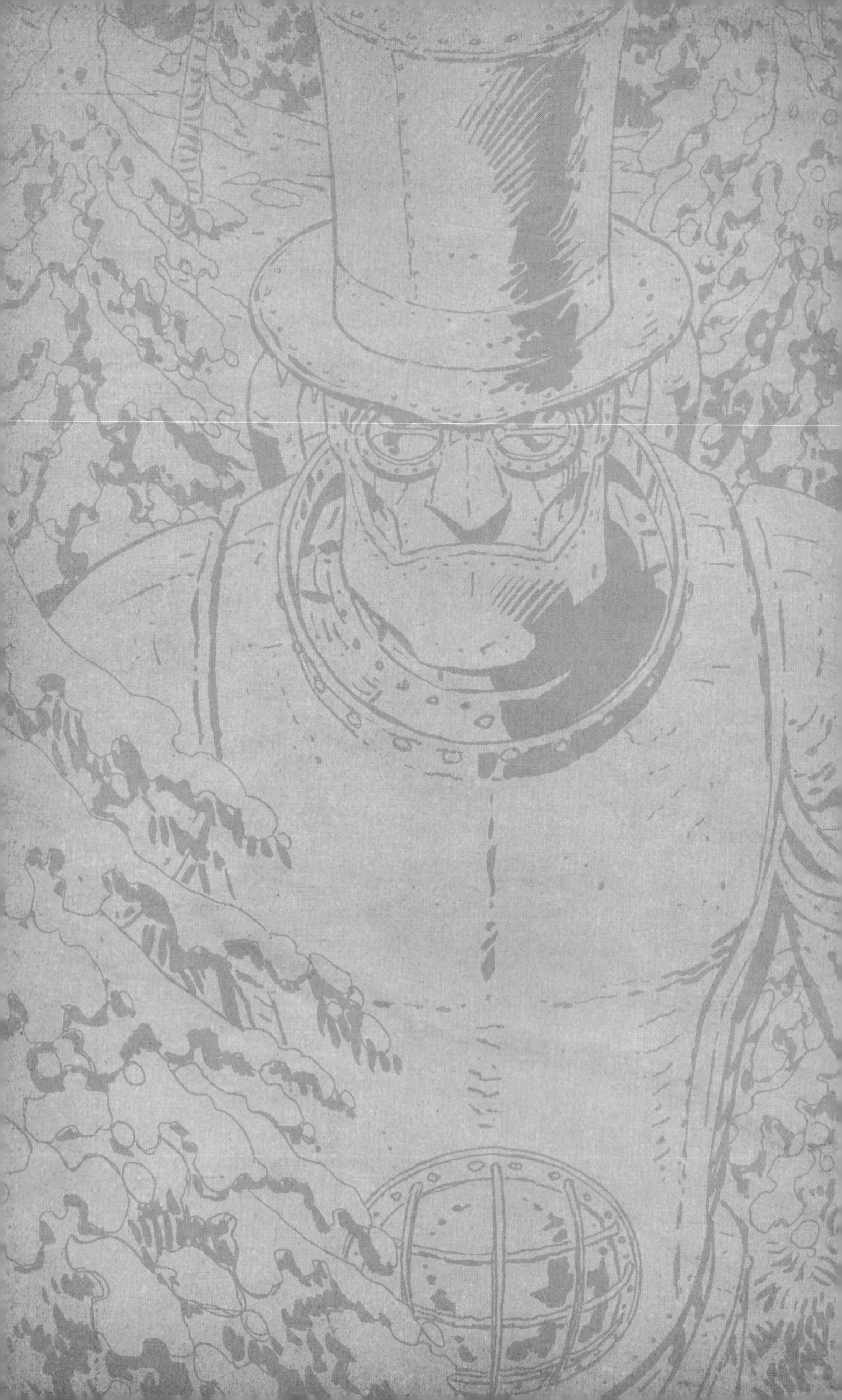

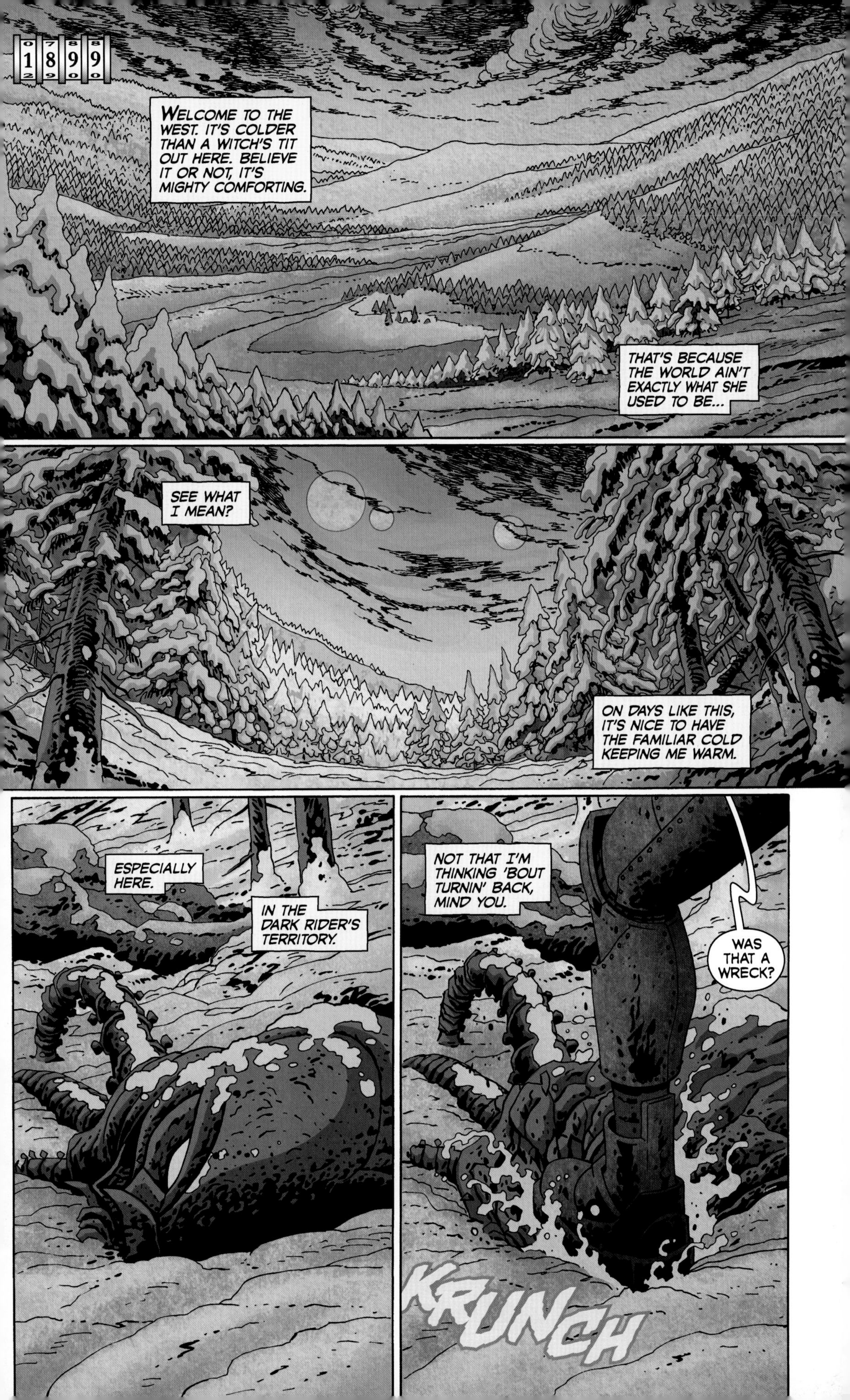
1899
WELCOME TO THE WEST. IT'S COLDER THAN A WITCH'S TIT OUT HERE. BELIEVE IT OR NOT, IT'S MIGHTY COMFORTING.
THAT'S BECAUSE THE WORLD AIN'T EXACTLY WHAT SHE USED TO BE...
SEE WHAT I MEAN?
ON DAYS LIKE THIS, IT'S NICE TO HAVE THE FAMILIAR COLD KEEPING ME WARM.
ESPECIALLY HERE.
IN THE DARK RIDER'S TERRITORY.
NOT THAT I'M THINKING 'BOUT TURNIN' BACK, MIND YOU.
WAS THAT A WRECK?
KRUNCH

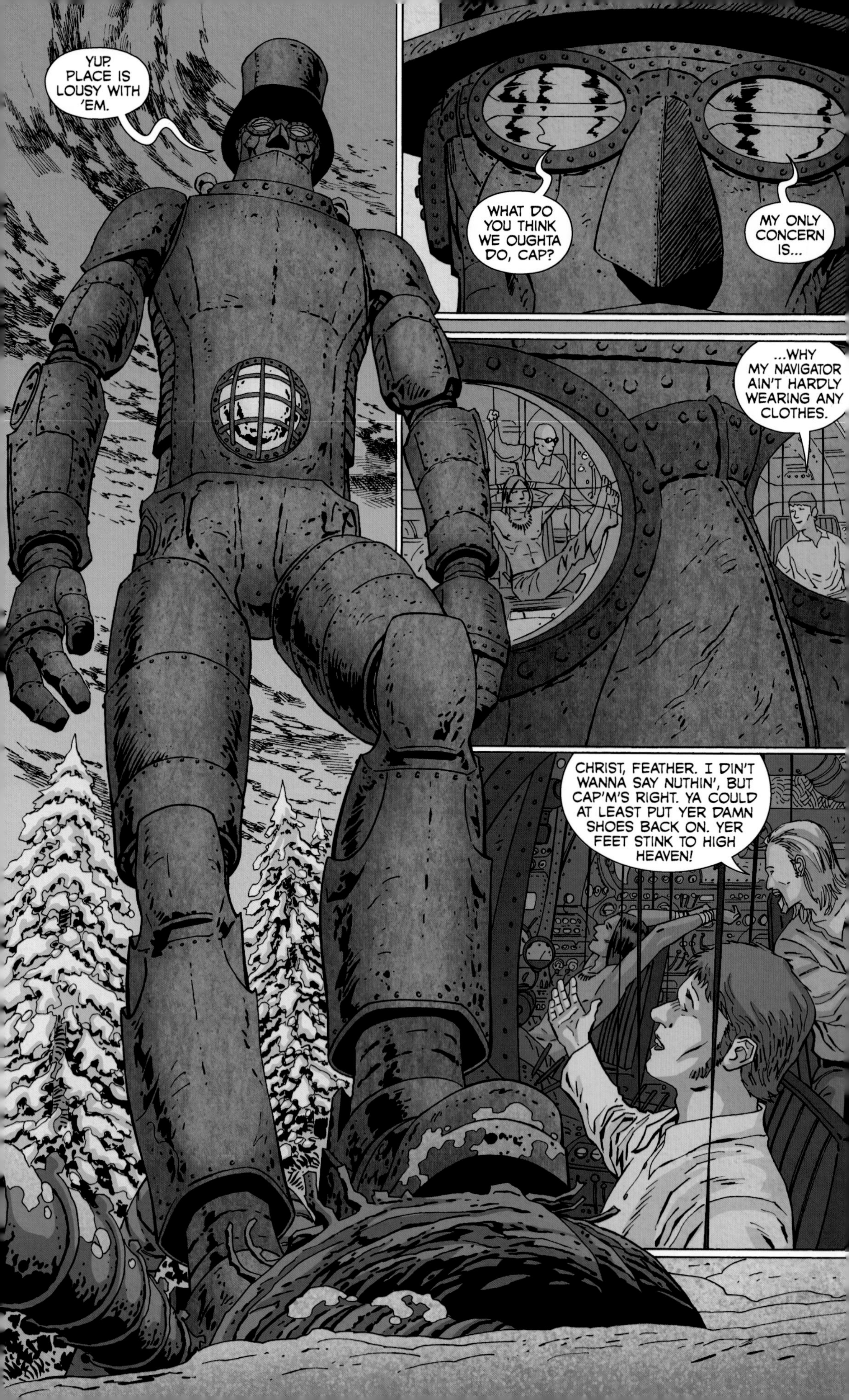
YUP. PLACE IS LOUSY WITH 'EM.
WHAT DO YOU THINK WE OUGHTA DO, CAP?
MY ONLY CONCERN IS...
...WHY MY NAVIGATOR AIN'T HARDLY WEARING ANY CLOTHES.
CHRIST, FEATHER. I DIN'T WANNA SAY NUTHIN', BUT CAP'M'S RIGHT. YA COULD AT LEAST PUT YER DAMN SHOES BACK ON. YER FEET STINK TO HIGH HEAVEN!

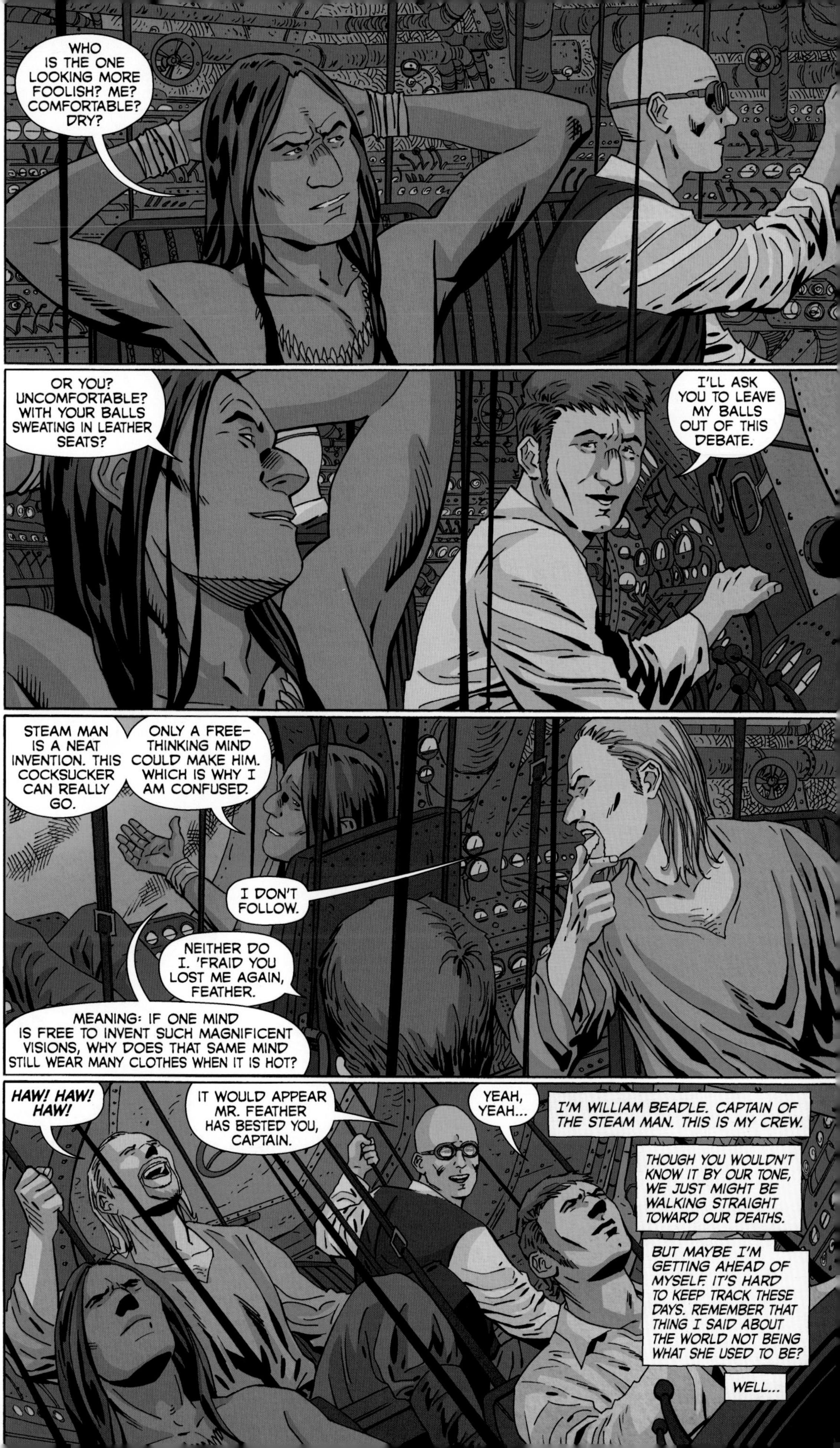
WHO IS THE ONE LOOKING MORE FOOLISH? ME? COMFORTABLE? DRY?
OR YOU? UNCOMFORTABLE? WITH YOUR BALLS SWEATING IN LEATHER SEATS?
I'LL ASK YOU TO LEAVE MY BALLS OUT OF THIS DEBATE.
STEAM MAN IS A NEAT INVENTION. THIS COCKSUCKER CAN REALLY GO.
ONLY A FREE-THINKING MIND COULD MAKE HIM. WHICH IS WHY I AM CONFUSED.
I DON'T FOLLOW.
NEITHER DO I. 'FRAID YOU LOST ME AGAIN, FEATHER.
MEANING: IF ONE MIND IS FREE TO INVENT SUCH MAGNIFICENT VISIONS, WHY DOES THAT SAME MIND STILL WEAR MANY CLOTHES WHEN IT IS HOT?
HAW! HAW! HAW!
IT WOULD APPEAR MR. FEATHER HAS BESTED YOU, CAPTAIN.
YEAH, YEAH...
I'M WILLIAM BEADLE. CAPTAIN OF THE STEAM MAN. THIS IS MY CREW.
THOUGH YOU WOULDN'T KNOW IT BY OUR TONE, WE JUST MIGHT BE WALKING STRAIGHT TOWARD OUR DEATHS.
BUT MAYBE I'M GETTING AHEAD OF MYSELF. IT'S HARD TO KEEP TRACK THESE DAYS. REMEMBER THAT THING I SAID ABOUT THE WORLD NOT BEING WHAT SHE USED TO BE?
WELL...

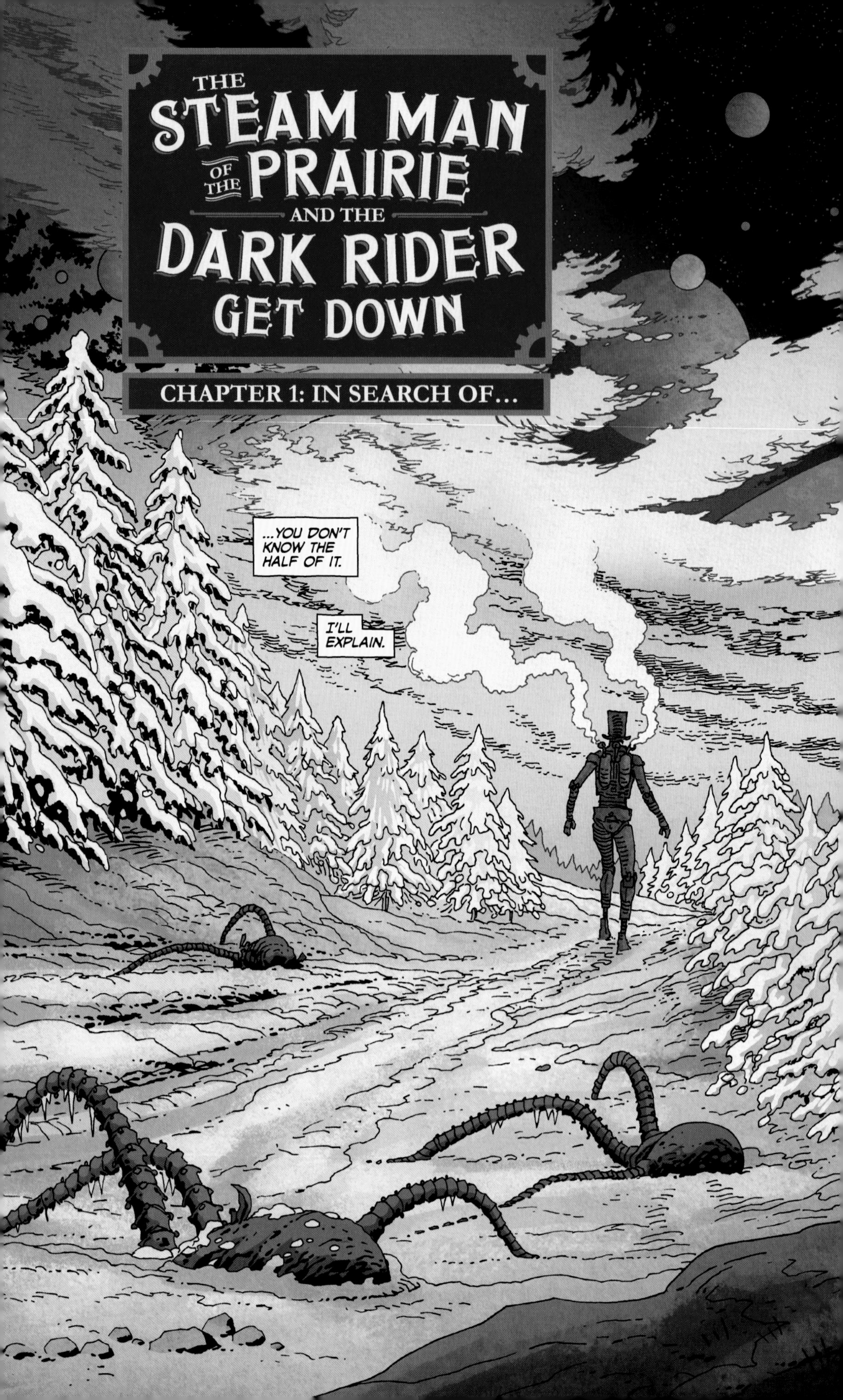
THE STEAM MAN OF THE PRAIRIE
AND THE
DARK RIDER
GET DOWN
CHAPTER 1: IN SEARCH OF...
...YOU DON'T KNOW THE HALF OF IT.
I'LL EXPLAIN.

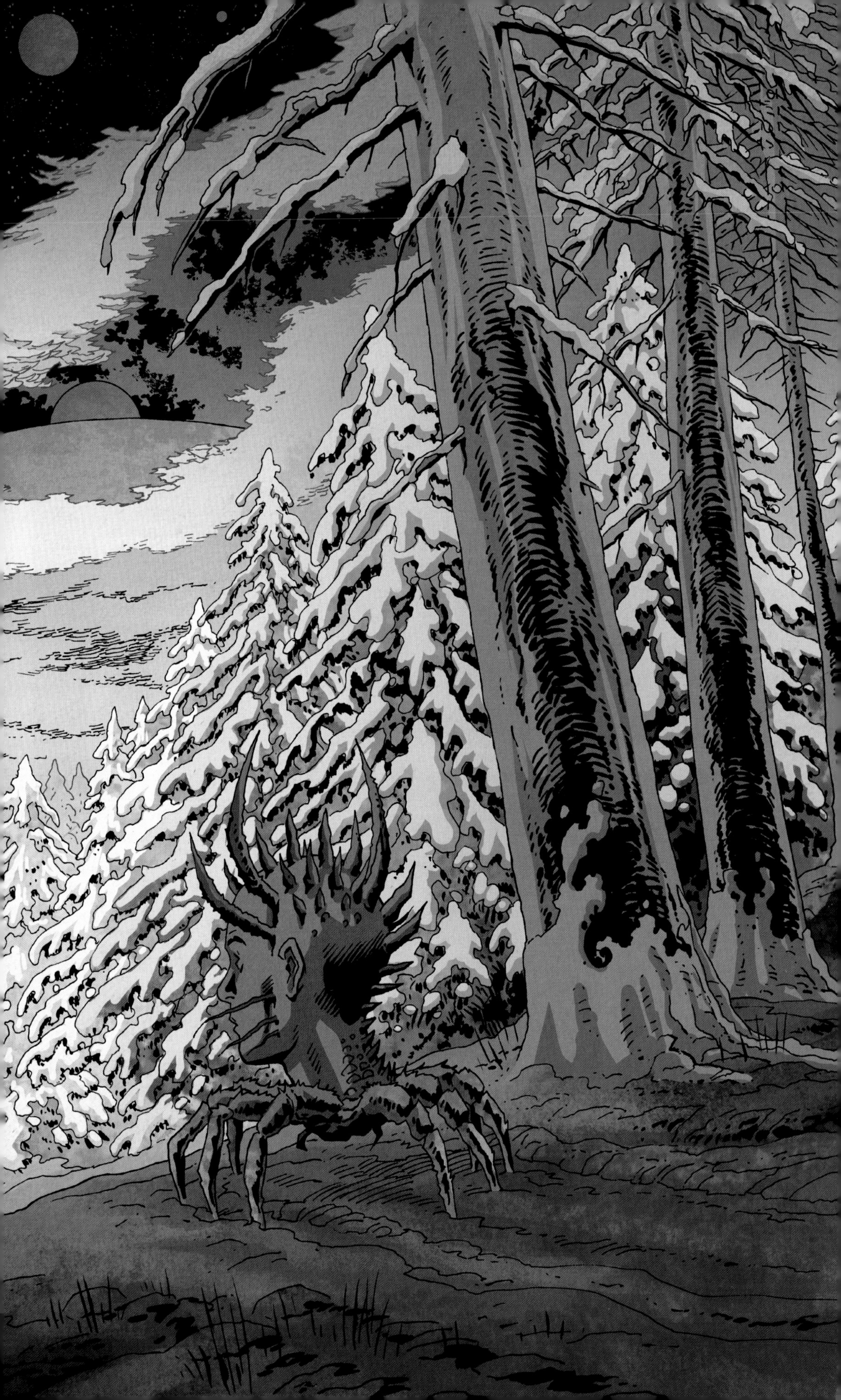

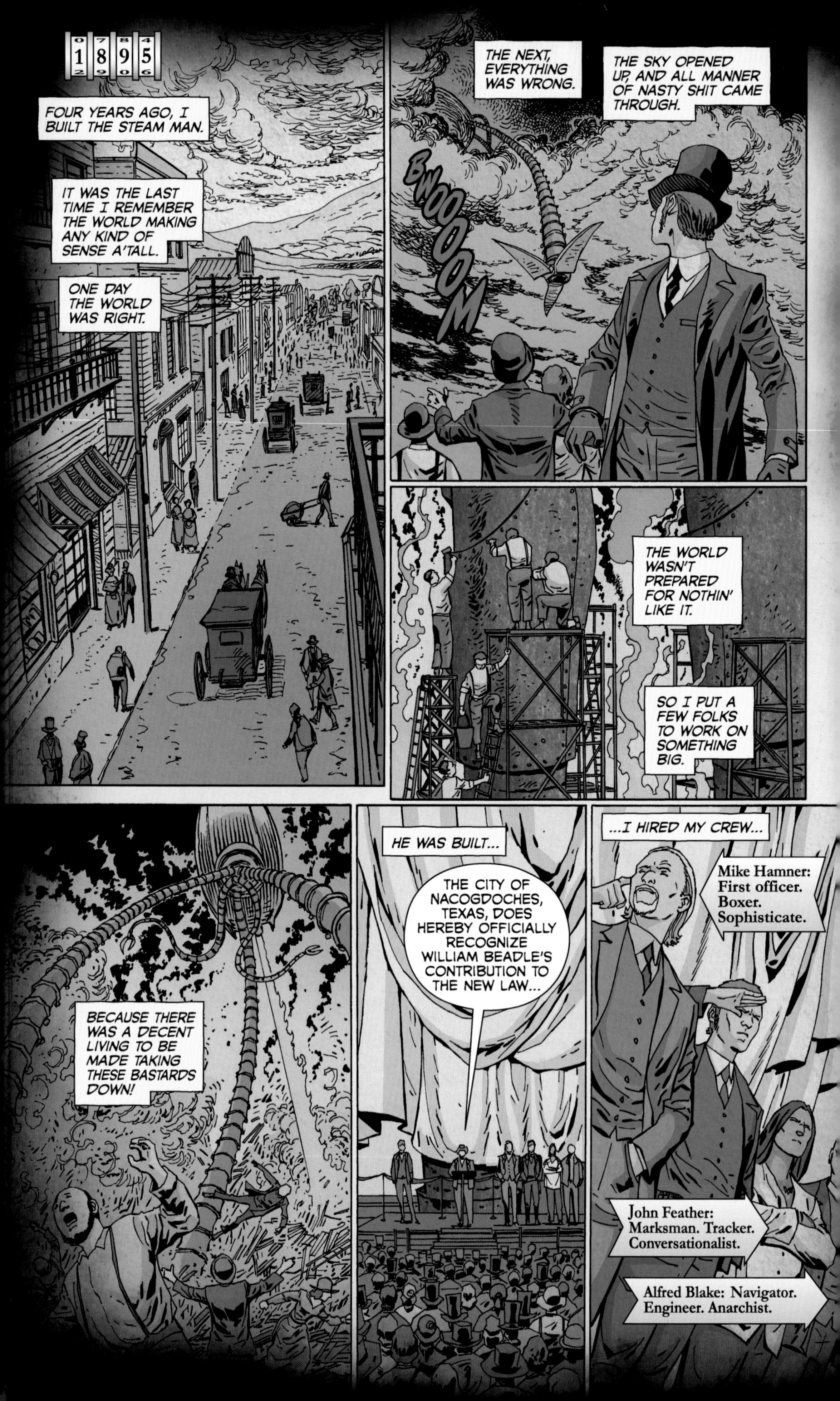
1895
FOUR YEARS AGO, I BUILT THE STEAM MAN.
IT WAS THE LAST TIME I REMEMBER THE WORLD MAKING ANY KIND OF SENSE A'TALL.
ONE DAY THE WORLD WAS RIGHT.
THE NEXT, EVERYTHING WAS WRONG.
THE SKY OPENED UP, AND ALL MANNER OF NASTY SHIT CAME THROUGH.
BWOOOOM
THE WORLD WASN'T PREPARED FOR NOTHIN' LIKE IT.
SO I PUT A FEW FOLKS TO WORK ON SOMETHING BIG.
BECAUSE THERE WAS A DECENT LIVING TO BE MADE TAKING THESE BASTARDS DOWN!
HE WAS BUILT...
THE CITY OF NACOGDOCHES, TEXAS, DOES HEREBY OFFICIALLY RECOGNIZE WILLIAM BEADLE'S CONTRIBUTION TO THE NEW LAW...
...I HIRED MY CREW...
Mike Hamner: First officer. Boxer. Sophisticate.
John Feather: Marksman. Tracker. Conversationalist.
Alfred Blake: Navigator. Engineer. Anarchist.

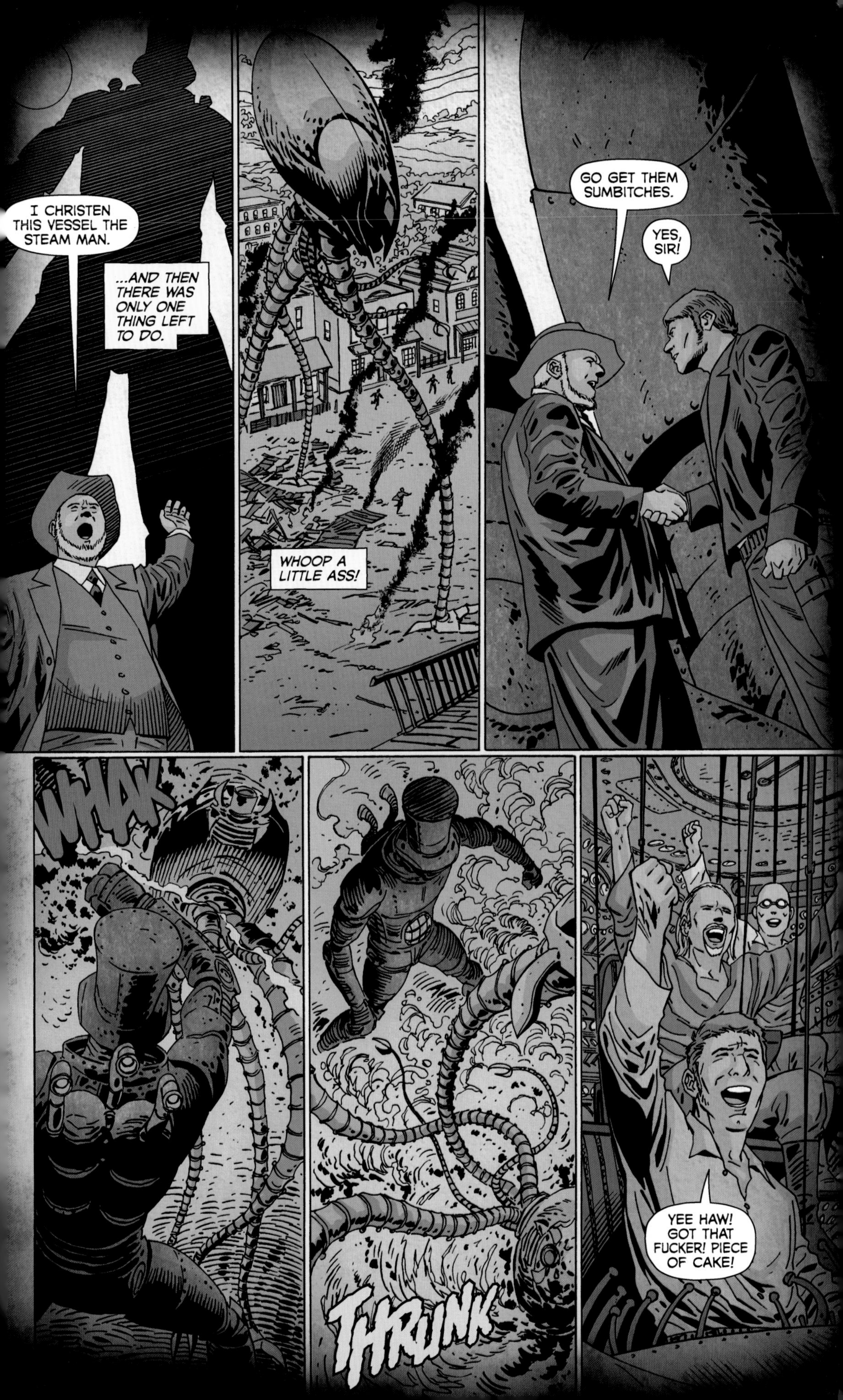
I CHRISTEN THIS VESSEL THE STEAM MAN.
...AND THEN THERE WAS ONLY ONE THING LEFT TO DO.
WHOOP A LITTLE ASS!
GO GET THEM SUMBITCHES.
YES, SIR!
WHAK
THRUNK
YEE HAW! GOT THAT FUCKER! PIECE OF CAKE!

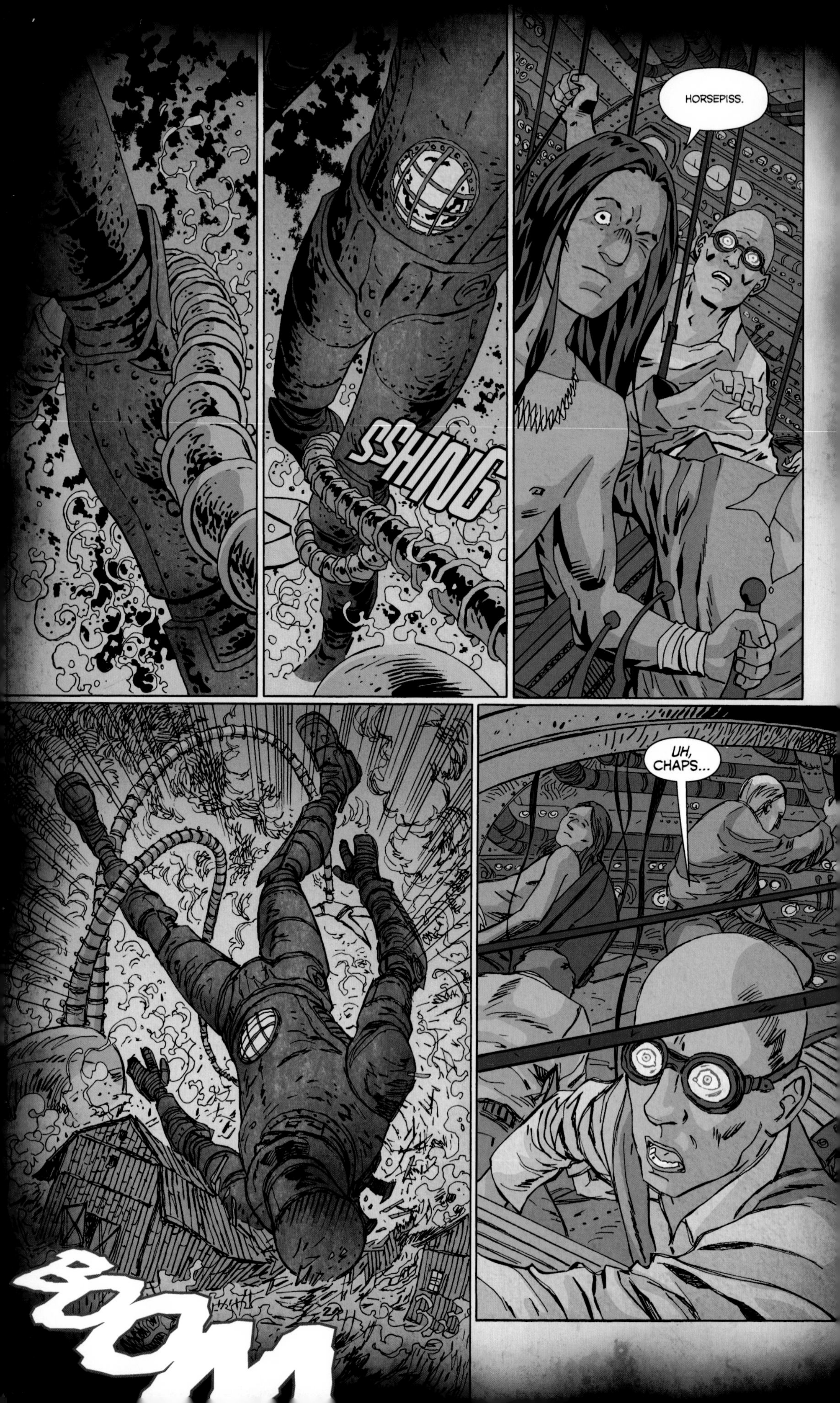

SSHING
HORSEPISS.
BOOM
UH, CHAPS...

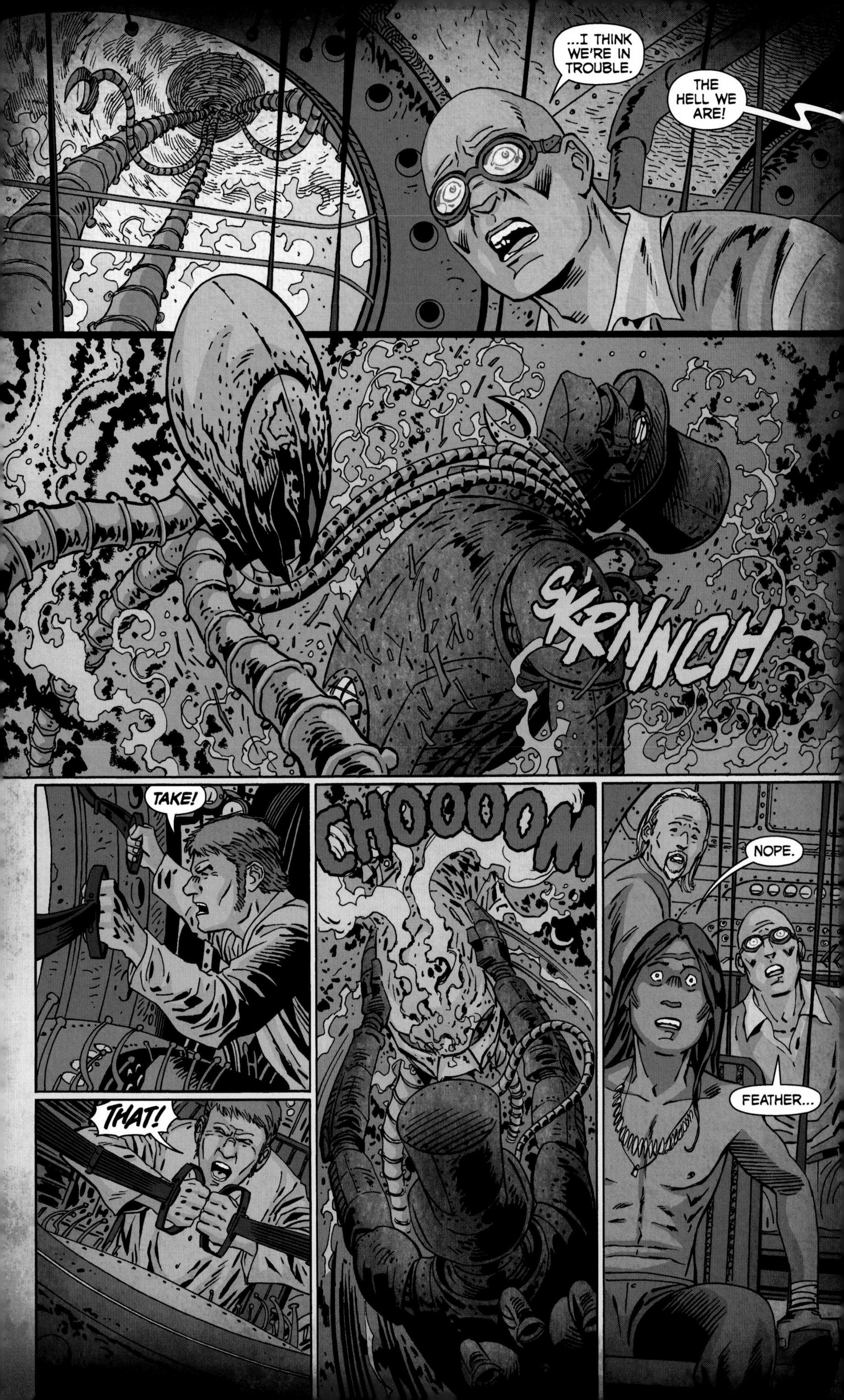
...I THINK WE'RE IN TROUBLE.
THE HELL WE ARE!
SKRNNCH
TAKE!
THAT!
CHOOOOOM
NOPE.
FEATHER...

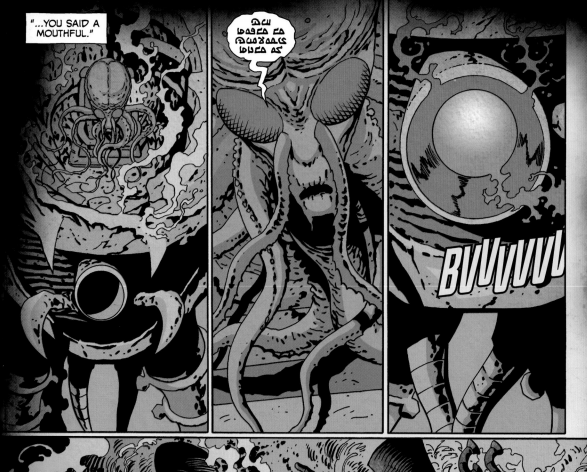

"...YOU SAID A MOUTHFUL."

ᎠᏯᎳ ᏂᏂ ᏓᎭᎦᎦ ᎠᏯᎾᎦᎦᏂ ᏓᎾᏓᏠᎦ ᎦᏂ

BVVVVVL

SHOOM

CAP! WHAT'S THE PLAN?

I HAVE A PLAN.

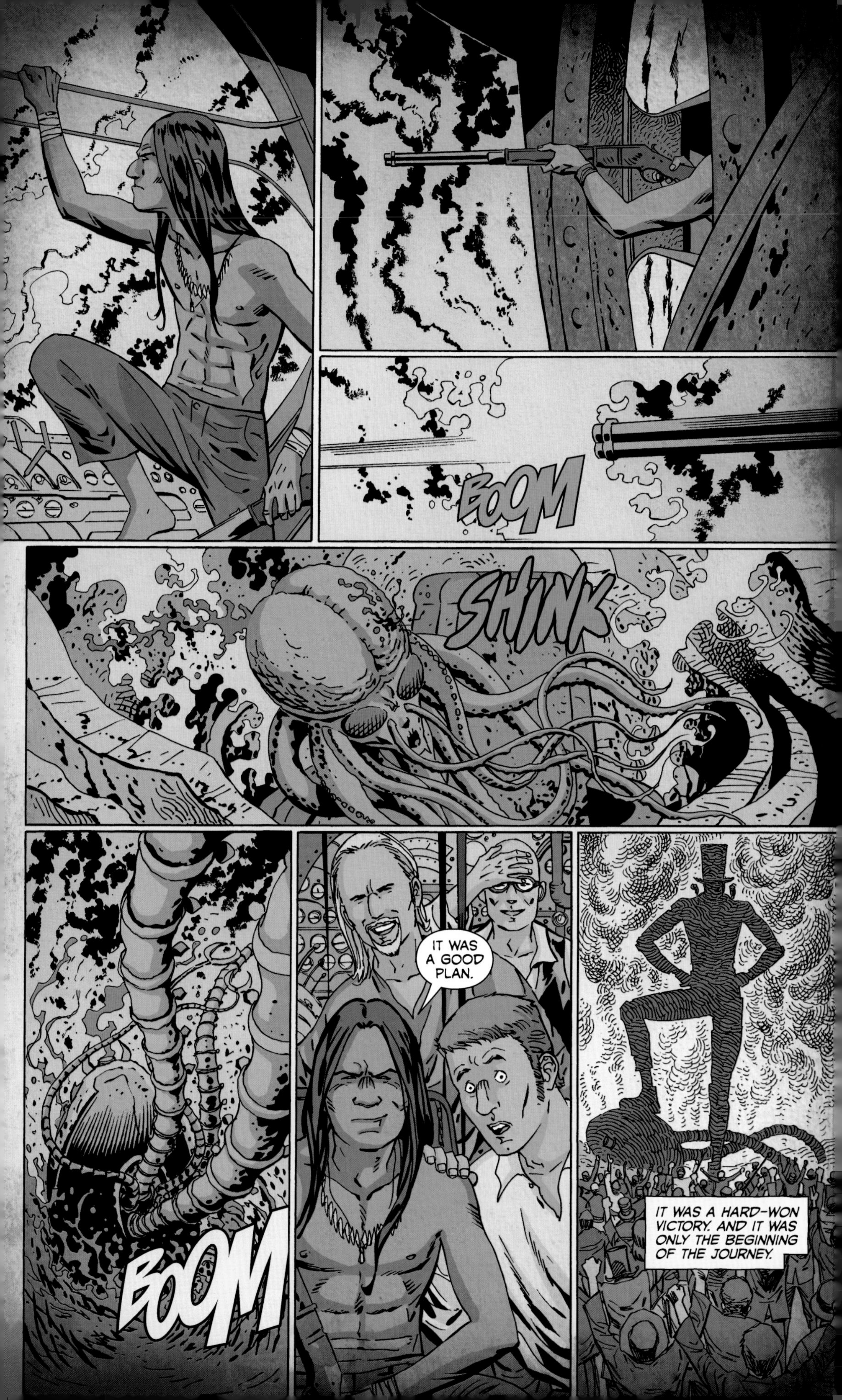
BOOM
SHINK
BOOM
IT WAS A GOOD PLAN.
IT WAS A HARD-WON VICTORY. AND IT WAS ONLY THE BEGINNING OF THE JOURNEY.

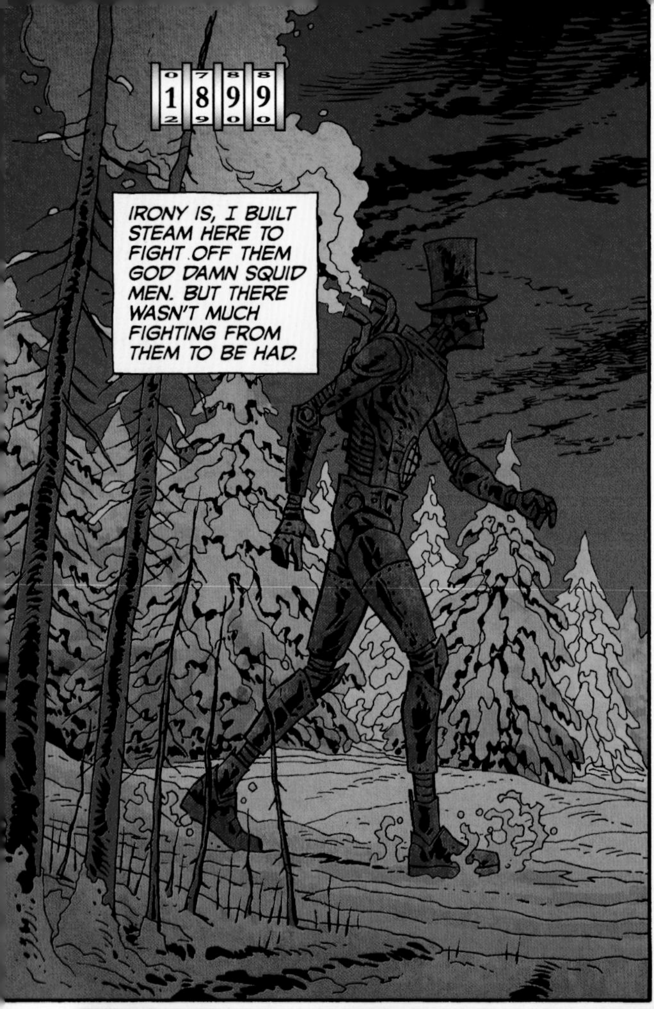
1899
IRONY IS, I BUILT STEAM HERE TO FIGHT OFF THEM GOD DAMN SQUID MEN. BUT THERE WASN'T MUCH FIGHTING FROM THEM TO BE HAD.

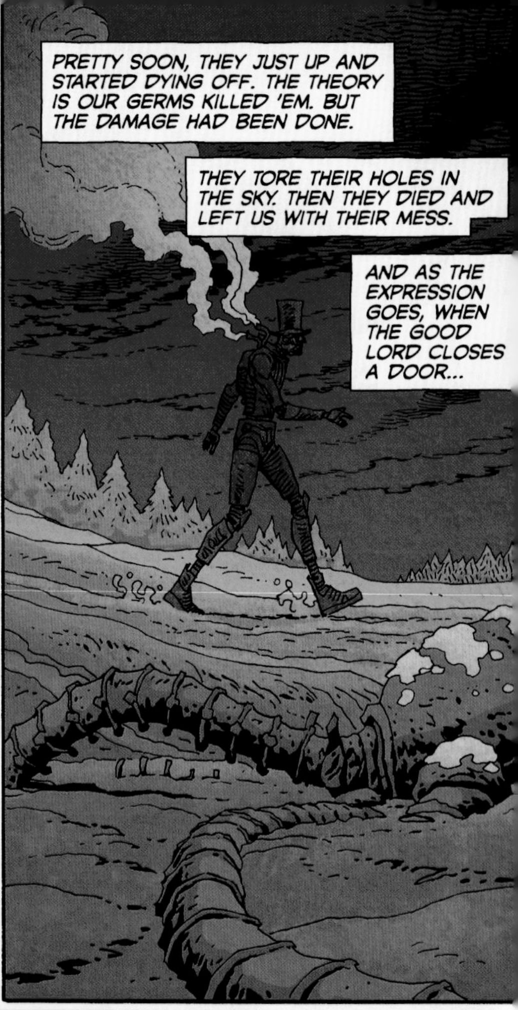
PRETTY SOON, THEY JUST UP AND STARTED DYING OFF. THE THEORY IS OUR GERMS KILLED 'EM. BUT THE DAMAGE HAD BEEN DONE.
THEY TORE THEIR HOLES IN THE SKY. THEN THEY DIED AND LEFT US WITH THEIR MESS.
AND AS THE EXPRESSION GOES, WHEN THE GOOD LORD CLOSES A DOOR...

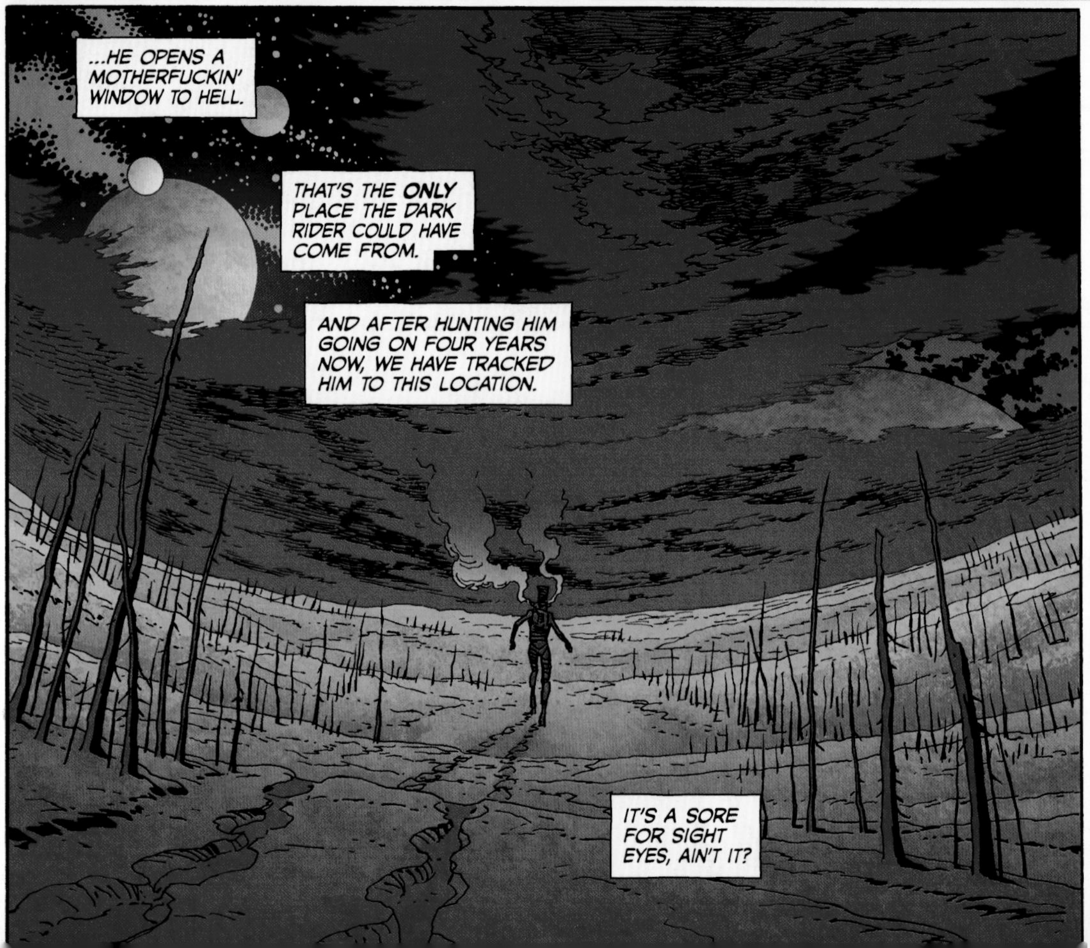
...HE OPENS A MOTHERFUCKIN' WINDOW TO HELL.
THAT'S THE ONLY PLACE THE DARK RIDER COULD HAVE COME FROM.
AND AFTER HUNTING HIM GOING ON FOUR YEARS NOW, WE HAVE TRACKED HIM TO THIS LOCATION.
IT'S A SORE FOR SIGHT EYES, AIN'T IT?

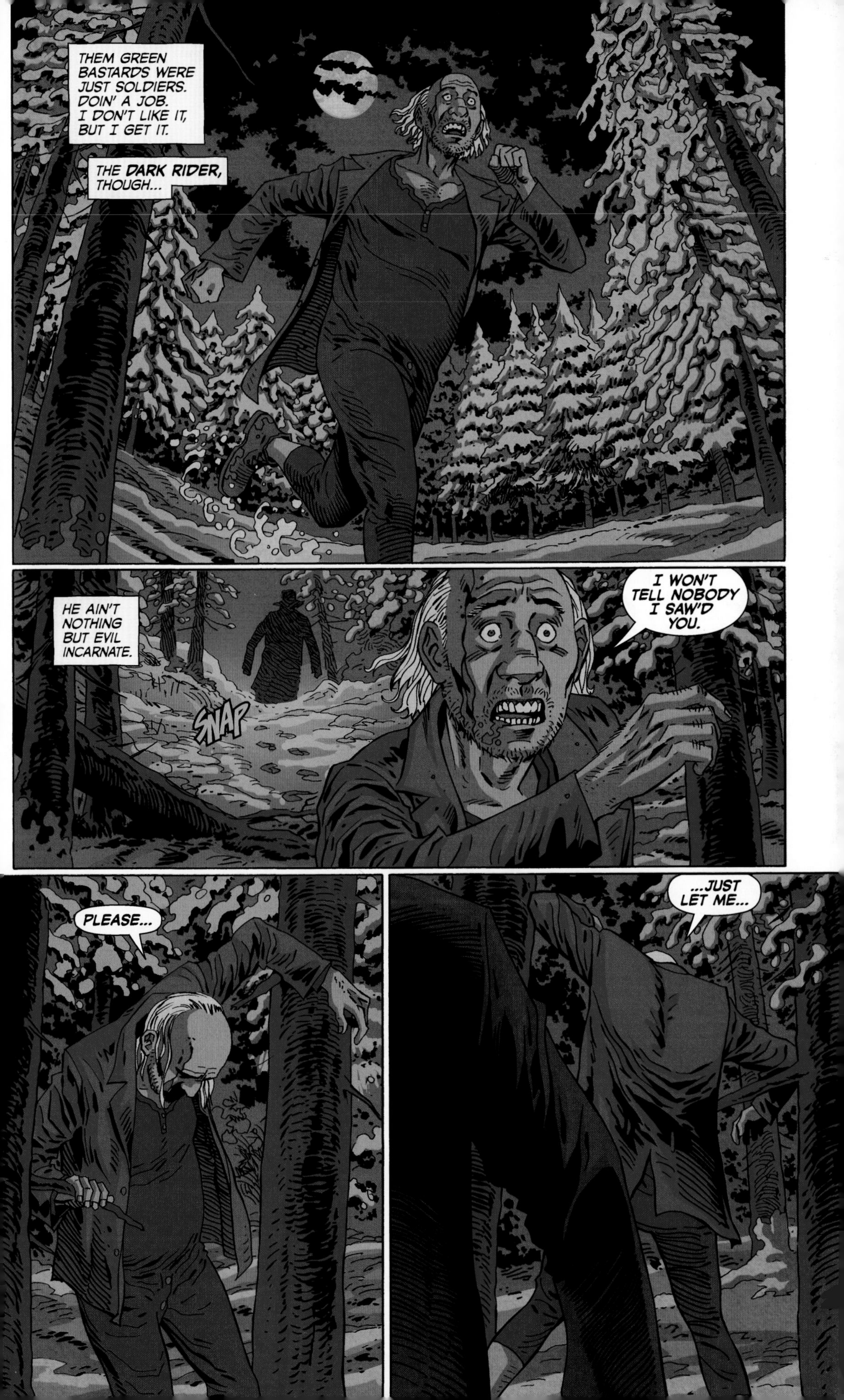
THEM GREEN BASTARDS WERE JUST SOLDIERS. DOIN' A JOB. I DON'T LIKE IT, BUT I GET IT.
THE **DARK RIDER,** THOUGH...
HE AIN'T NOTHING BUT EVIL INCARNATE.
I WON'T TELL NOBODY I SAW'D YOU.
SNAP
PLEASE...
...JUST LET ME...

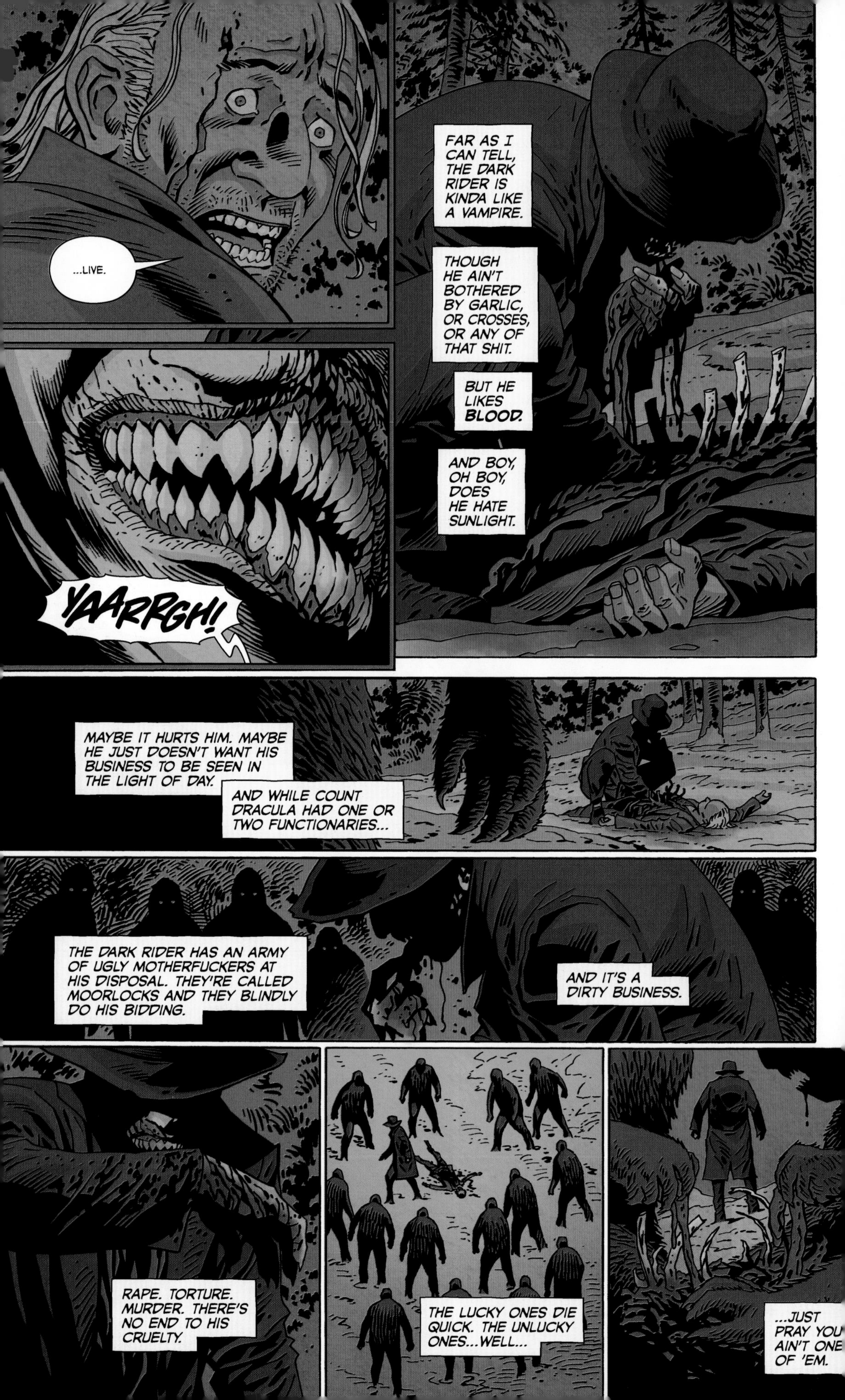
...LIVE.
YAARRGH!
FAR AS I CAN TELL, THE DARK RIDER IS KINDA LIKE A VAMPIRE.
THOUGH HE AIN'T BOTHERED BY GARLIC, OR CROSSES, OR ANY OF THAT SHIT.
BUT HE LIKES BLOOD.
AND BOY, OH BOY, DOES HE HATE SUNLIGHT.
MAYBE IT HURTS HIM. MAYBE HE JUST DOESN'T WANT HIS BUSINESS TO BE SEEN IN THE LIGHT OF DAY.
AND WHILE COUNT DRACULA HAD ONE OR TWO FUNCTIONARIES...
THE DARK RIDER HAS AN ARMY OF UGLY MOTHERFUCKERS AT HIS DISPOSAL. THEY'RE CALLED MOORLOCKS AND THEY BLINDLY DO HIS BIDDING.
AND IT'S A DIRTY BUSINESS.
RAPE. TORTURE. MURDER. THERE'S NO END TO HIS CRUELTY.
THE LUCKY ONES DIE QUICK. THE UNLUCKY ONES...WELL...
...JUST PRAY YOU AIN'T ONE OF 'EM.

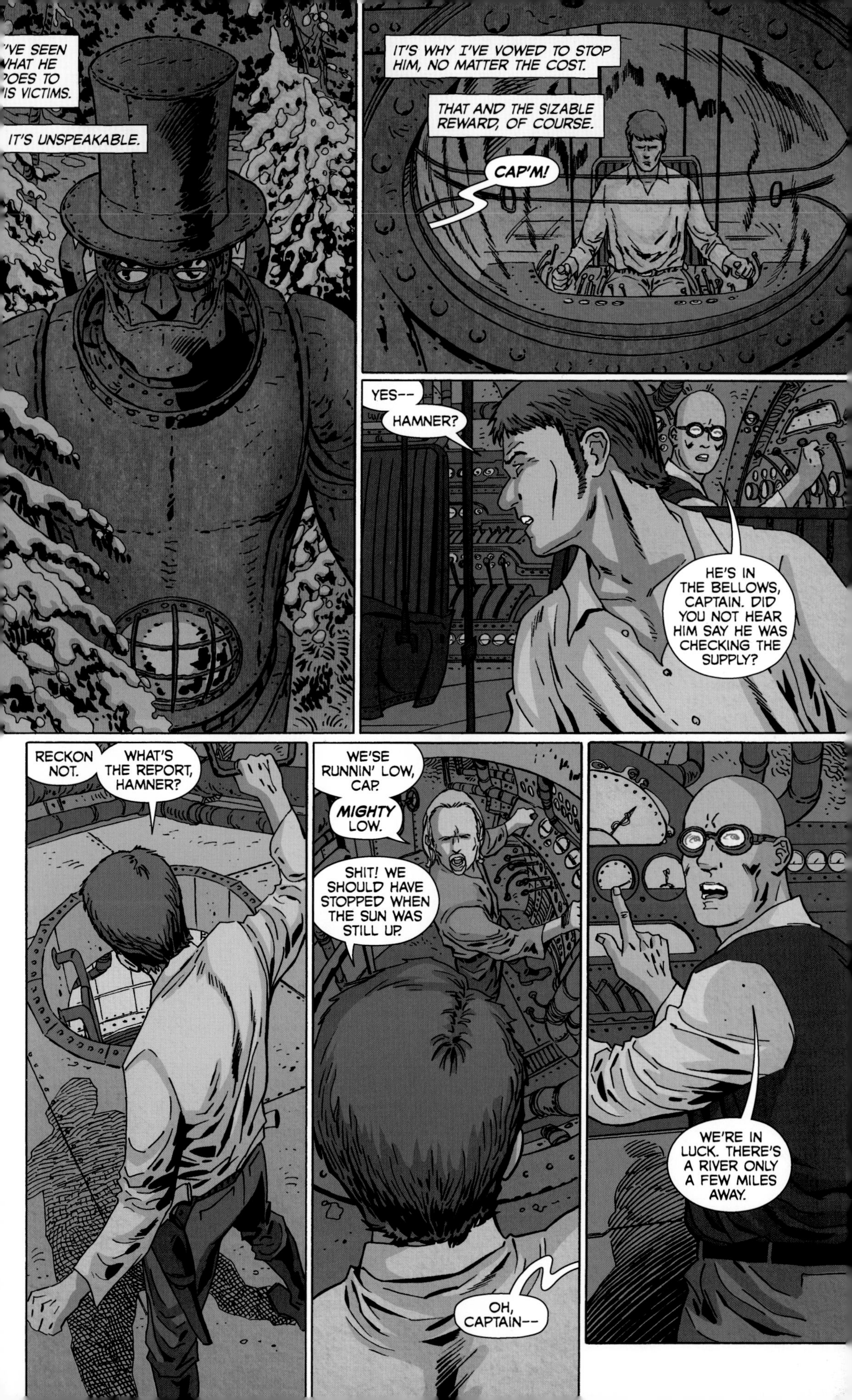

'VE SEEN
VHAT HE
DOES TO
IS VICTIMS.
IT'S UNSPEAKABLE.
IT'S WHY I'VE VOWED TO STOP HIM, NO MATTER THE COST.
THAT AND THE SIZABLE REWARD, OF COURSE.
CAP'M!
YES--
HAMNER?
HE'S IN THE BELLOWS, CAPTAIN. DID YOU NOT HEAR HIM SAY HE WAS CHECKING THE SUPPLY?
RECKON NOT.
WHAT'S THE REPORT, HAMNER?
WE'SE RUNNIN' LOW, CAP.
MIGHTY LOW.
SHIT! WE SHOULD HAVE STOPPED WHEN THE SUN WAS STILL UP.
OH, CAPTAIN--
WE'RE IN LUCK. THERE'S A RIVER ONLY A FEW MILES AWAY.

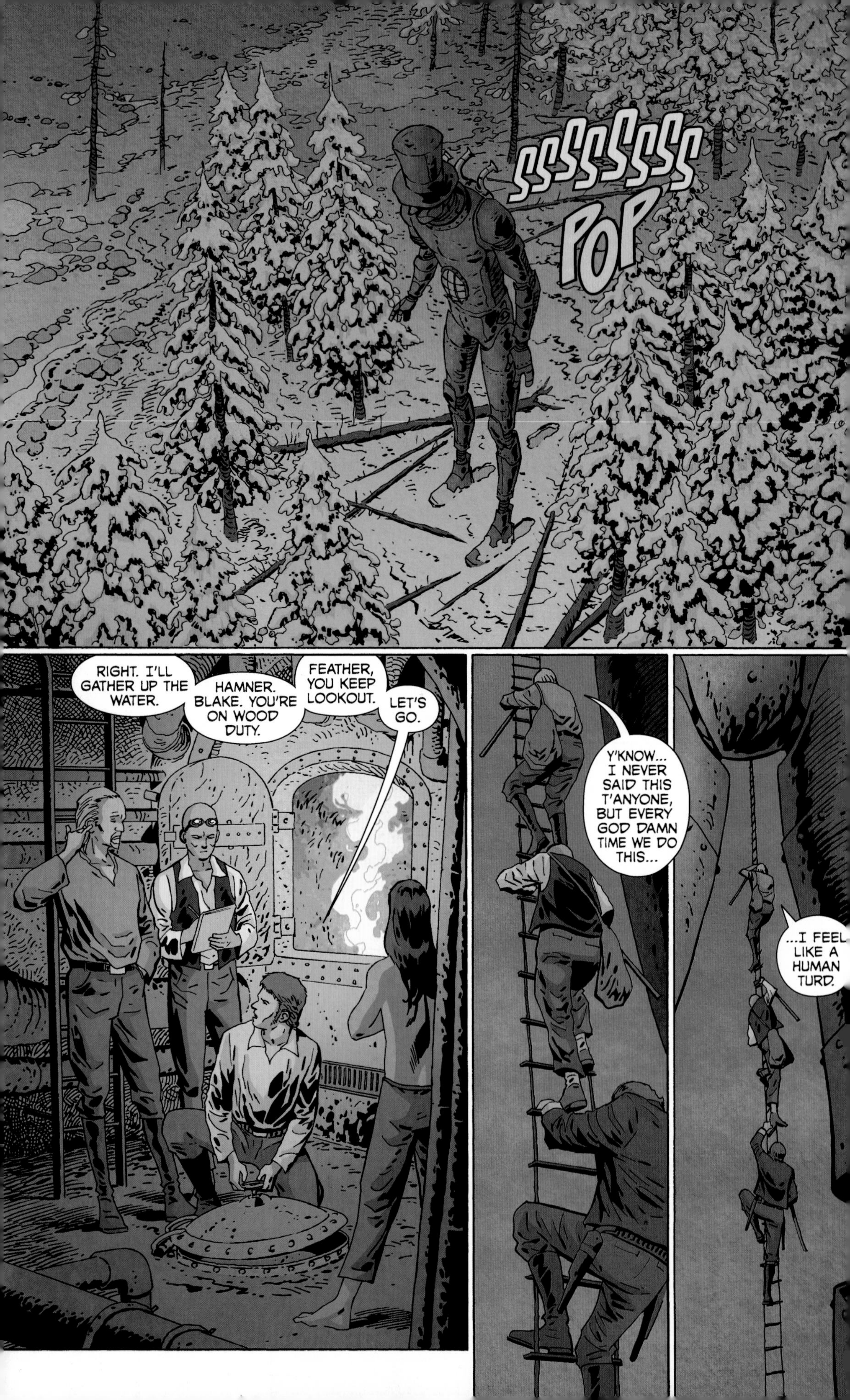
SSSSSSSS
POP
RIGHT. I'LL GATHER UP THE WATER.
HAMNER. BLAKE. YOU'RE ON WOOD DUTY.
FEATHER, YOU KEEP LOOKOUT.
LET'S GO.
Y'KNOW... I NEVER SAID THIS T'ANYONE, BUT EVERY GOD DAMN TIME WE DO THIS...
...I FEEL LIKE A HUMAN TURD.

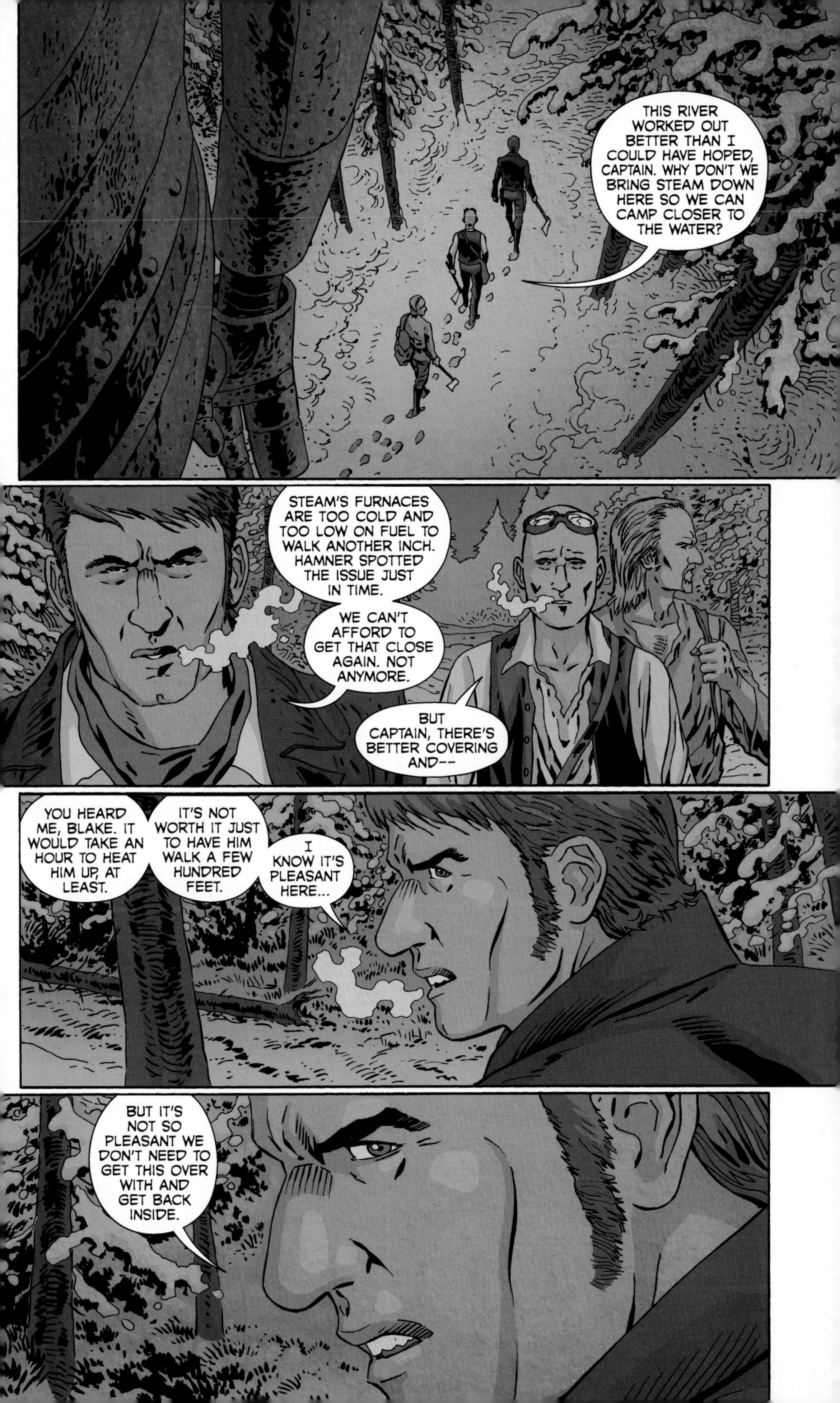

THIS RIVER WORKED OUT BETTER THAN I COULD HAVE HOPED, CAPTAIN. WHY DON'T WE BRING STEAM DOWN HERE SO WE CAN CAMP CLOSER TO THE WATER?
STEAM'S FURNACES ARE TOO COLD AND TOO LOW ON FUEL TO WALK ANOTHER INCH. HAMNER SPOTTED THE ISSUE JUST IN TIME.
WE CAN'T AFFORD TO GET THAT CLOSE AGAIN. NOT ANYMORE.
BUT CAPTAIN, THERE'S BETTER COVERING AND--
YOU HEARD ME, BLAKE. IT WOULD TAKE AN HOUR TO HEAT HIM UP, AT LEAST.
IT'S NOT WORTH IT JUST TO HAVE HIM WALK A FEW HUNDRED FEET.
I KNOW IT'S PLEASANT HERE...
BUT IT'S NOT SO PLEASANT WE DON'T NEED TO GET THIS OVER WITH AND GET BACK INSIDE.

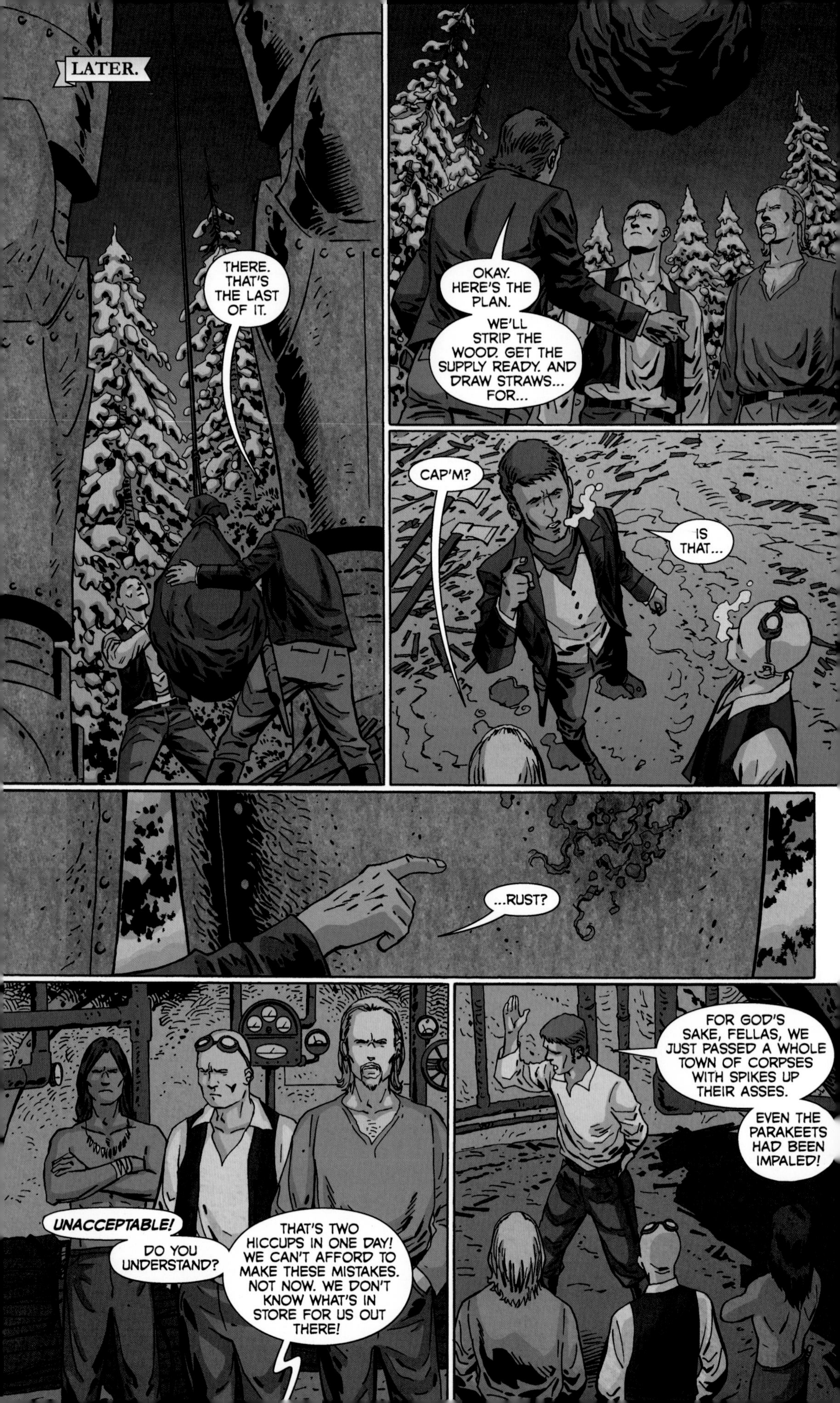
LATER.
THERE. THAT'S THE LAST OF IT.
OKAY. HERE'S THE PLAN.
WE'LL STRIP THE WOOD. GET THE SUPPLY READY. AND DRAW STRAWS... FOR...
CAP'M?
IS THAT...
...RUST?
UNACCEPTABLE!
DO YOU UNDERSTAND?
THAT'S TWO HICCUPS IN ONE DAY! WE CAN'T AFFORD TO MAKE THESE MISTAKES. NOT NOW. WE DON'T KNOW WHAT'S IN STORE FOR US OUT THERE!
FOR GOD'S SAKE, FELLAS, WE JUST PASSED A WHOLE TOWN OF CORPSES WITH SPIKES UP THEIR ASSES.
EVEN THE PARAKEETS HAD BEEN IMPALED!

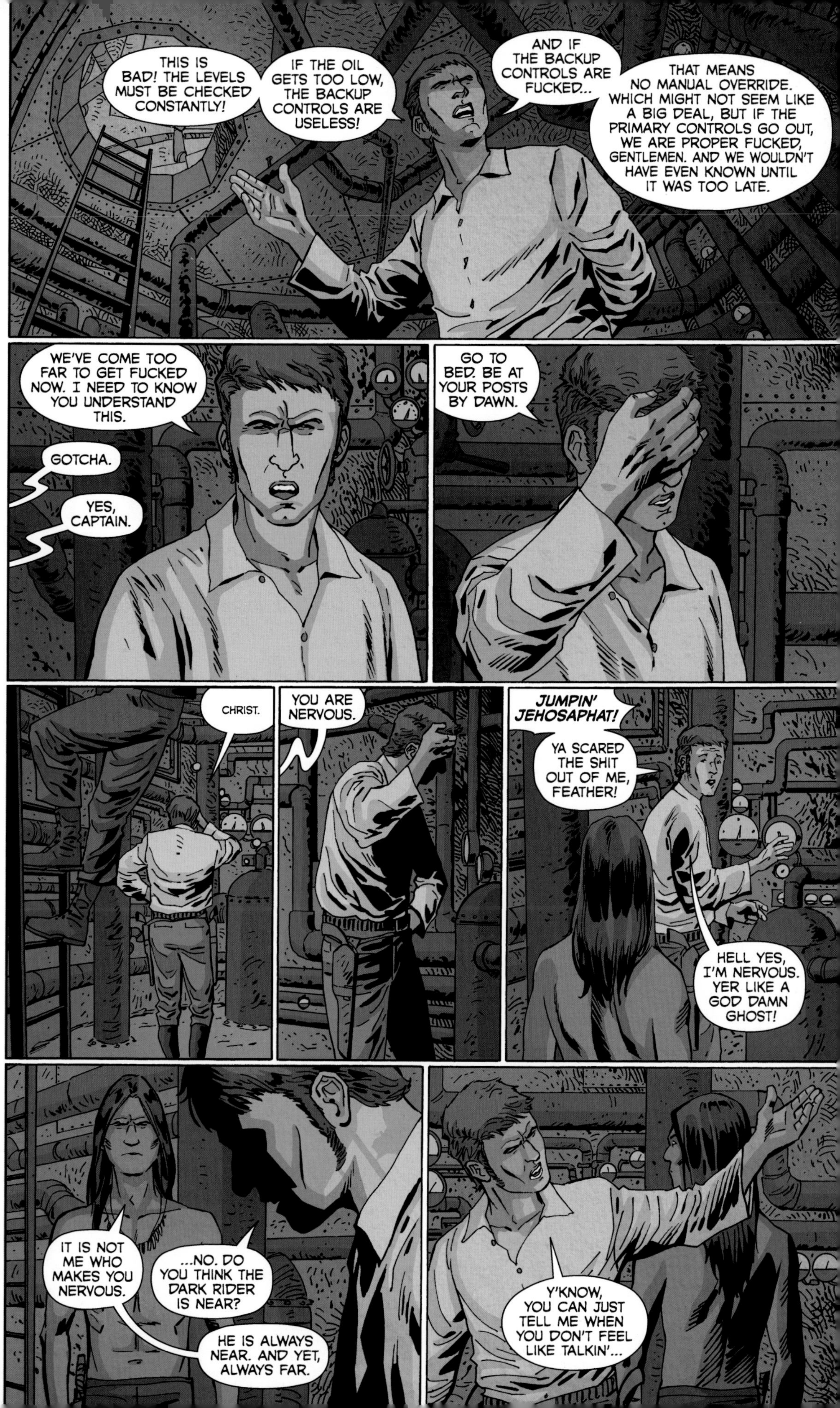
THIS IS BAD! THE LEVELS MUST BE CHECKED CONSTANTLY!
IF THE OIL GETS TOO LOW, THE BACKUP CONTROLS ARE USELESS!
AND IF THE BACKUP CONTROLS ARE FUCKED...
THAT MEANS NO MANUAL OVERRIDE. WHICH MIGHT NOT SEEM LIKE A BIG DEAL, BUT IF THE PRIMARY CONTROLS GO OUT, WE ARE PROPER FUCKED, GENTLEMEN. AND WE WOULDN'T HAVE EVEN KNOWN UNTIL IT WAS TOO LATE.
WE'VE COME TOO FAR TO GET FUCKED NOW. I NEED TO KNOW YOU UNDERSTAND THIS.
GOTCHA.
YES, CAPTAIN.
GO TO BED. BE AT YOUR POSTS BY DAWN.
CHRIST.
YOU ARE NERVOUS.
JUMPIN' JEHOSAPHAT!
YA SCARED THE SHIT OUT OF ME, FEATHER!
HELL YES, I'M NERVOUS. YER LIKE A GOD DAMN GHOST!
IT IS NOT ME WHO MAKES YOU NERVOUS.
...NO. DO YOU THINK THE DARK RIDER IS NEAR?
HE IS ALWAYS NEAR. AND YET, ALWAYS FAR.
Y'KNOW, YOU CAN JUST TELL ME WHEN YOU DON'T FEEL LIKE TALKIN'...

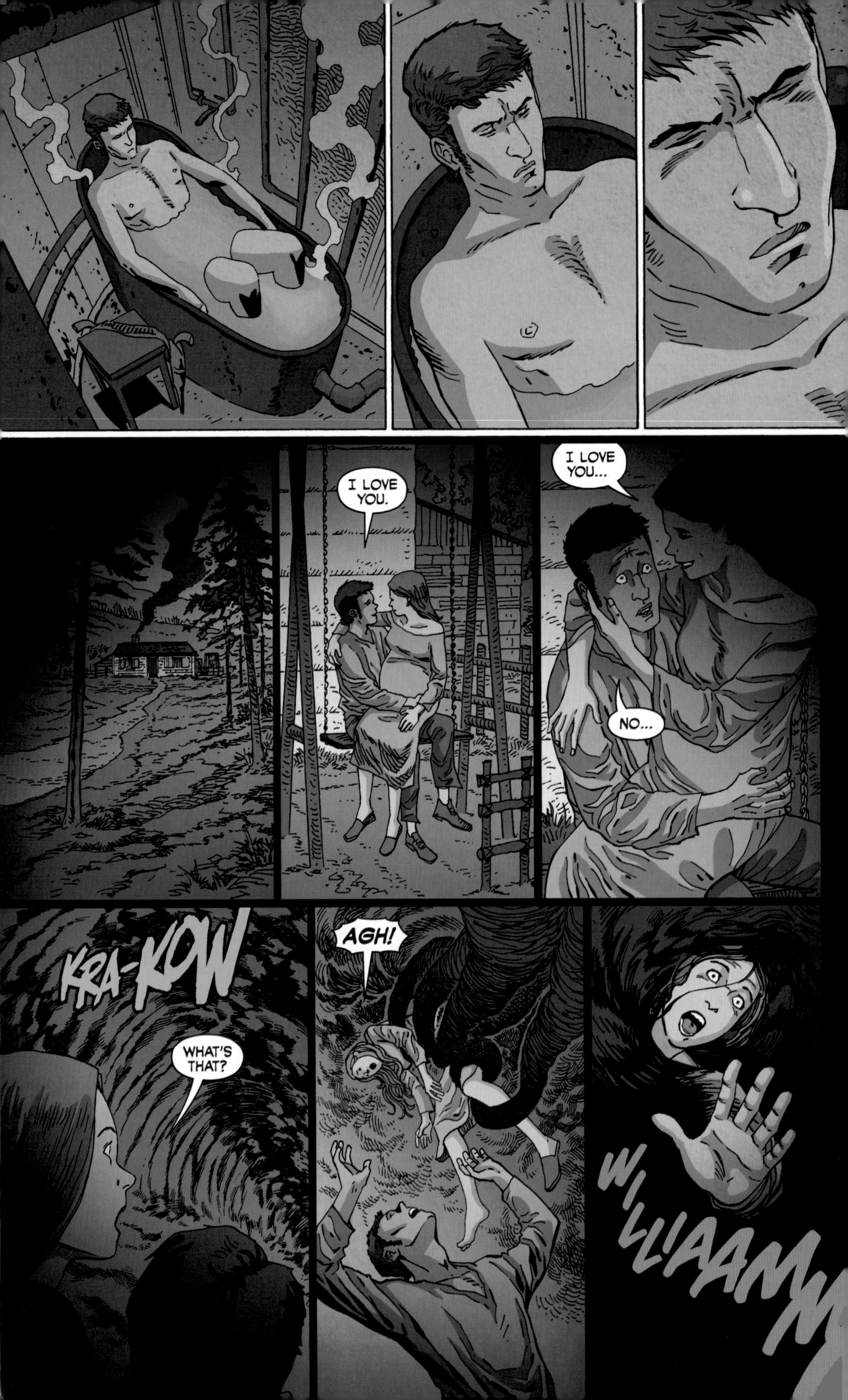
I LOVE YOU.
I LOVE YOU...
NO...
KRA-KOW
WHAT'S THAT?
AGH!
WILLIAAMM

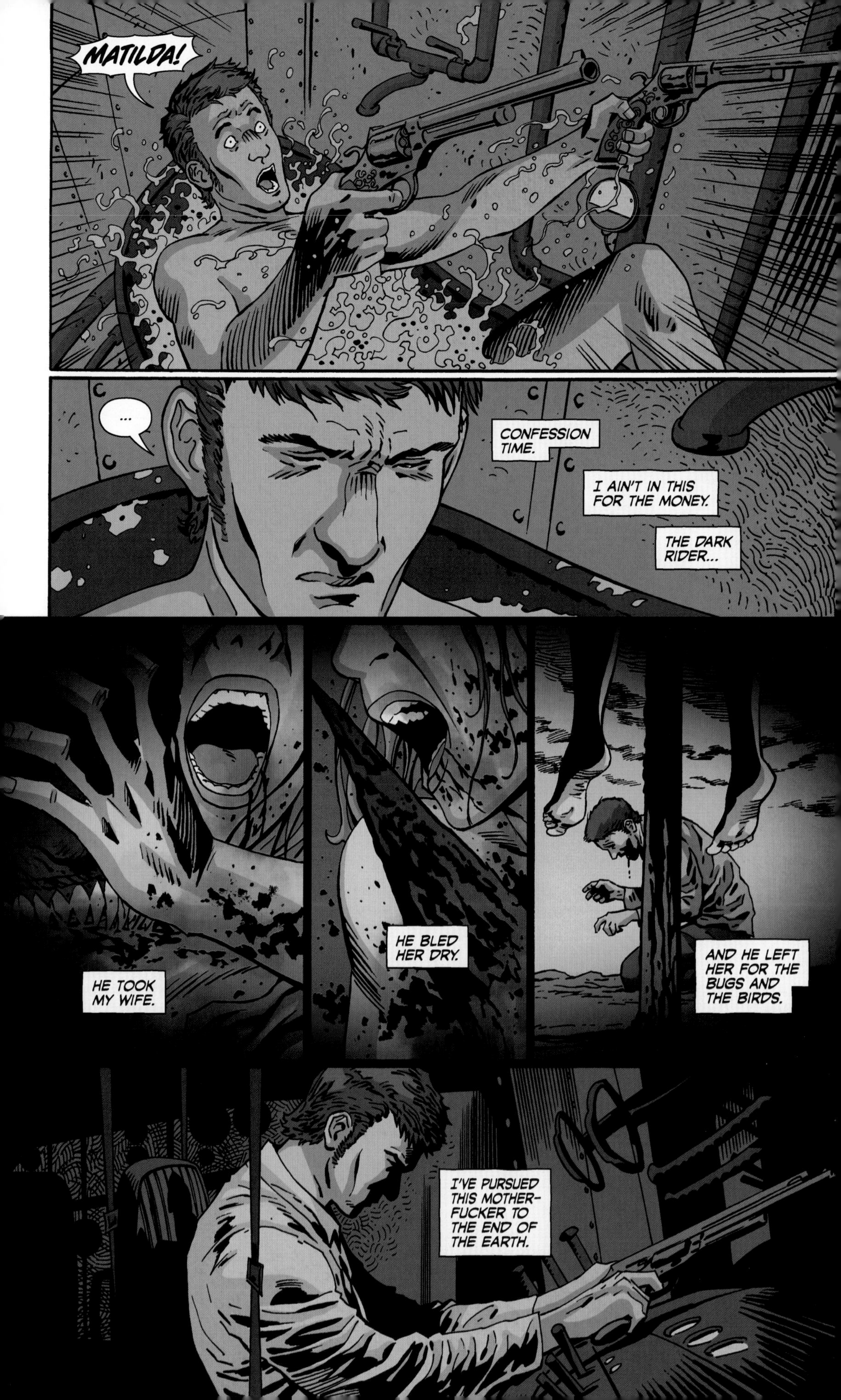
MATILDA!
...
CONFESSION TIME.
I AIN'T IN THIS FOR THE MONEY.
THE DARK RIDER...
HE TOOK MY WIFE.
HE BLED HER DRY.
AND HE LEFT HER FOR THE BUGS AND THE BIRDS.
I'VE PURSUED THIS MOTHER-FUCKER TO THE END OF THE EARTH.

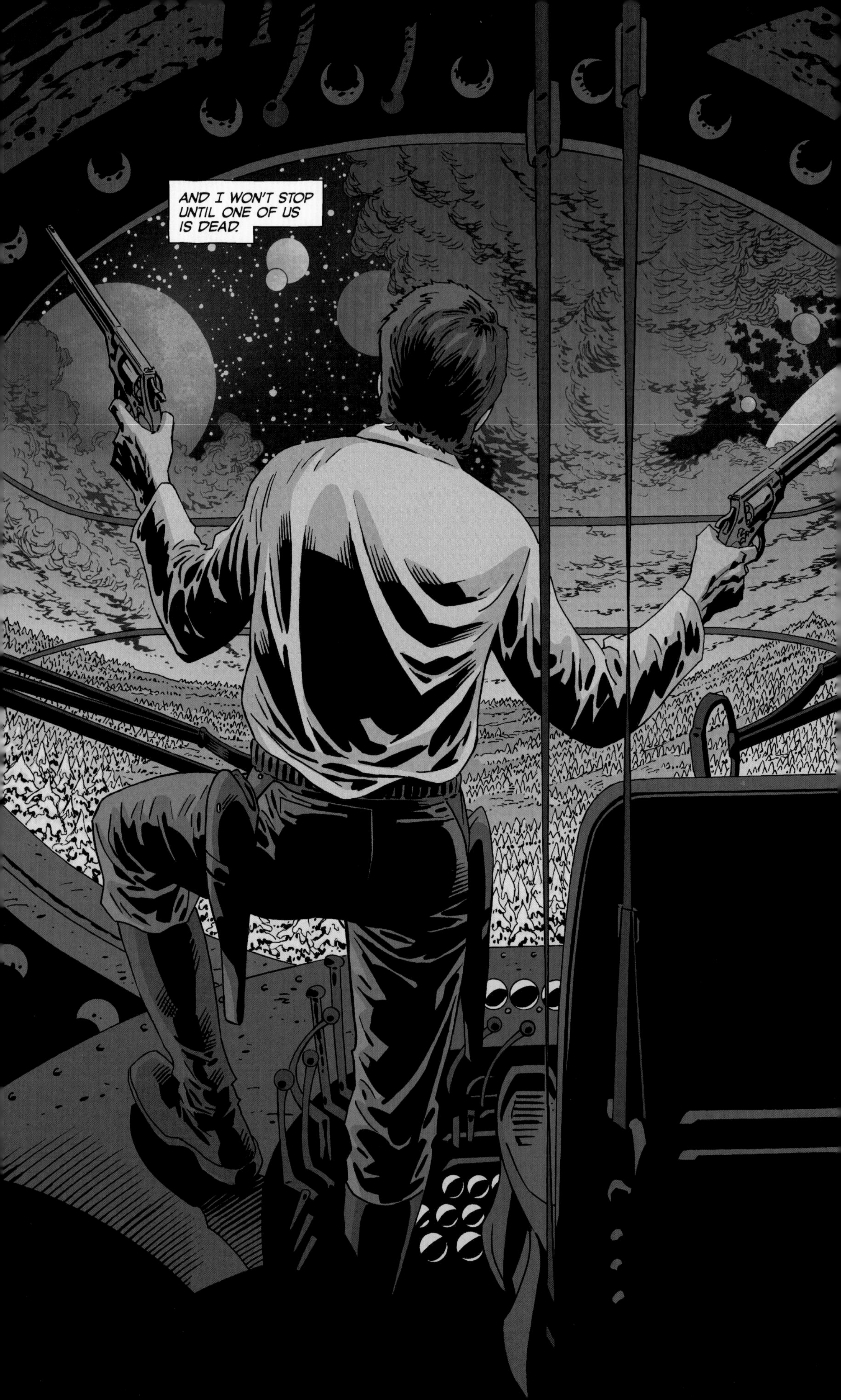
AND I WON'T STOP
UNTIL ONE OF US
IS DEAD.

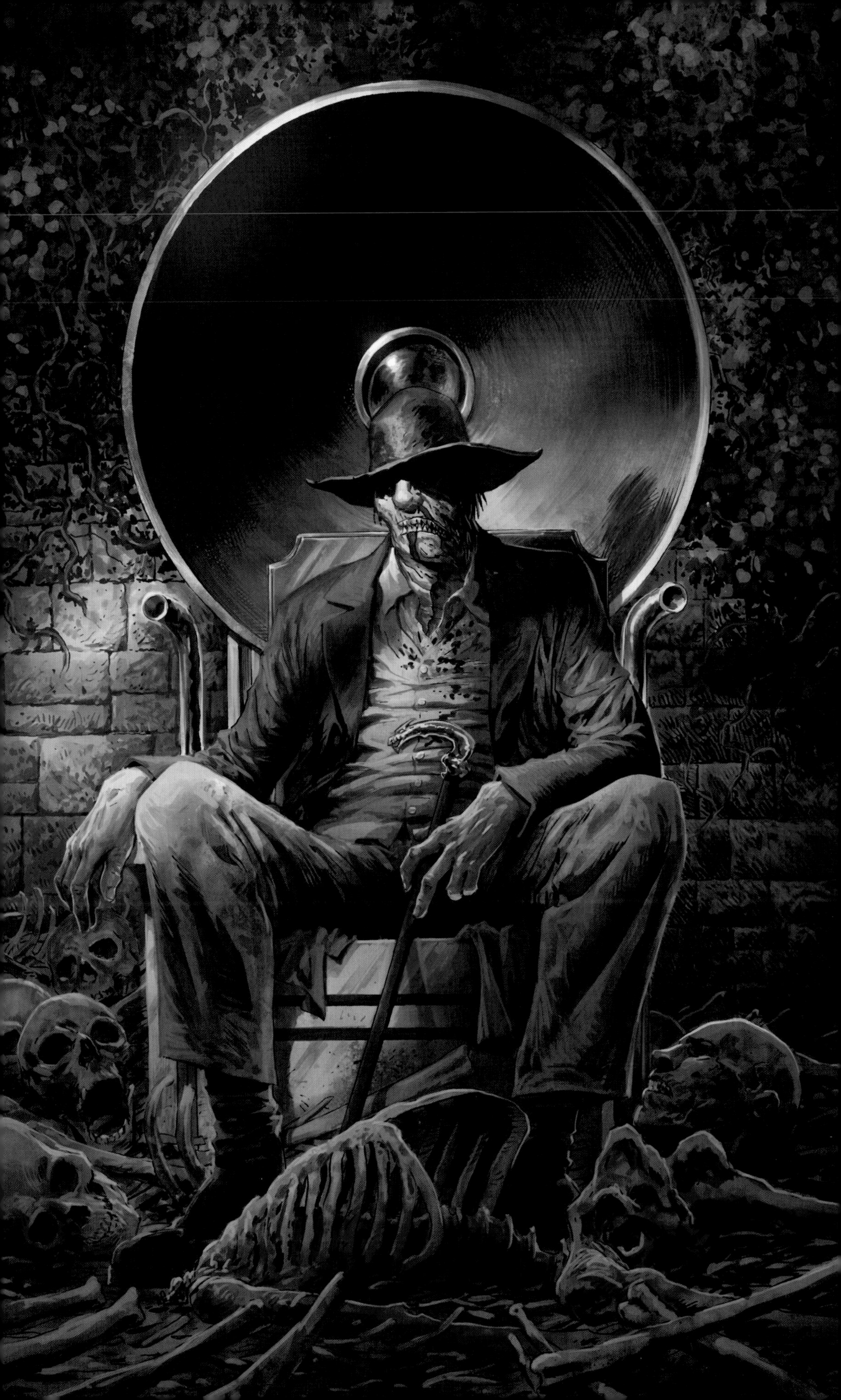

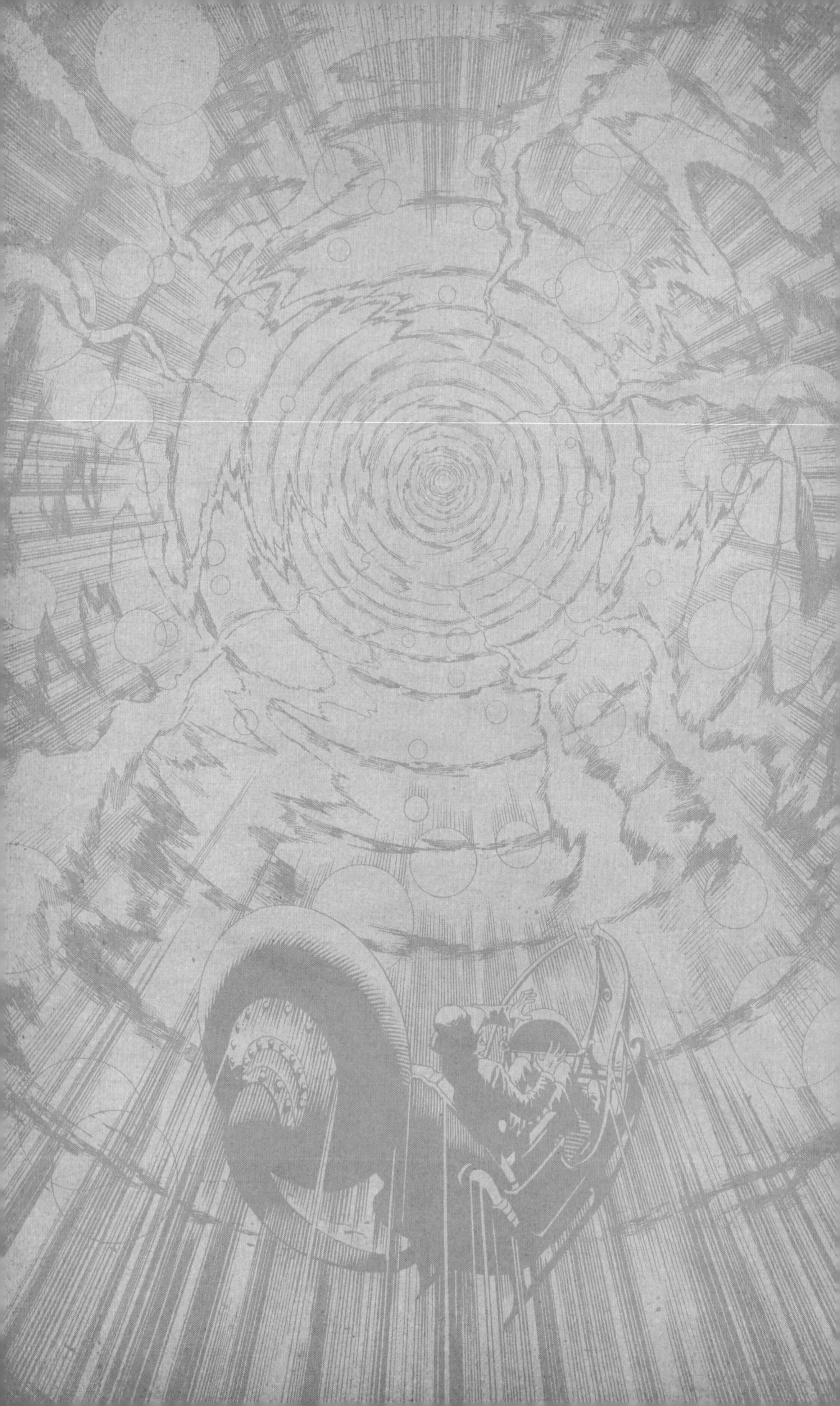

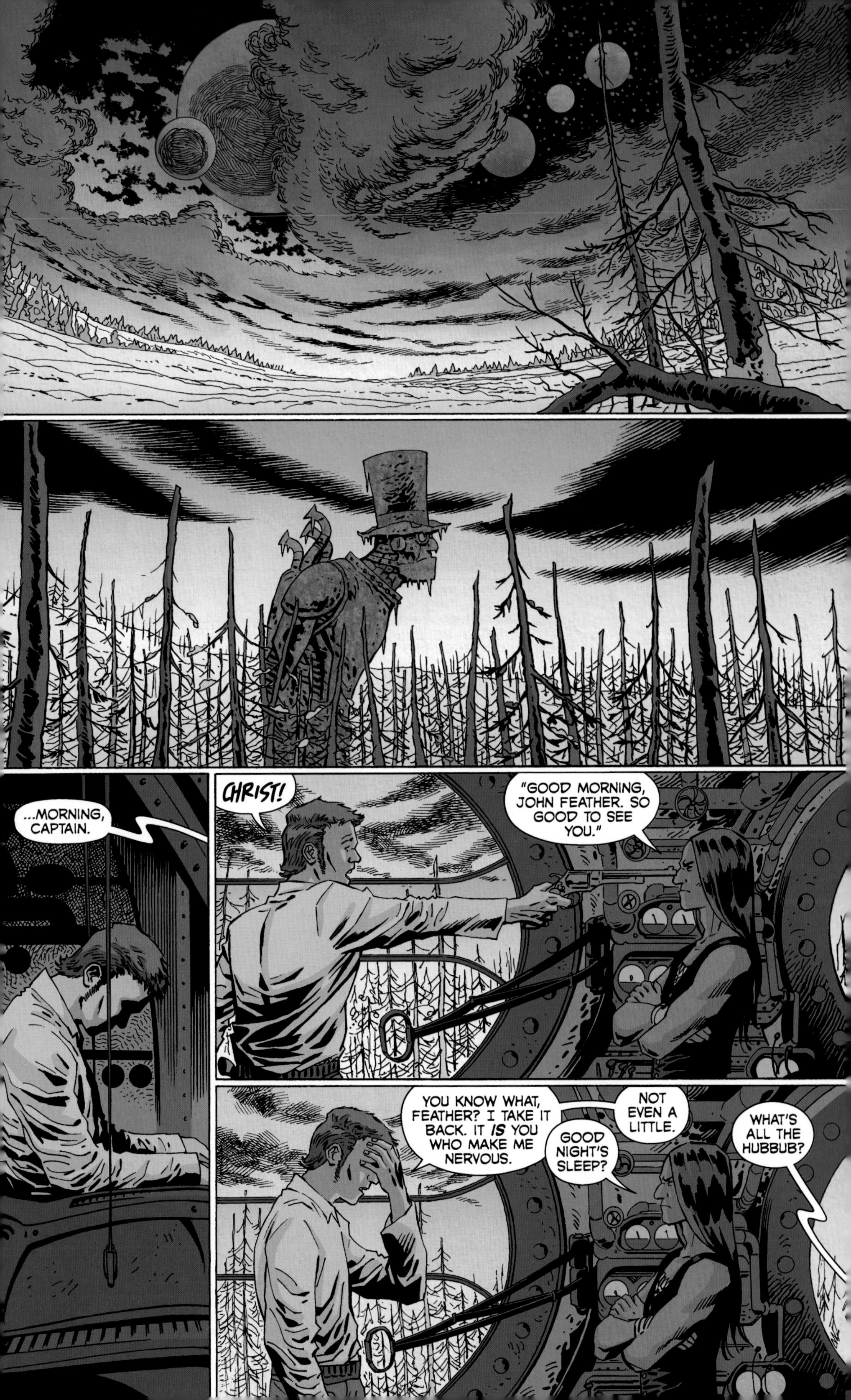
...MORNING, CAPTAIN.
CHRIST!
"GOOD MORNING, JOHN FEATHER. SO GOOD TO SEE YOU."
YOU KNOW WHAT, FEATHER? I TAKE IT BACK. IT *IS* YOU WHO MAKE ME NERVOUS.
NOT EVEN A LITTLE.
GOOD NIGHT'S SLEEP?
WHAT'S ALL THE HUBBUB?

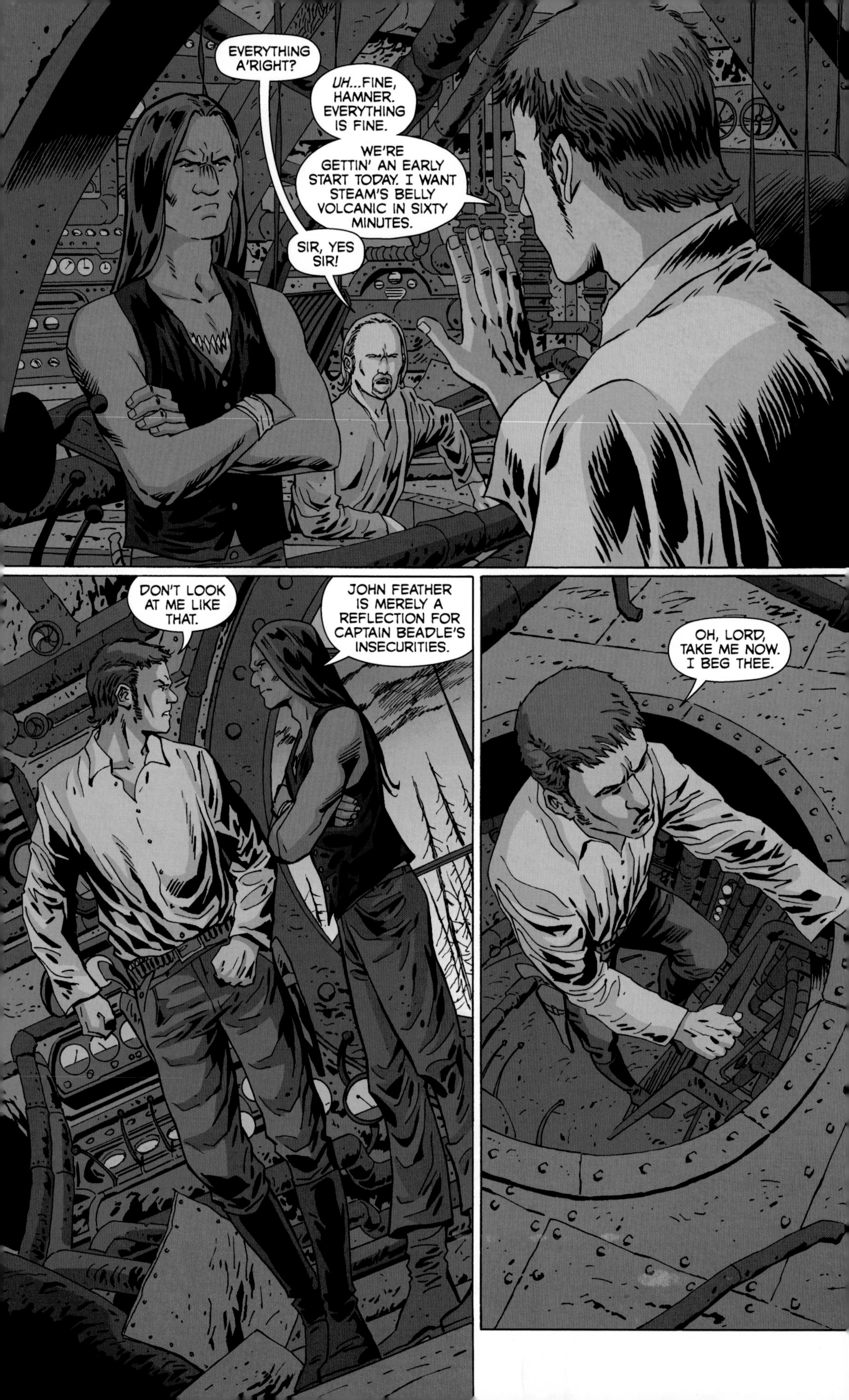
EVERYTHING A'RIGHT?
UH...FINE, HAMNER. EVERYTHING IS FINE.
WE'RE GETTIN' AN EARLY START TODAY. I WANT STEAM'S BELLY VOLCANIC IN SIXTY MINUTES.
SIR, YES SIR!
DON'T LOOK AT ME LIKE THAT.
JOHN FEATHER IS MERELY A REFLECTION FOR CAPTAIN BEADLE'S INSECURITIES.
OH, LORD, TAKE ME NOW. I BEG THEE.

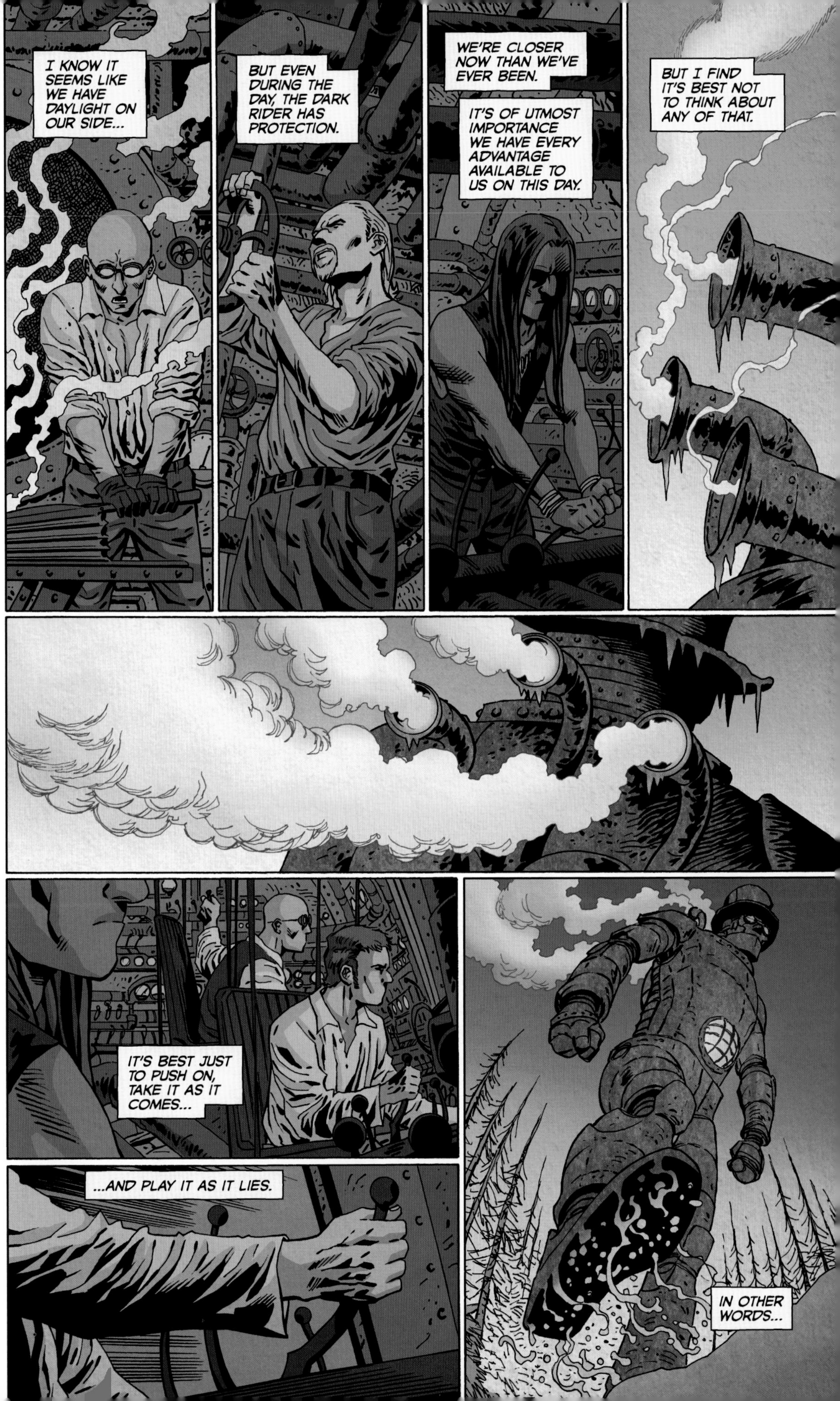
I KNOW IT SEEMS LIKE WE HAVE DAYLIGHT ON OUR SIDE...
BUT EVEN DURING THE DAY, THE DARK RIDER HAS PROTECTION.
WE'RE CLOSER NOW THAN WE'VE EVER BEEN.
IT'S OF UTMOST IMPORTANCE WE HAVE EVERY ADVANTAGE AVAILABLE TO US ON THIS DAY.
BUT I FIND IT'S BEST NOT TO THINK ABOUT ANY OF THAT.
IT'S BEST JUST TO PUSH ON, TAKE IT AS IT COMES...
...AND PLAY IT AS IT LIES.
IN OTHER WORDS...

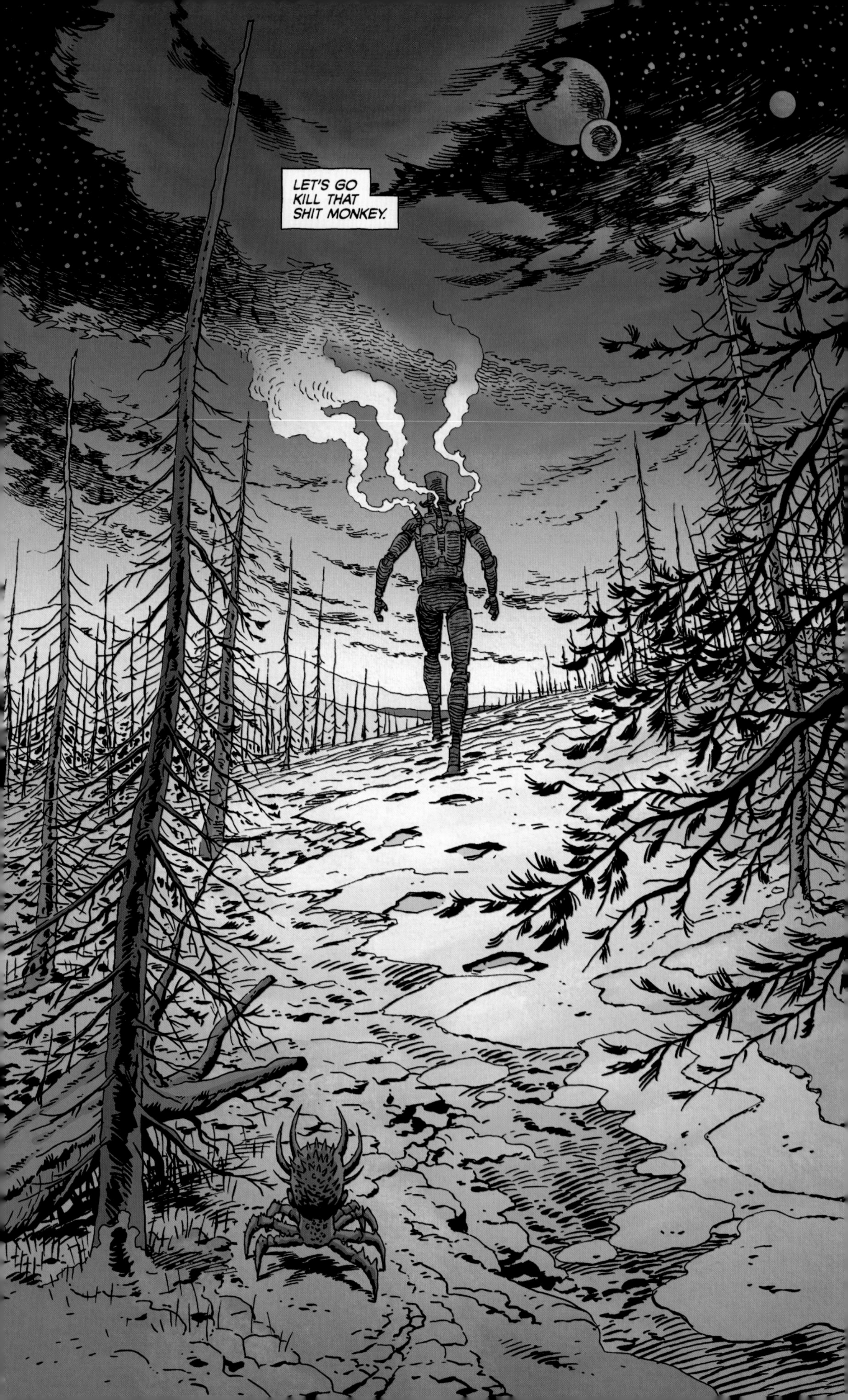
LET'S GO KILL THAT SHIT MONKEY.

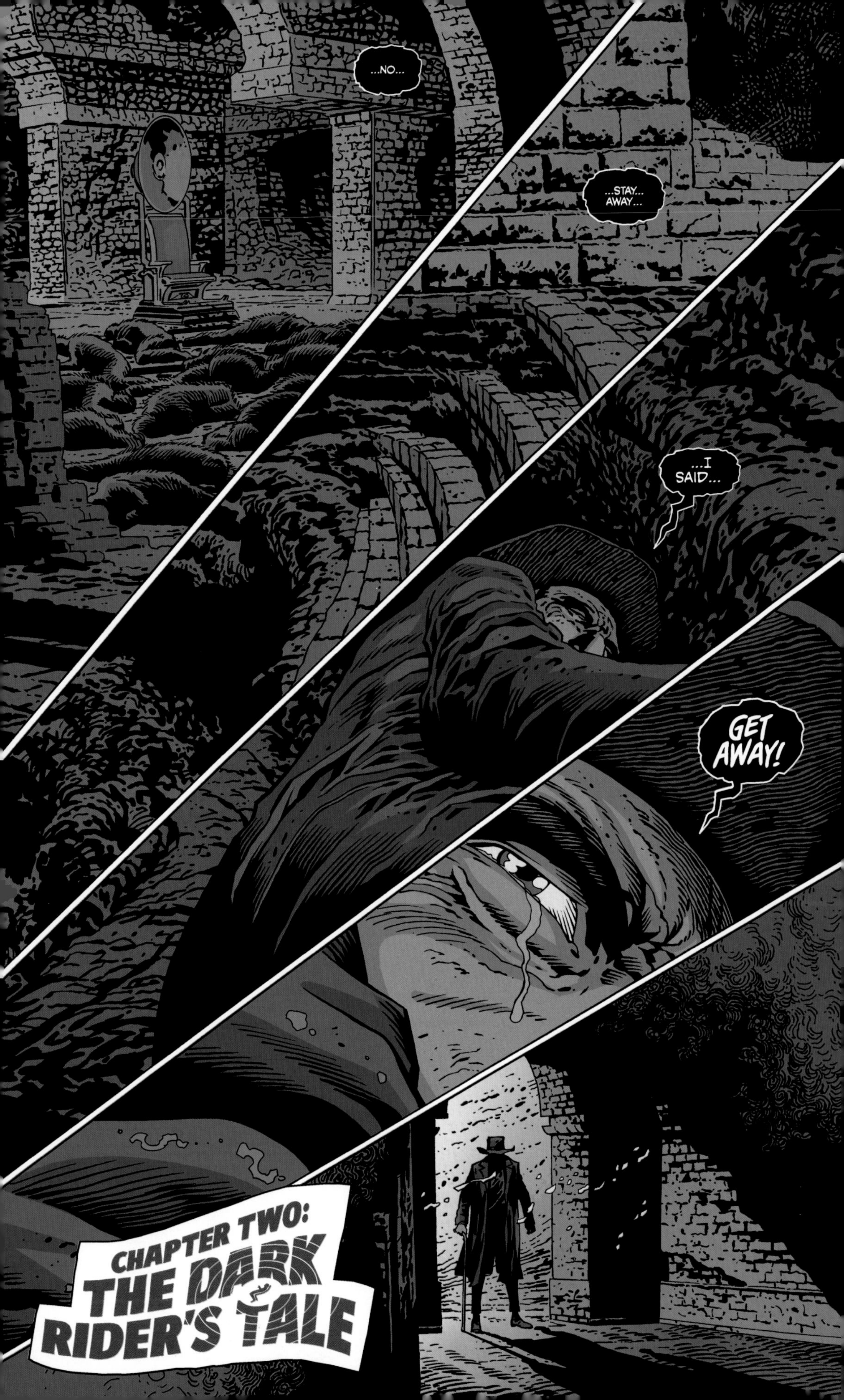
...NO...
...STAY... AWAY...
...I SAID...
GET AWAY!
CHAPTER TWO: THE DARK RIDER'S TALE

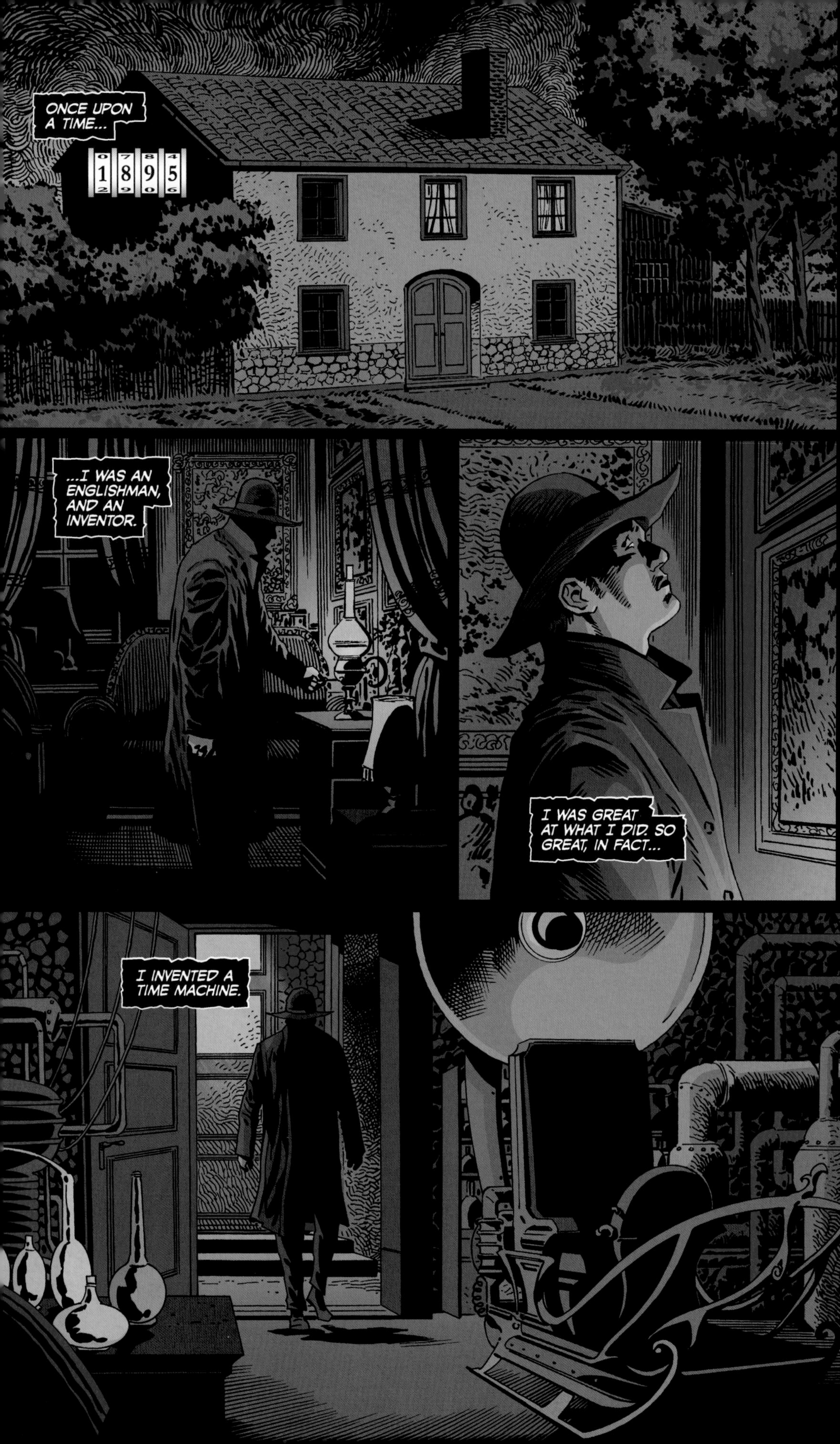
ONCE UPON A TIME...
1895
...I WAS AN ENGLISHMAN, AND AN INVENTOR.
I WAS GREAT AT WHAT I DID. SO GREAT, IN FACT...
I INVENTED A TIME MACHINE.

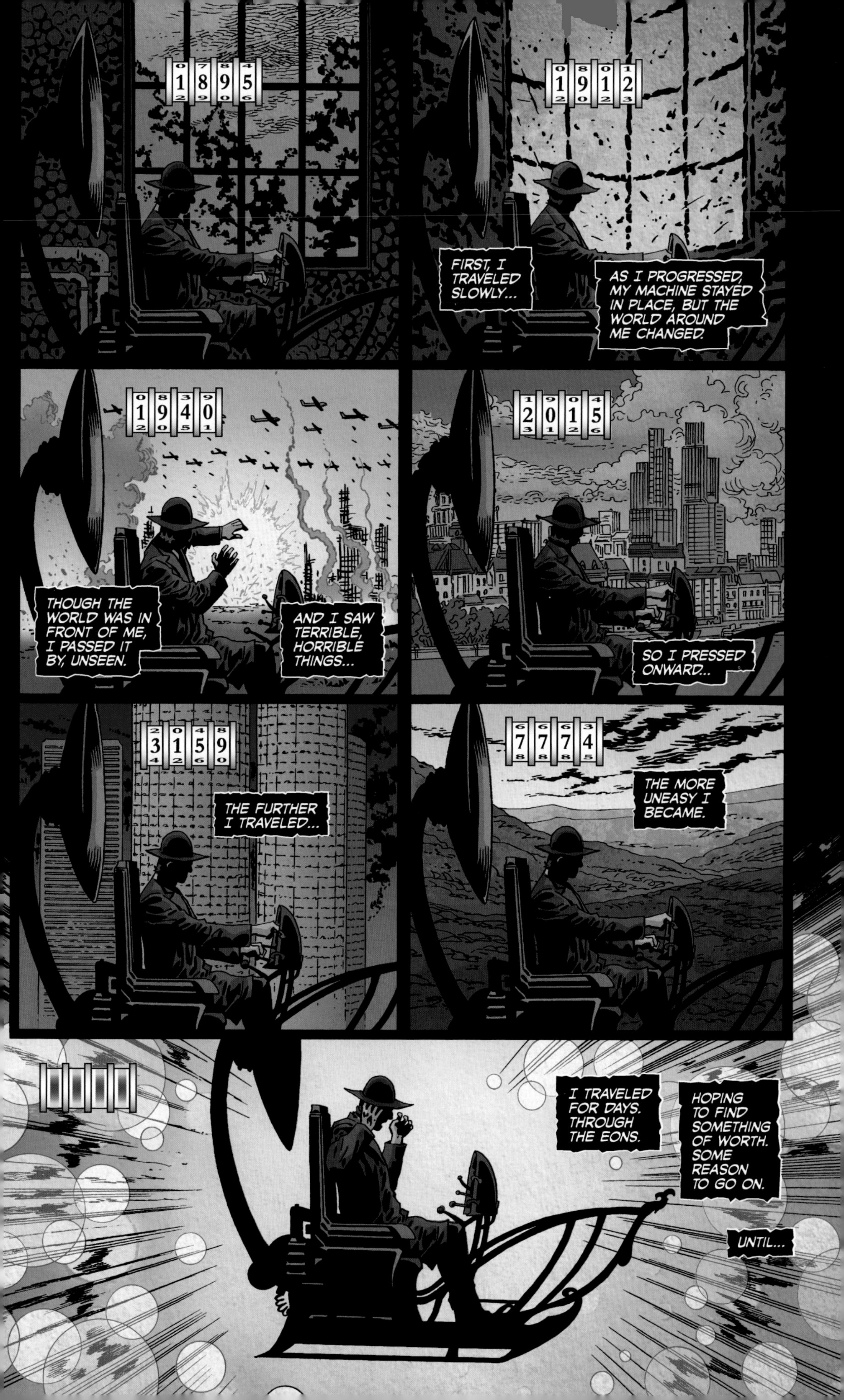
1895
1912
FIRST, I TRAVELED SLOWLY...
AS I PROGRESSED, MY MACHINE STAYED IN PLACE, BUT THE WORLD AROUND ME CHANGED.
1940
THOUGH THE WORLD WAS IN FRONT OF ME, I PASSED IT BY, UNSEEN.
AND I SAW TERRIBLE, HORRIBLE THINGS...
2015
SO I PRESSED ONWARD...
3159
THE FURTHER I TRAVELED...
7774
THE MORE UNEASY I BECAME.
I TRAVELED FOR DAYS. THROUGH THE EONS.
HOPING TO FIND SOMETHING OF WORTH. SOME REASON TO GO ON.
UNTIL...

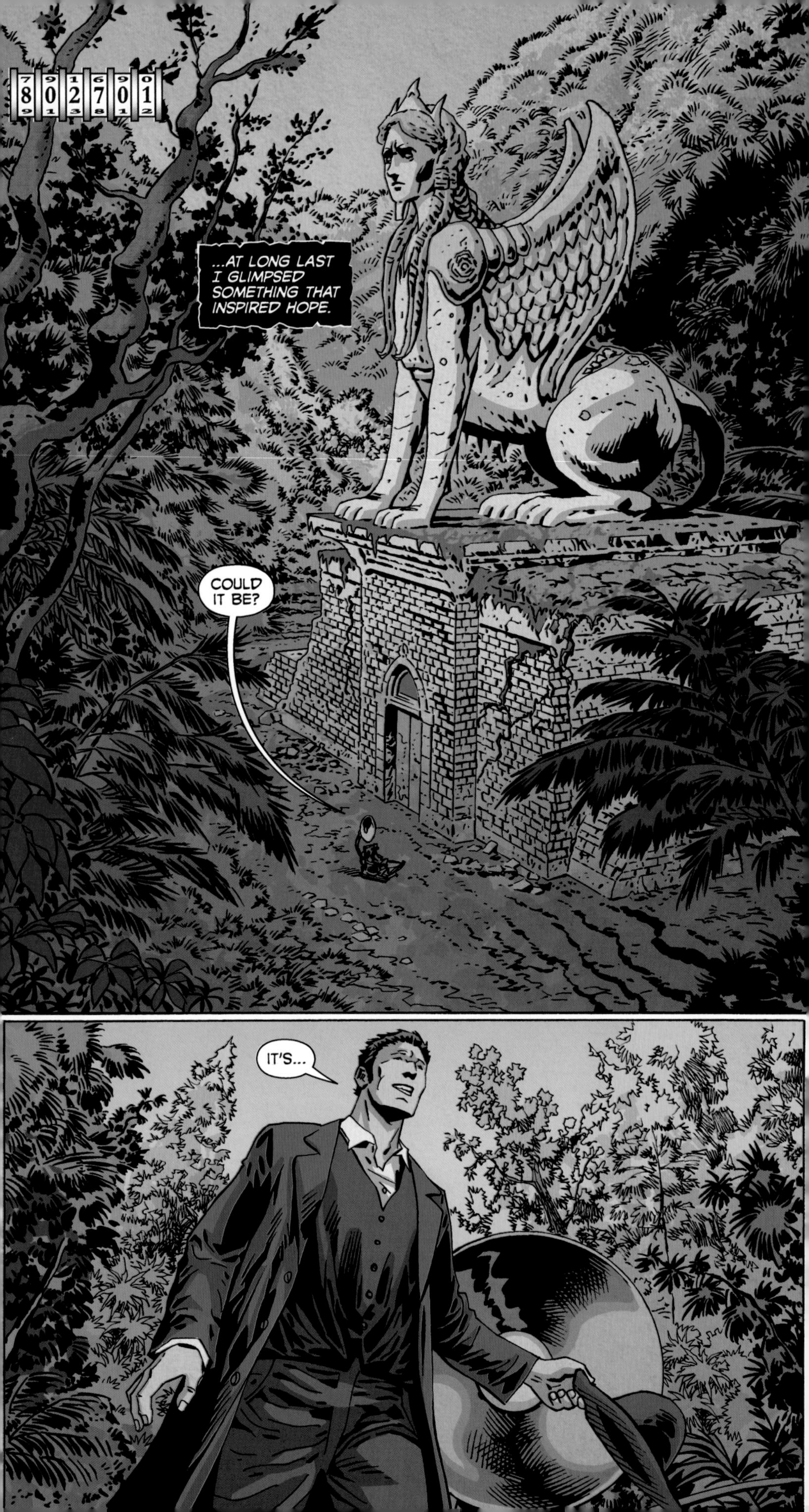
802701
...AT LONG LAST I GLIMPSED SOMETHING THAT INSPIRED HOPE.
COULD IT BE?
IT'S...

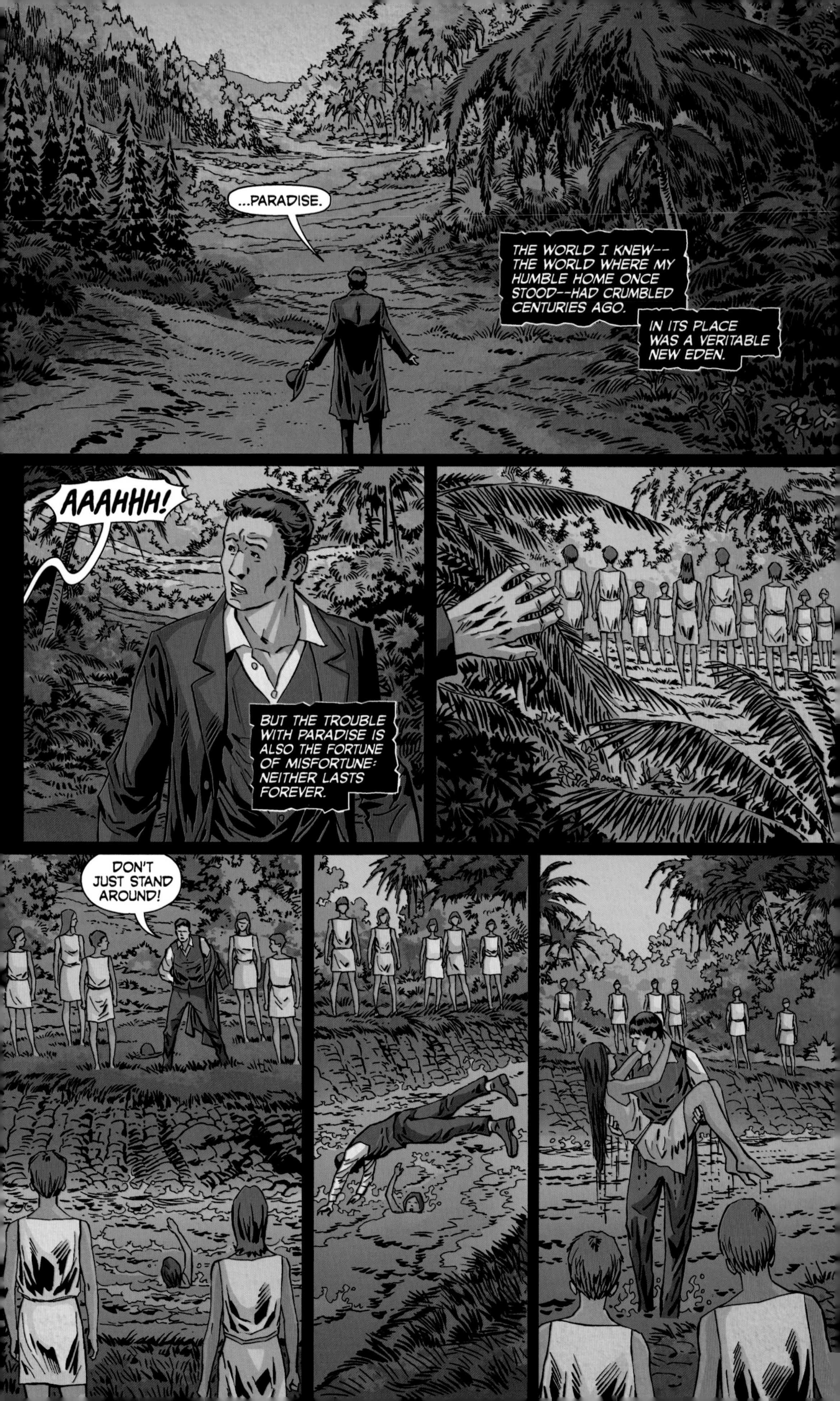
...PARADISE.
THE WORLD I KNEW-- THE WORLD WHERE MY HUMBLE HOME ONCE STOOD--HAD CRUMBLED CENTURIES AGO.
IN ITS PLACE WAS A VERITABLE NEW EDEN.
AAAHHH!
BUT THE TROUBLE WITH PARADISE IS ALSO THE FORTUNE OF MISFORTUNE: NEITHER LASTS FOREVER.
DON'T JUST STAND AROUND!

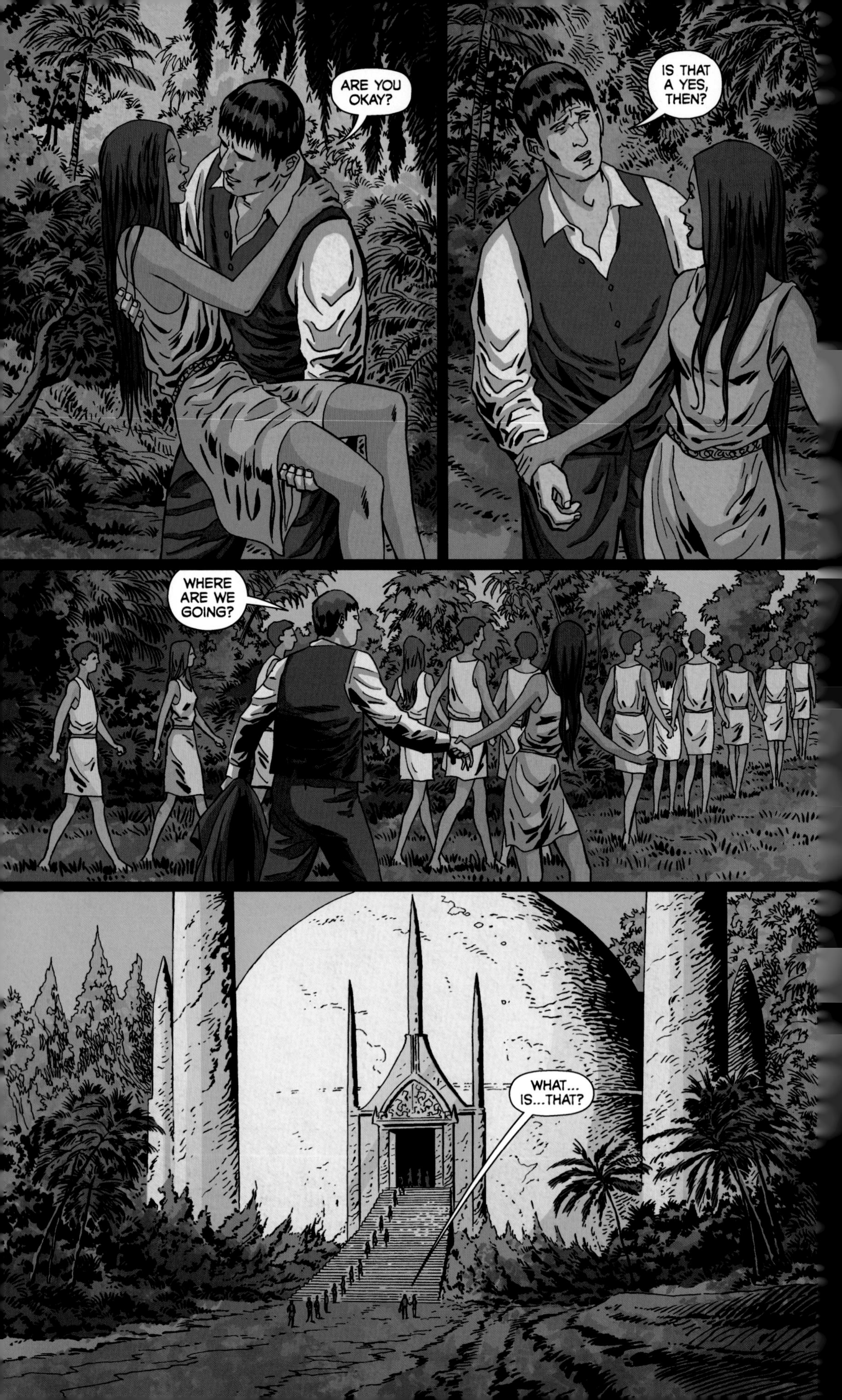
ARE YOU OKAY?
IS THAT A YES, THEN?
WHERE ARE WE GOING?
WHAT... IS...THAT?

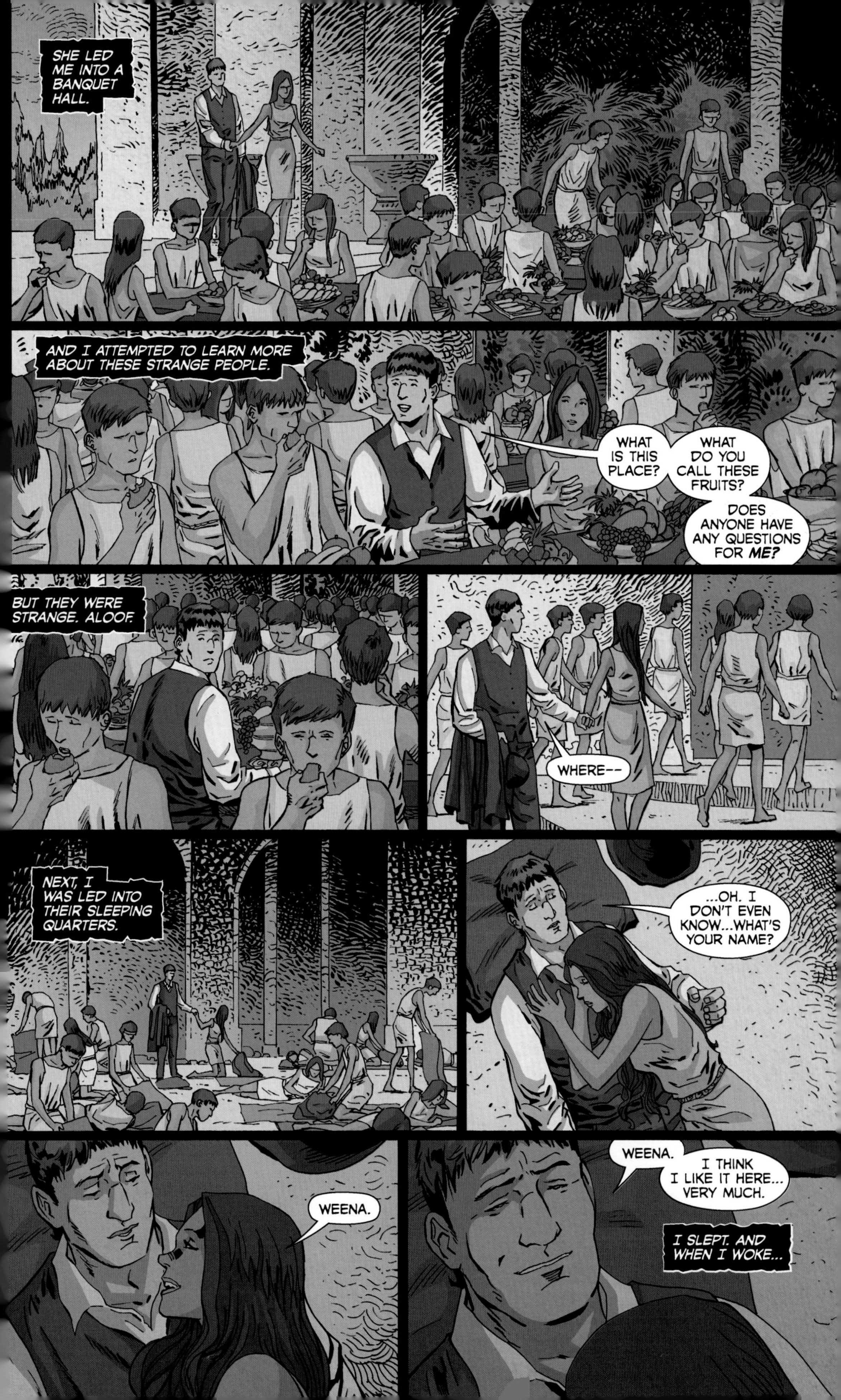
SHE LED ME INTO A BANQUET HALL.
AND I ATTEMPTED TO LEARN MORE ABOUT THESE STRANGE PEOPLE.
WHAT IS THIS PLACE?
WHAT DO YOU CALL THESE FRUITS?
DOES ANYONE HAVE ANY QUESTIONS FOR ME?
BUT THEY WERE STRANGE. ALOOF.
WHERE--
NEXT, I WAS LED INTO THEIR SLEEPING QUARTERS.
...OH. I DON'T EVEN KNOW...WHAT'S YOUR NAME?
WEENA.
WEENA.
I THINK I LIKE IT HERE... VERY MUCH.
I SLEPT. AND WHEN I WOKE...

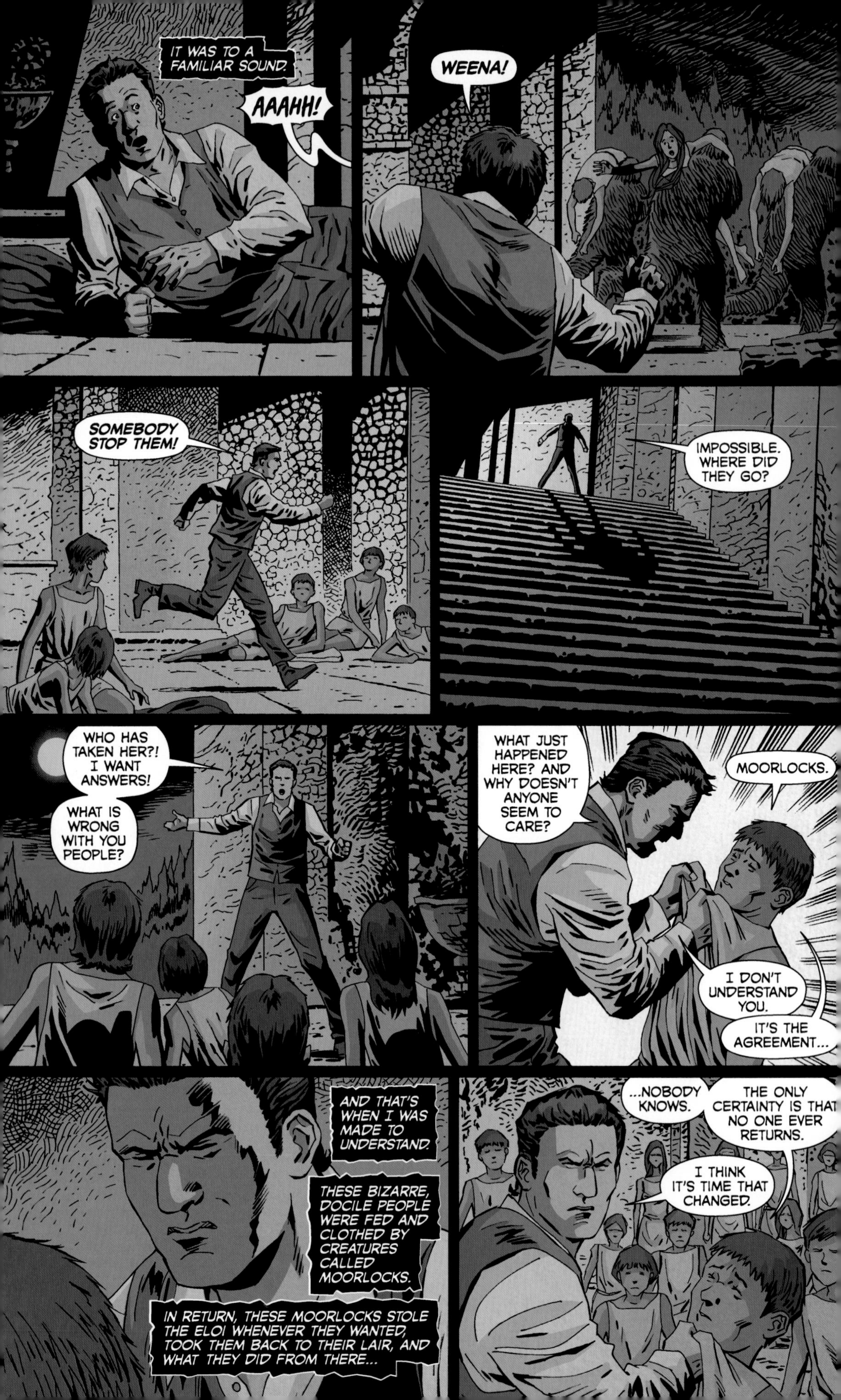
IT WAS TO A FAMILIAR SOUND.
AAAHH!
WEENA!
SOMEBODY STOP THEM!
IMPOSSIBLE. WHERE DID THEY GO?
WHO HAS TAKEN HER?! I WANT ANSWERS!
WHAT IS WRONG WITH YOU PEOPLE?
WHAT JUST HAPPENED HERE? AND WHY DOESN'T ANYONE SEEM TO CARE?
MOORLOCKS.
I DON'T UNDERSTAND YOU.
IT'S THE AGREEMENT...
AND THAT'S WHEN I WAS MADE TO UNDERSTAND.
THESE BIZARRE, DOCILE PEOPLE WERE FED AND CLOTHED BY CREATURES CALLED MOORLOCKS.
IN RETURN, THESE MOORLOCKS STOLE THE ELOI WHENEVER THEY WANTED, TOOK THEM BACK TO THEIR LAIR, AND WHAT THEY DID FROM THERE...
...NOBODY KNOWS.
THE ONLY CERTAINTY IS THAT NO ONE EVER RETURNS.
I THINK IT'S TIME THAT CHANGED.

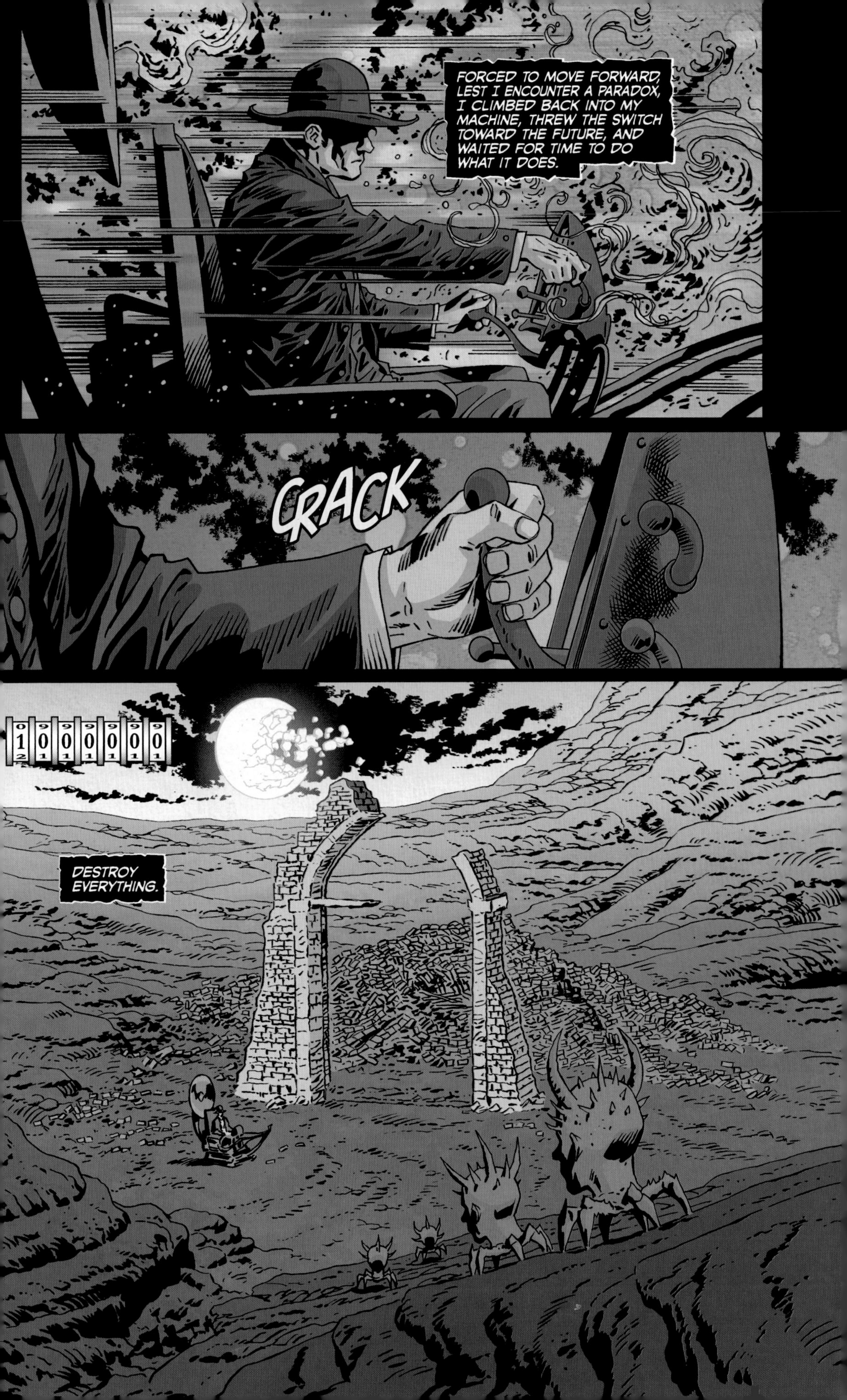
FORCED TO MOVE FORWARD, LEST I ENCOUNTER A PARADOX, I CLIMBED BACK INTO MY MACHINE, THREW THE SWITCH TOWARD THE FUTURE, AND WAITED FOR TIME TO DO WHAT IT DOES.
CRACK
1000000
DESTROY EVERYTHING.

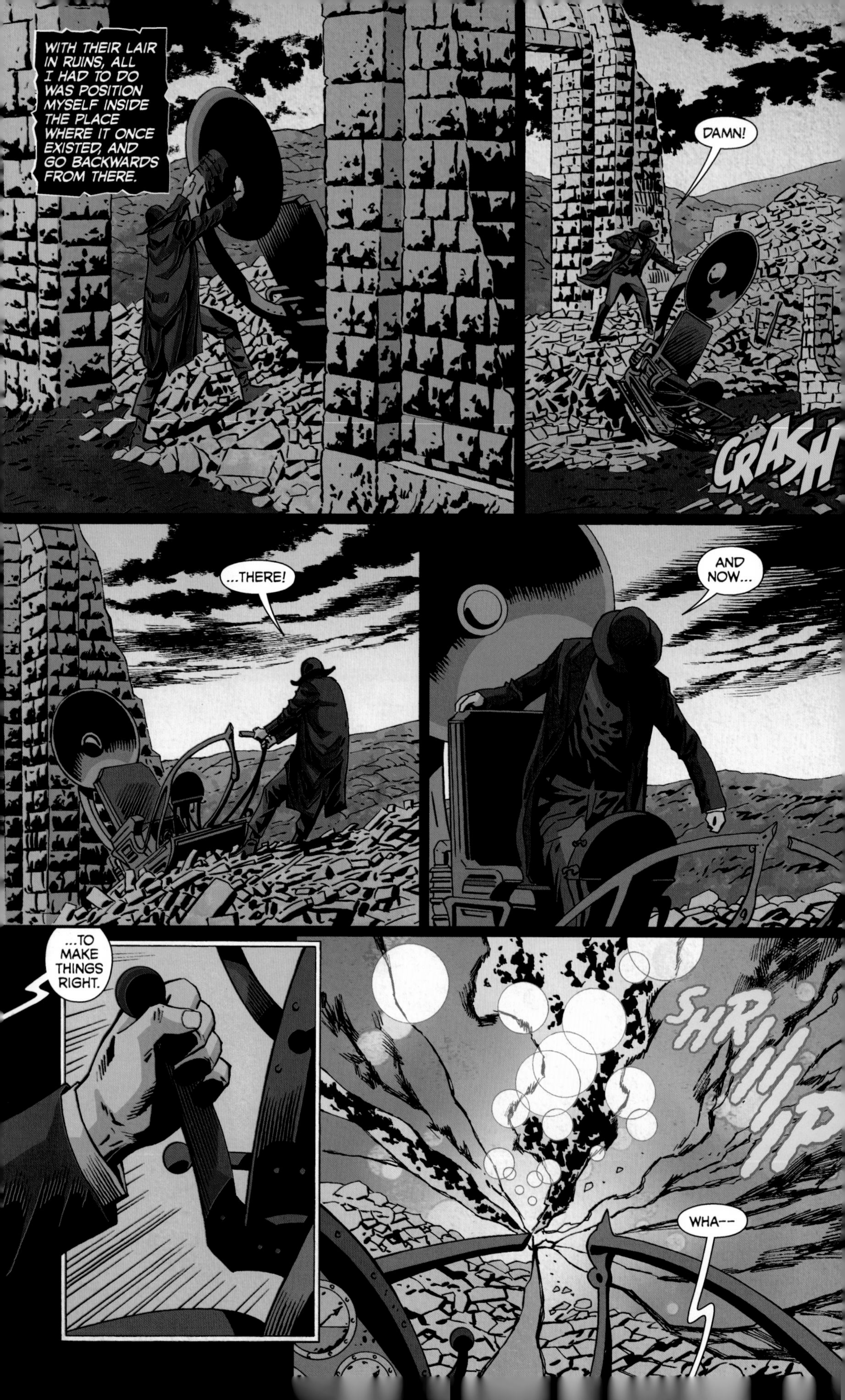
WITH THEIR LAIR IN RUINS, ALL I HAD TO DO WAS POSITION MYSELF INSIDE THE PLACE WHERE IT ONCE EXISTED, AND GO BACKWARDS FROM THERE.
DAMN!
CRASH
...THERE!
AND NOW...
...TO MAKE THINGS RIGHT.
SHRIIIP
WHA--

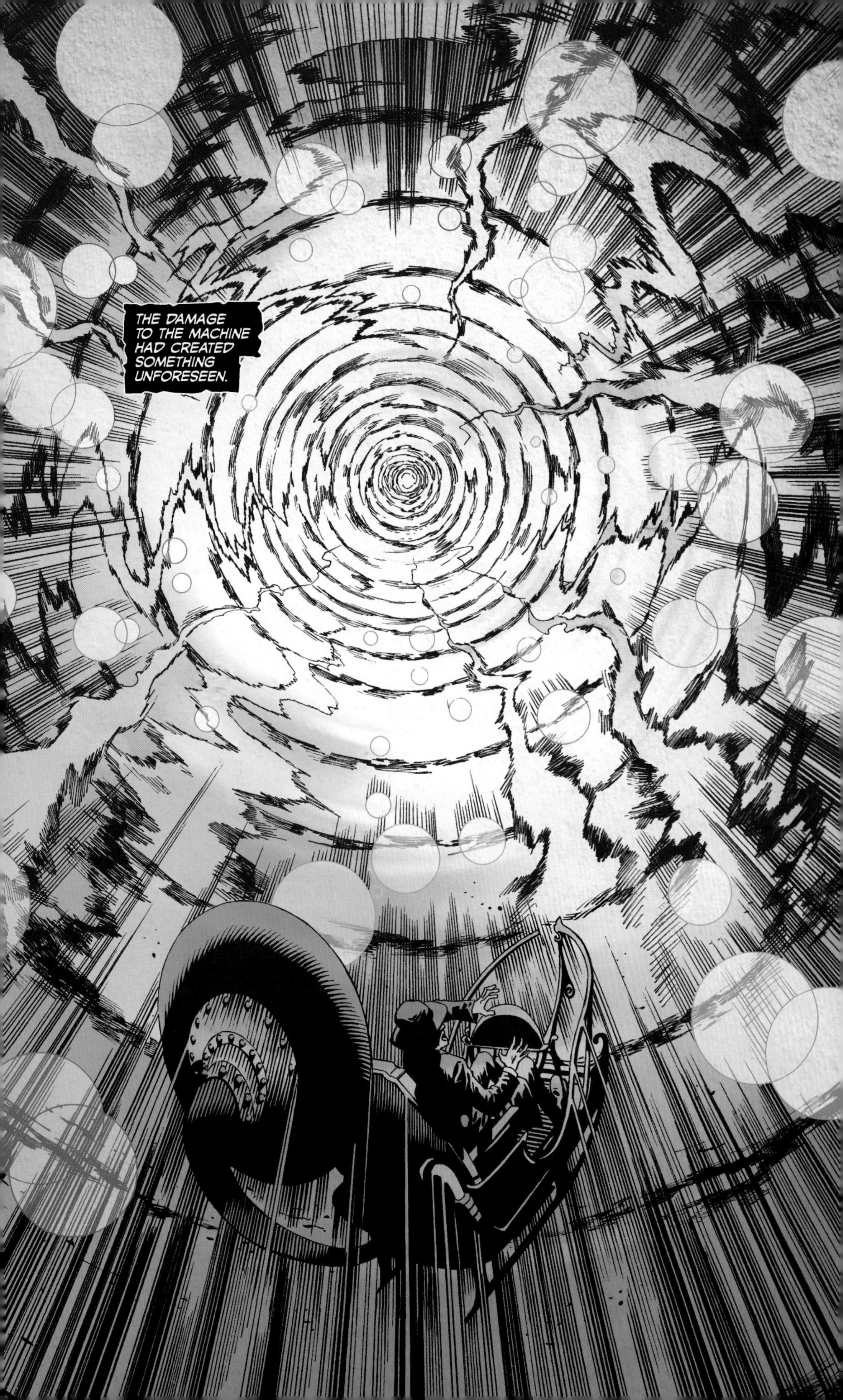
THE DAMAGE TO THE MACHINE HAD CREATED SOMETHING UNFORESEEN.

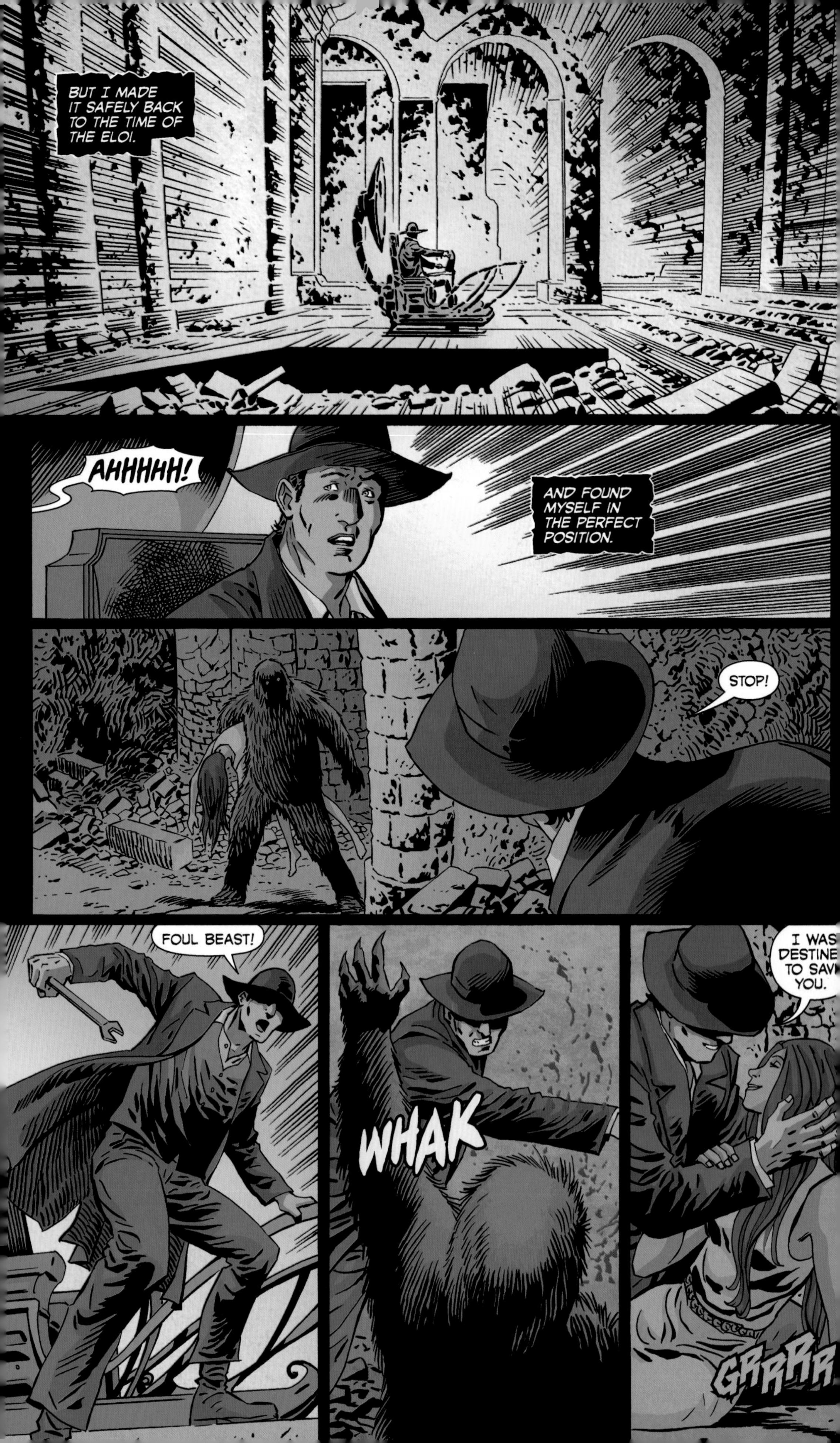
BUT I MADE IT SAFELY BACK TO THE TIME OF THE ELOI.
AHHHHH!
AND FOUND MYSELF IN THE PERFECT POSITION.
STOP!
FOUL BEAST!
WHAK
GRRRR

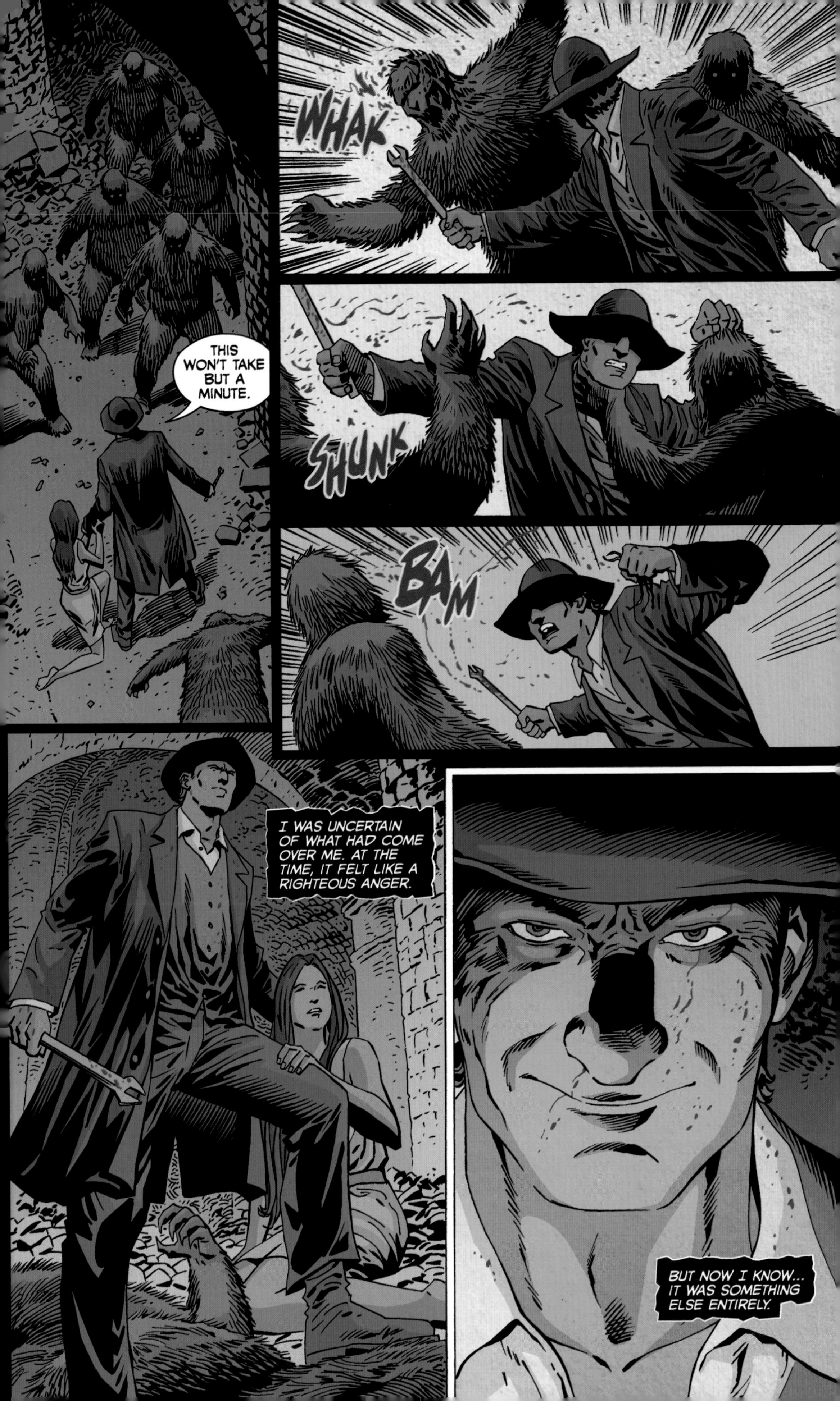

THIS WON'T TAKE BUT A MINUTE.
WHAK
SHUNK
BAM
I WAS UNCERTAIN OF WHAT HAD COME OVER ME. AT THE TIME, IT FELT LIKE A RIGHTEOUS ANGER.
BUT NOW I KNOW... IT WAS SOMETHING ELSE ENTIRELY.

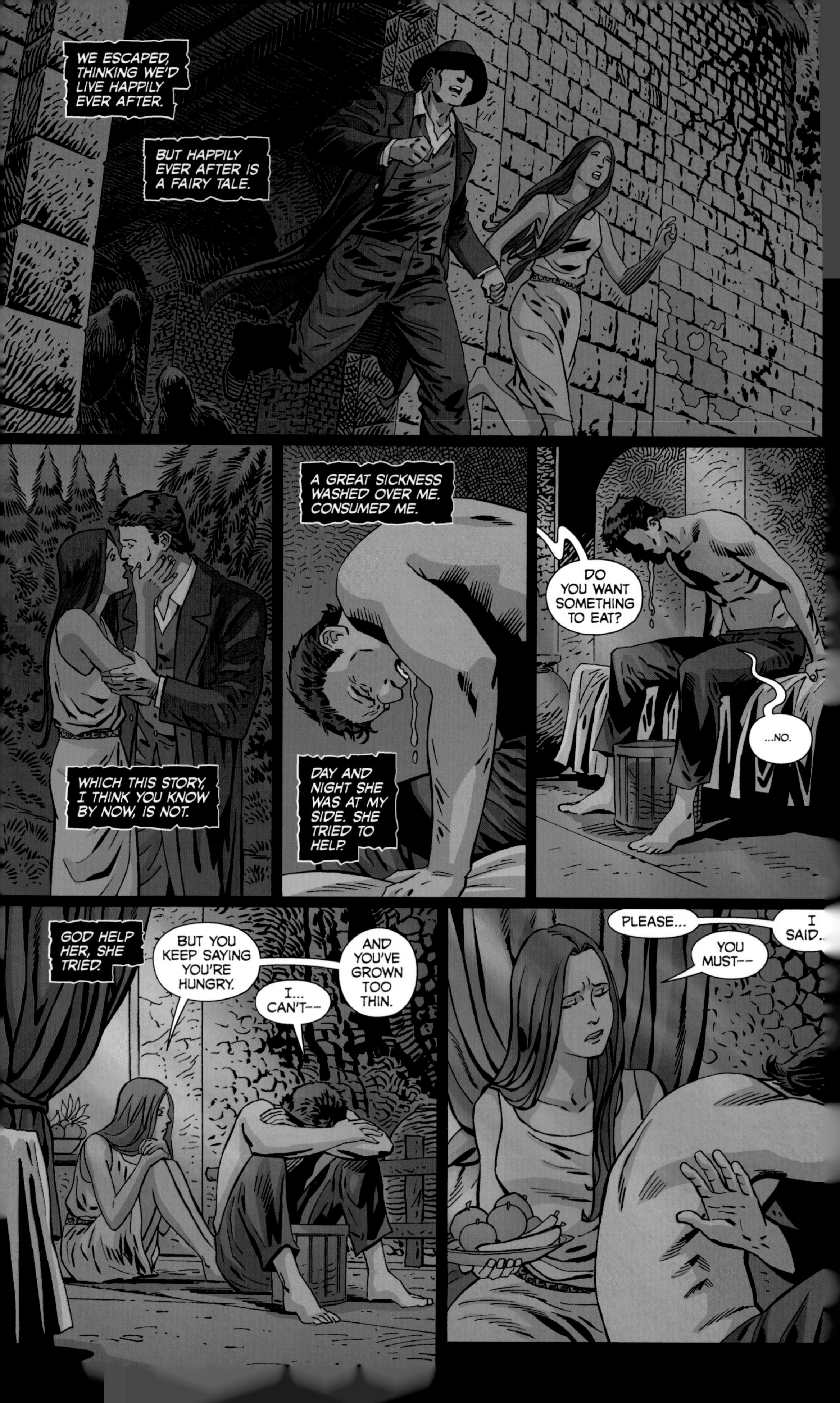
WE ESCAPED, THINKING WE'D LIVE HAPPILY EVER AFTER.
BUT HAPPILY EVER AFTER IS A FAIRY TALE.
WHICH THIS STORY, I THINK YOU KNOW BY NOW, IS NOT.
A GREAT SICKNESS WASHED OVER ME. CONSUMED ME.
DAY AND NIGHT SHE WAS AT MY SIDE. SHE TRIED TO HELP.
DO YOU WANT SOMETHING TO EAT?
...NO.
GOD HELP HER, SHE TRIED.
BUT YOU KEEP SAYING YOU'RE HUNGRY.
AND YOU'VE GROWN TOO THIN.
I... CAN'T--
PLEASE...
YOU MUST--
I SAID.

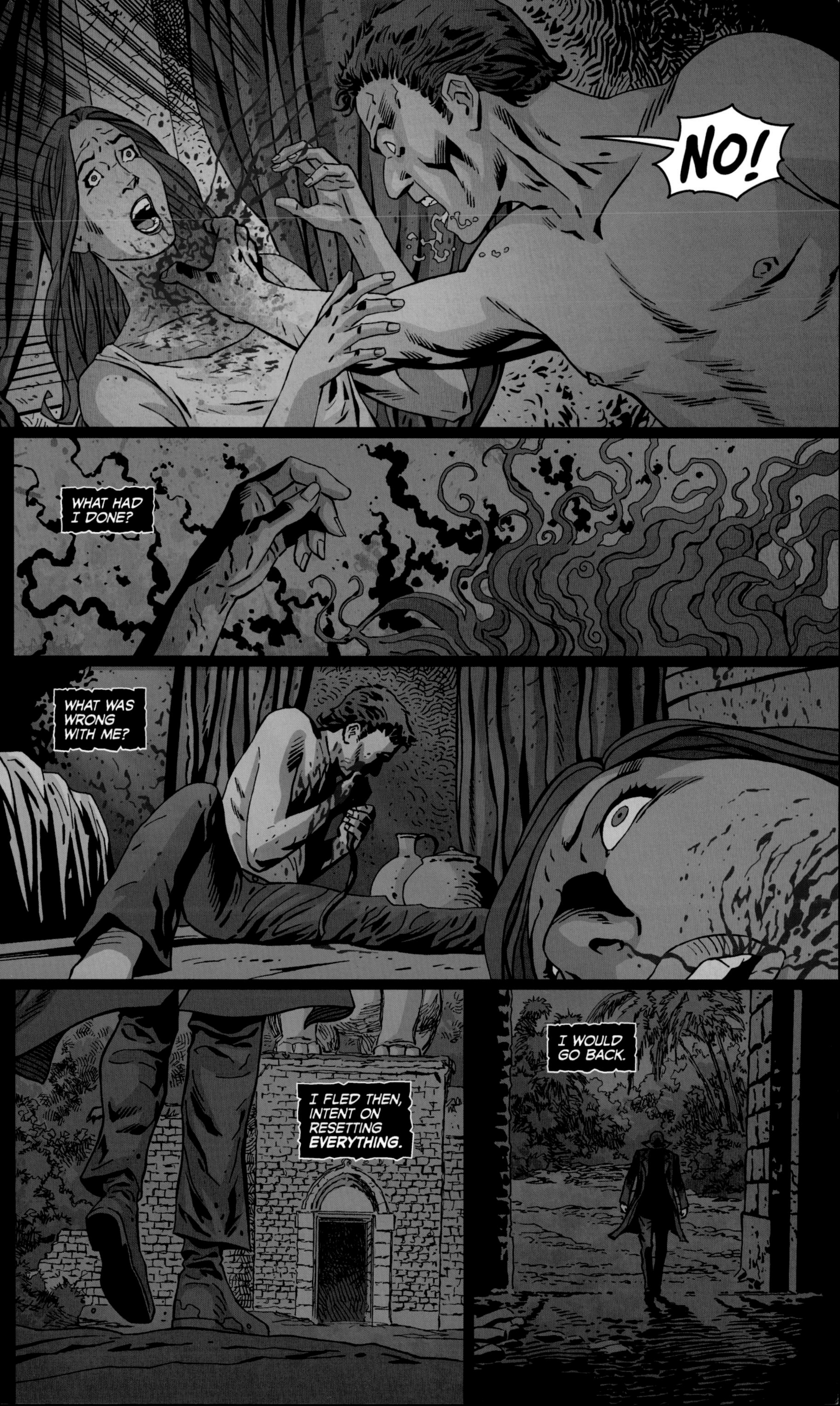
NO!
WHAT HAD I DONE?
WHAT WAS WRONG WITH ME?
I FLED THEN, INTENT ON RESETTING EVERYTHING.
I WOULD GO BACK.

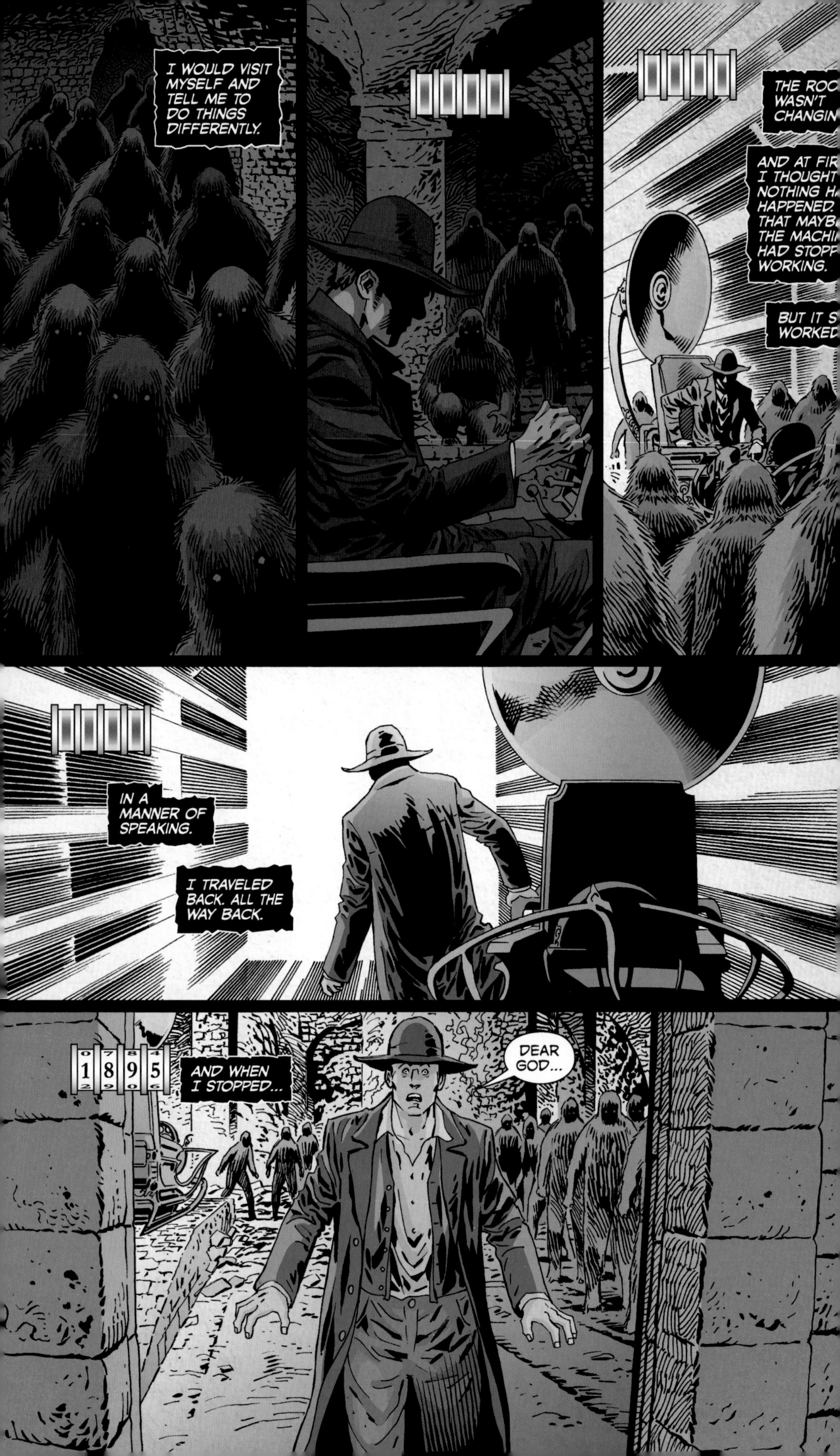

I WOULD VISIT MYSELF AND TELL ME TO DO THINGS DIFFERENTLY.
THE ROO
WASN'T CHANGIN
AND AT FIR
I THOUGHT
NOTHING HA
HAPPENED.
THAT MAYB
THE MACHI
HAD STOPP
WORKING.
BUT IT S
WORKED
IN A MANNER OF SPEAKING.
I TRAVELED BACK. ALL THE WAY BACK.
1895
AND WHEN I STOPPED...
DEAR GOD...

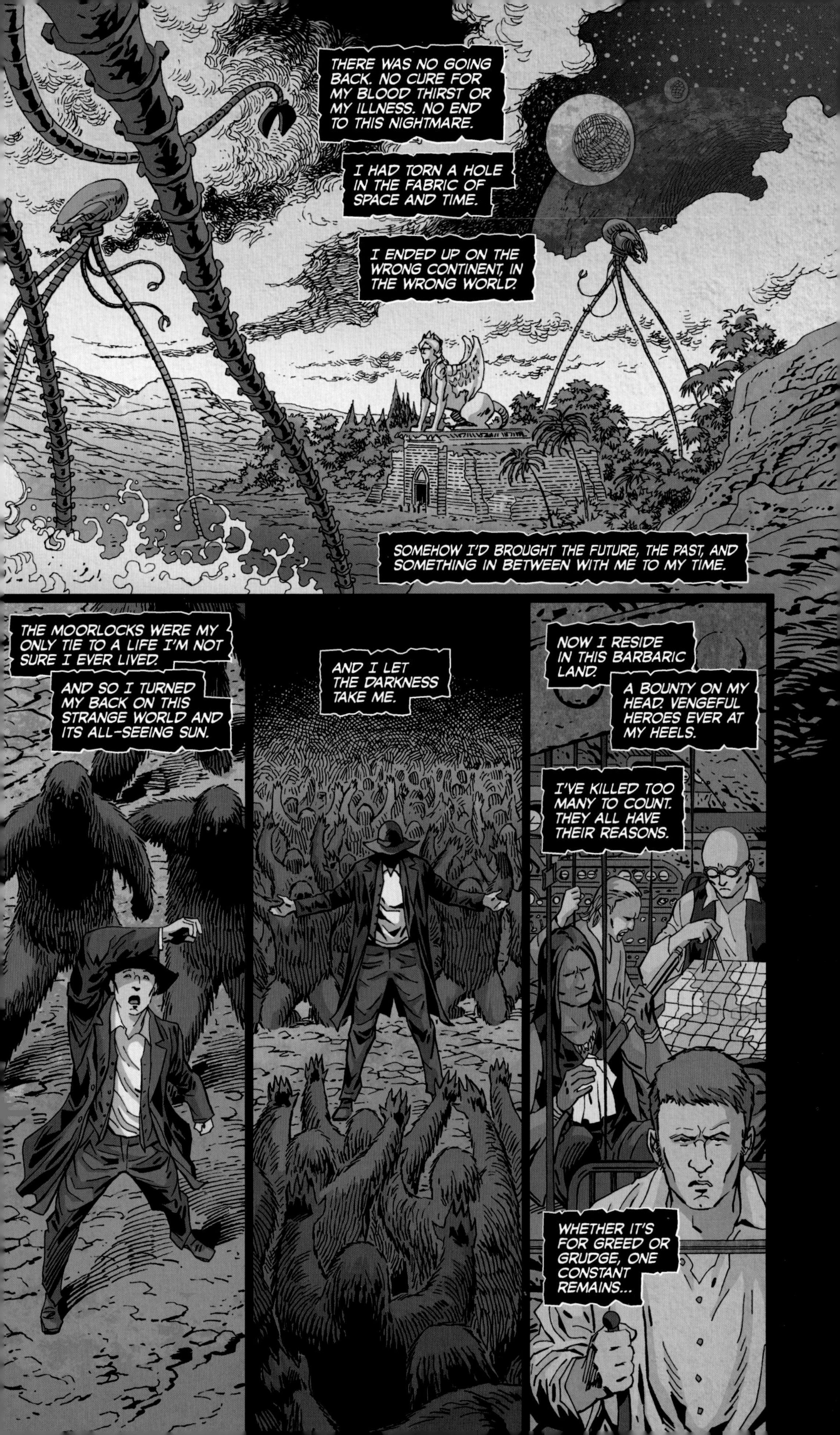
THERE WAS NO GOING BACK. NO CURE FOR MY BLOOD THIRST OR MY ILLNESS. NO END TO THIS NIGHTMARE.
I HAD TORN A HOLE IN THE FABRIC OF SPACE AND TIME.
I ENDED UP ON THE WRONG CONTINENT, IN THE WRONG WORLD.
SOMEHOW I'D BROUGHT THE FUTURE, THE PAST, AND SOMETHING IN BETWEEN WITH ME TO MY TIME.
THE MOORLOCKS WERE MY ONLY TIE TO A LIFE I'M NOT SURE I EVER LIVED.
AND SO I TURNED MY BACK ON THIS STRANGE WORLD AND ITS ALL-SEEING SUN.
AND I LET THE DARKNESS TAKE ME.
NOW I RESIDE IN THIS BARBARIC LAND.
A BOUNTY ON MY HEAD. VENGEFUL HEROES EVER AT MY HEELS.
I'VE KILLED TOO MANY TO COUNT. THEY ALL HAVE THEIR REASONS.
WHETHER IT'S FOR GREED OR GRUDGE, ONE CONSTANT REMAINS...

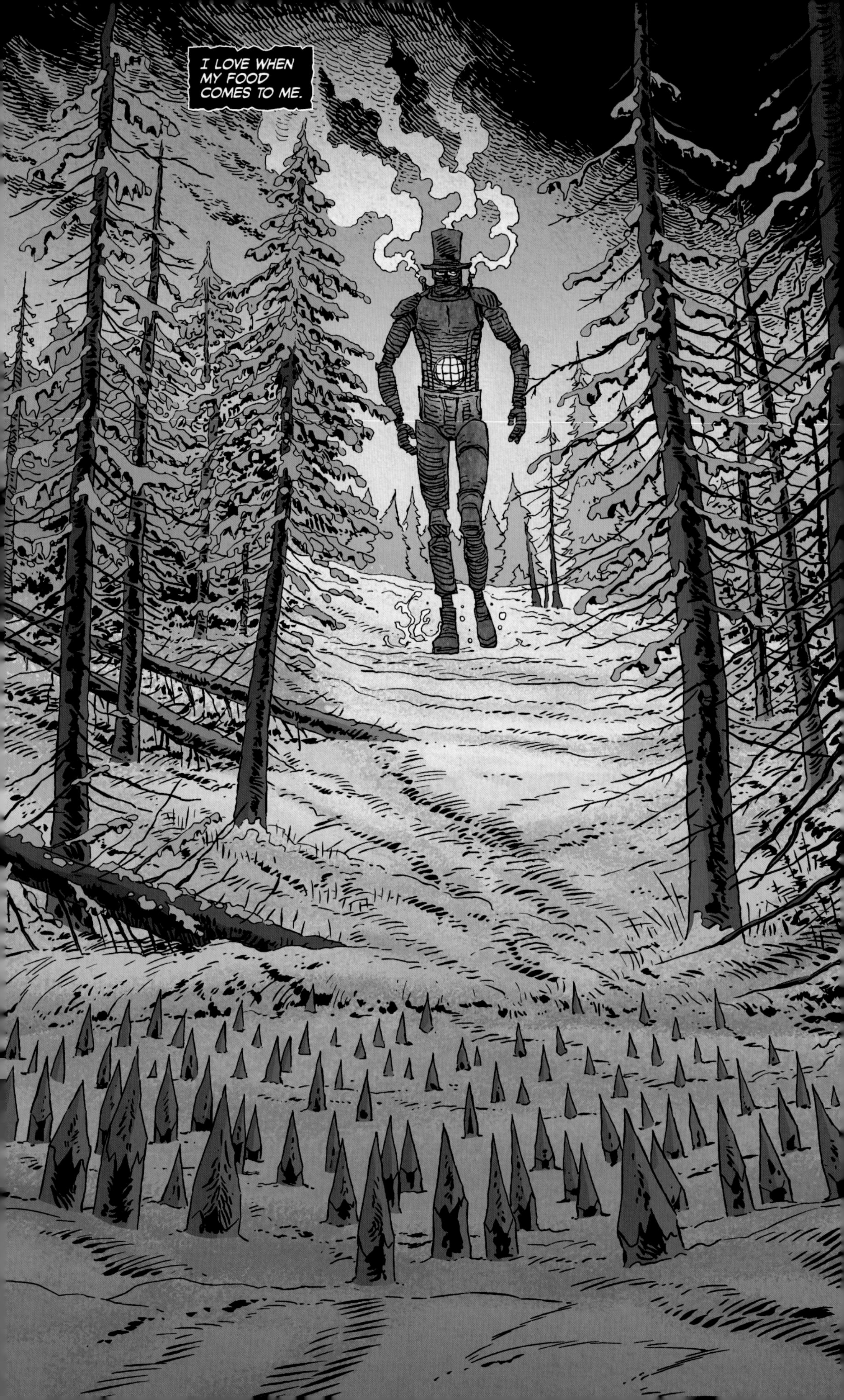
I LOVE WHEN MY FOOD COMES TO ME.

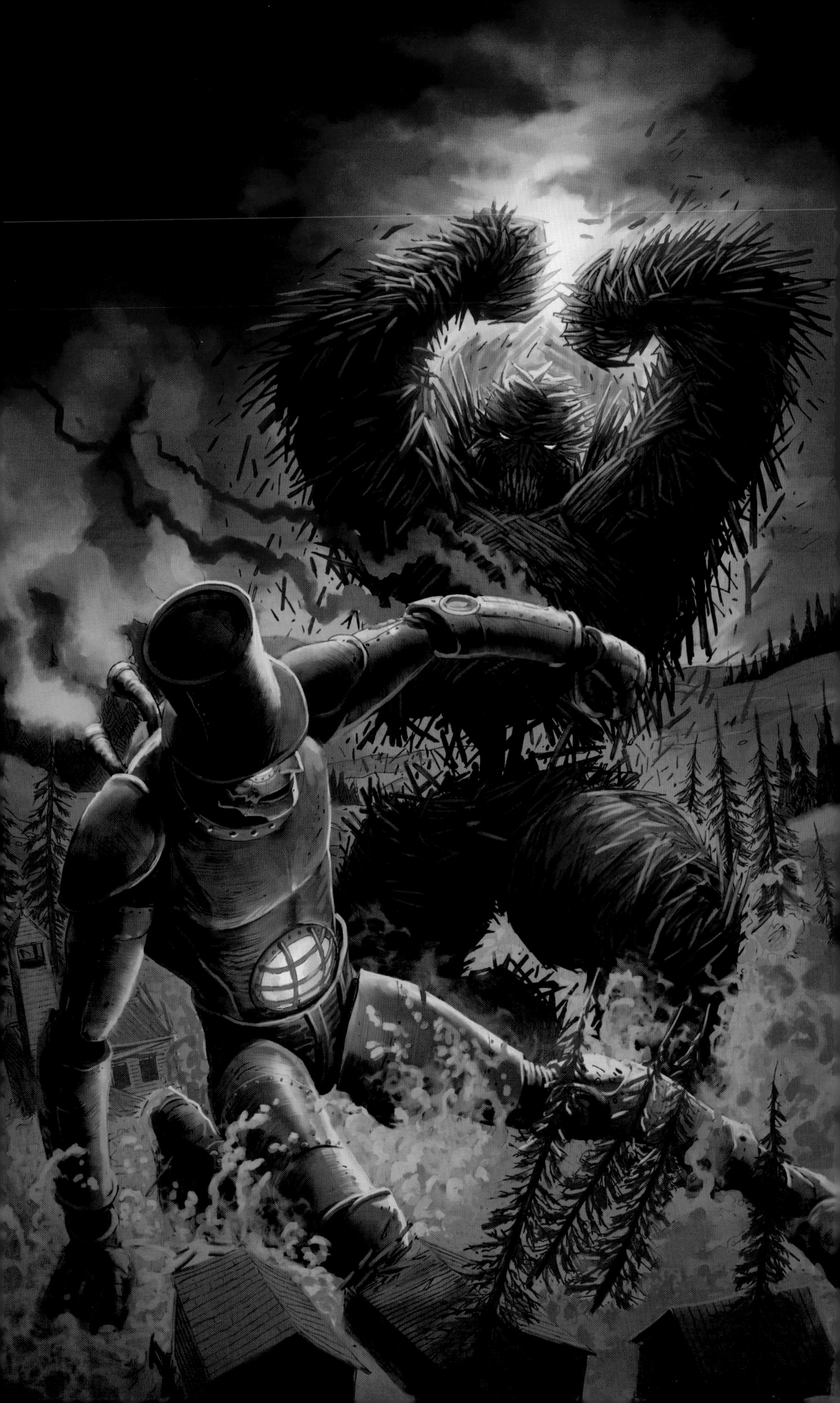

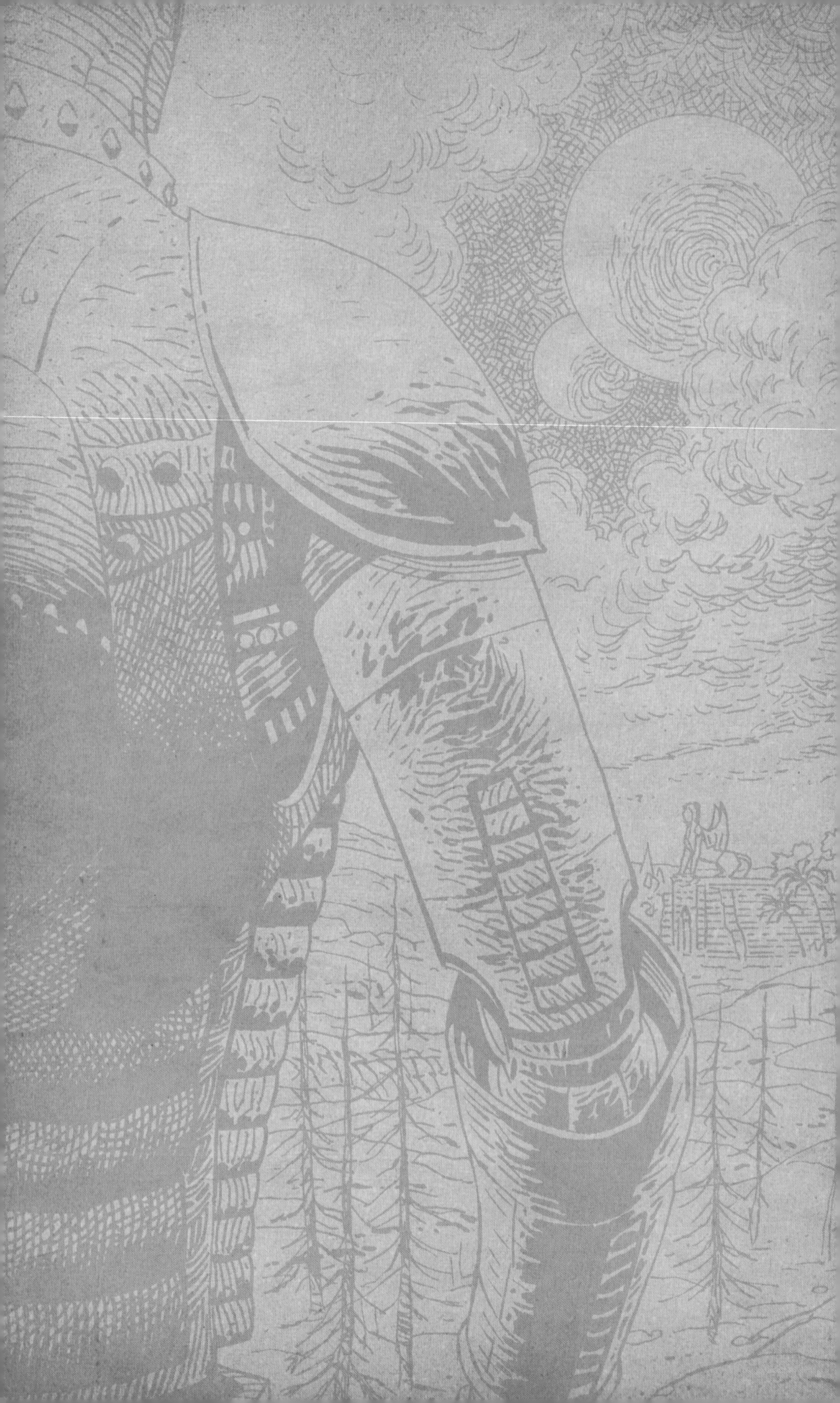

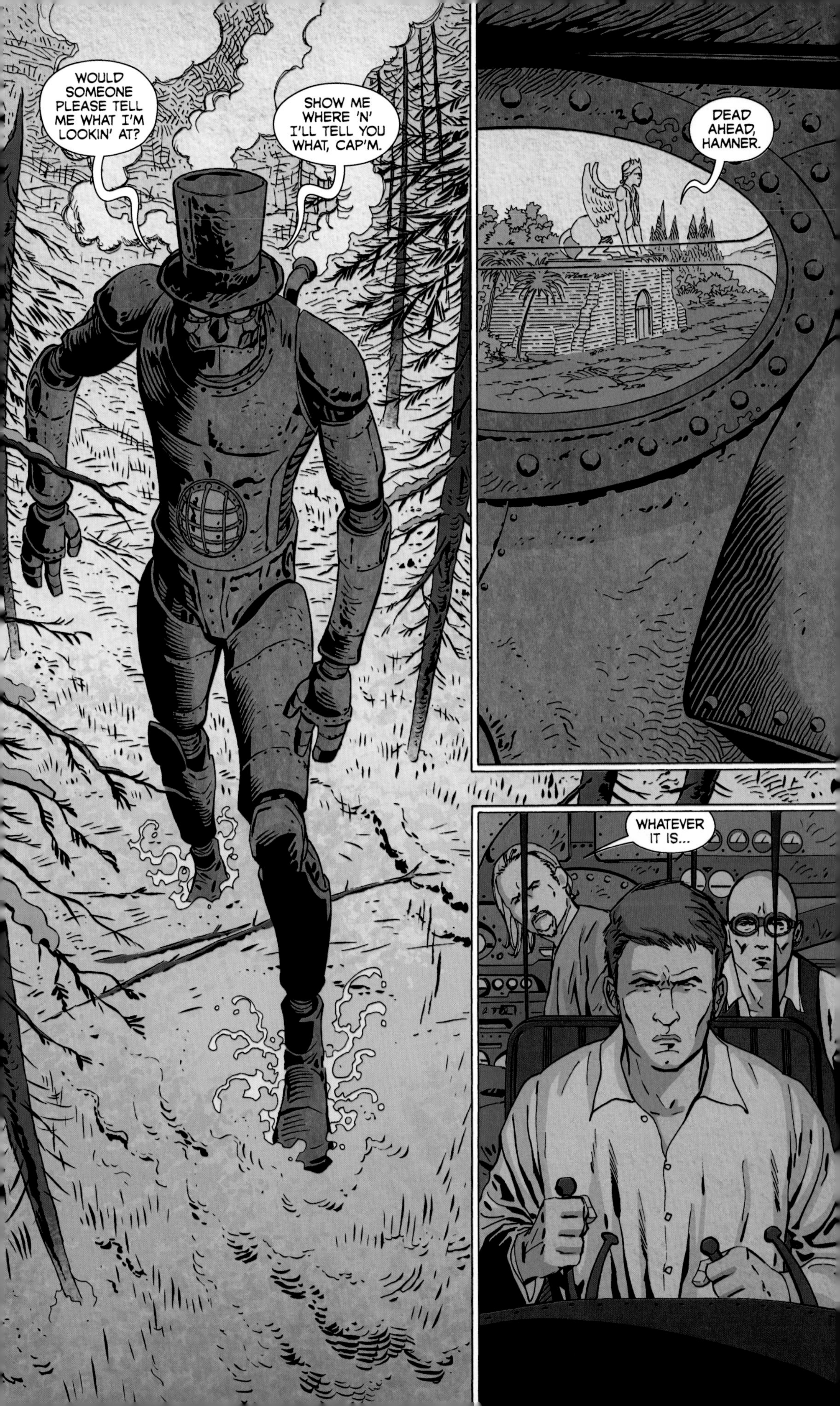
WOULD SOMEONE PLEASE TELL ME WHAT I'M LOOKIN' AT?
SHOW ME WHERE 'N' I'LL TELL YOU WHAT, CAP'M.
DEAD AHEAD, HAMNER.
WHATEVER IT IS...

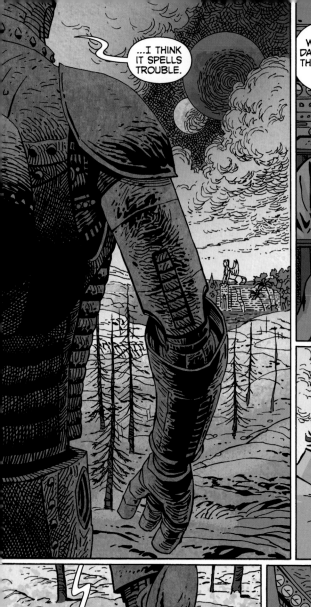

...I THINK IT SPELLS TROUBLE.

IF I WERE THE DARK RIDER, THAT WOULD BE MY DEN.

WELL IF IT AIN'T, I'LL LIKE TO LAY CLAIM TO IT!

HAMNER, WHAT WOULD *YOU* DO WITH A PLACE LIKE *THAT*?

WHAT EVERY MAN'D DO GIVEN HALF THE CHANCE!

NOTHIN'!

SPEAK FOR YOURSELF, HAMNER. I'M A WORKING MAN. I'LL PROBABLY DIE DOING WHAT I LOVE.

AND I WOULDN'T HAVE IT ANY OTHER--

WHAT--

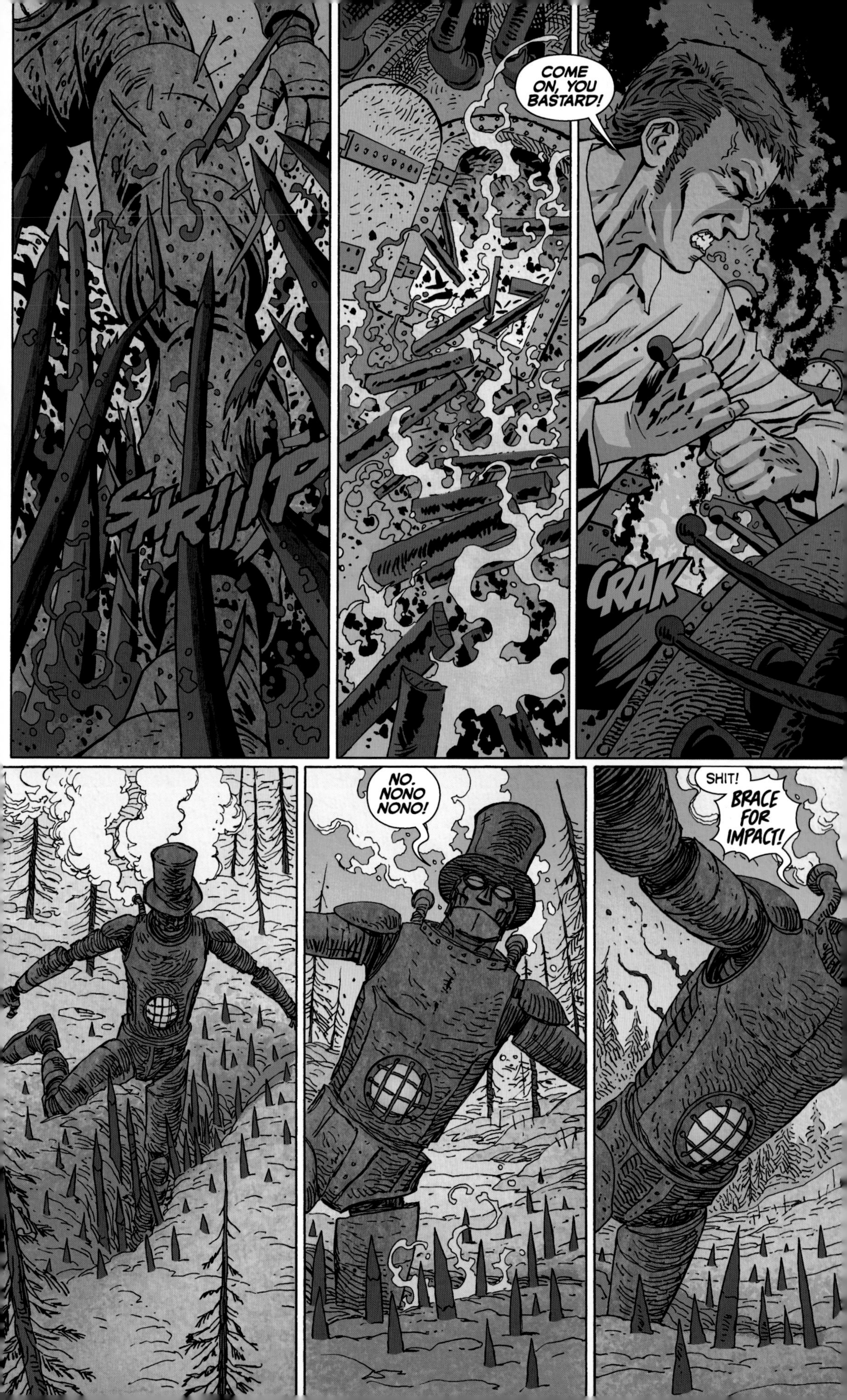
SHRIIIP
COME ON, YOU BASTARD!
CRAK
NO. NONO NONO!
SHIT!
BRACE FOR IMPACT!

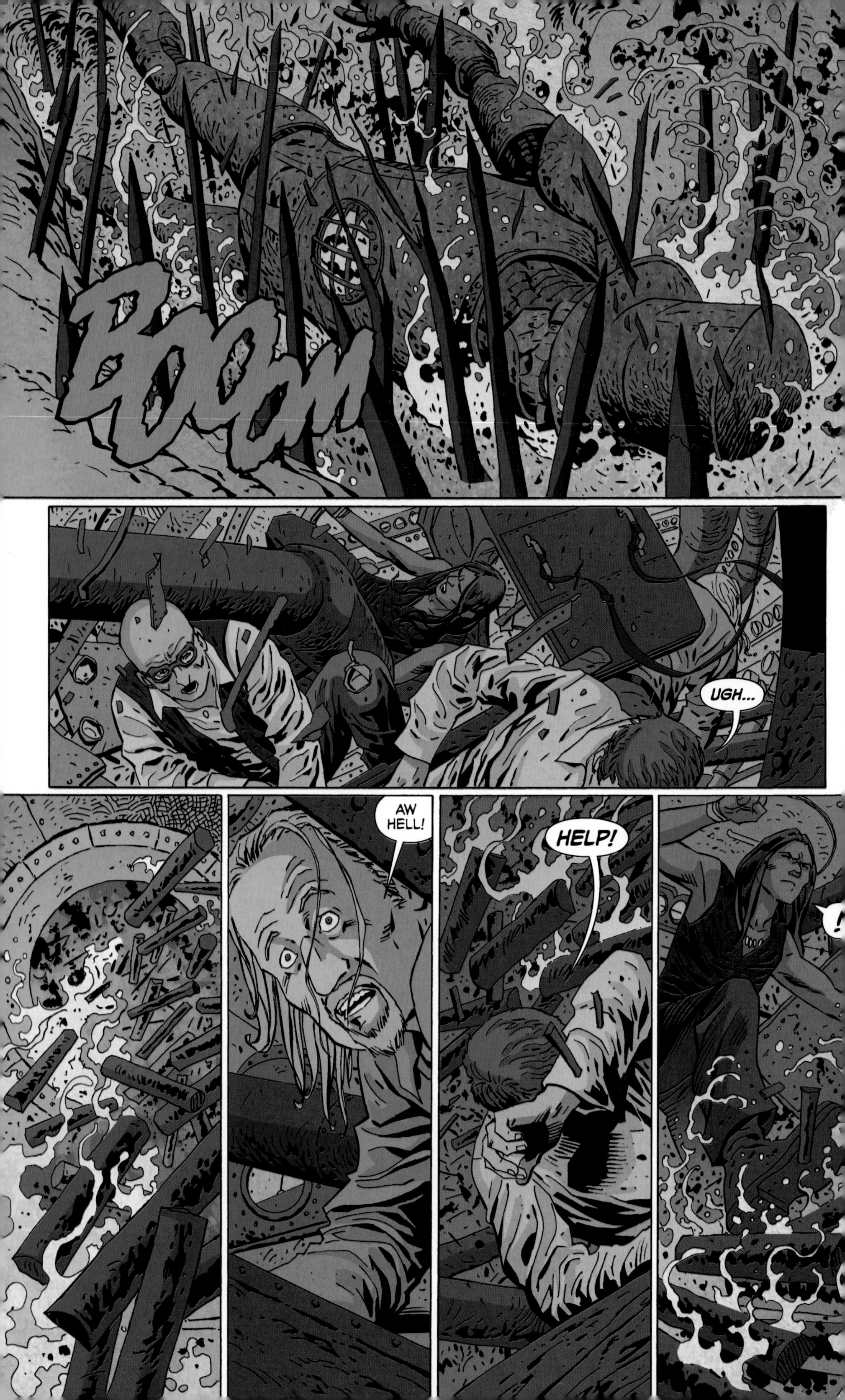
BOOM
UGH...
AW HELL!
HELP!
!

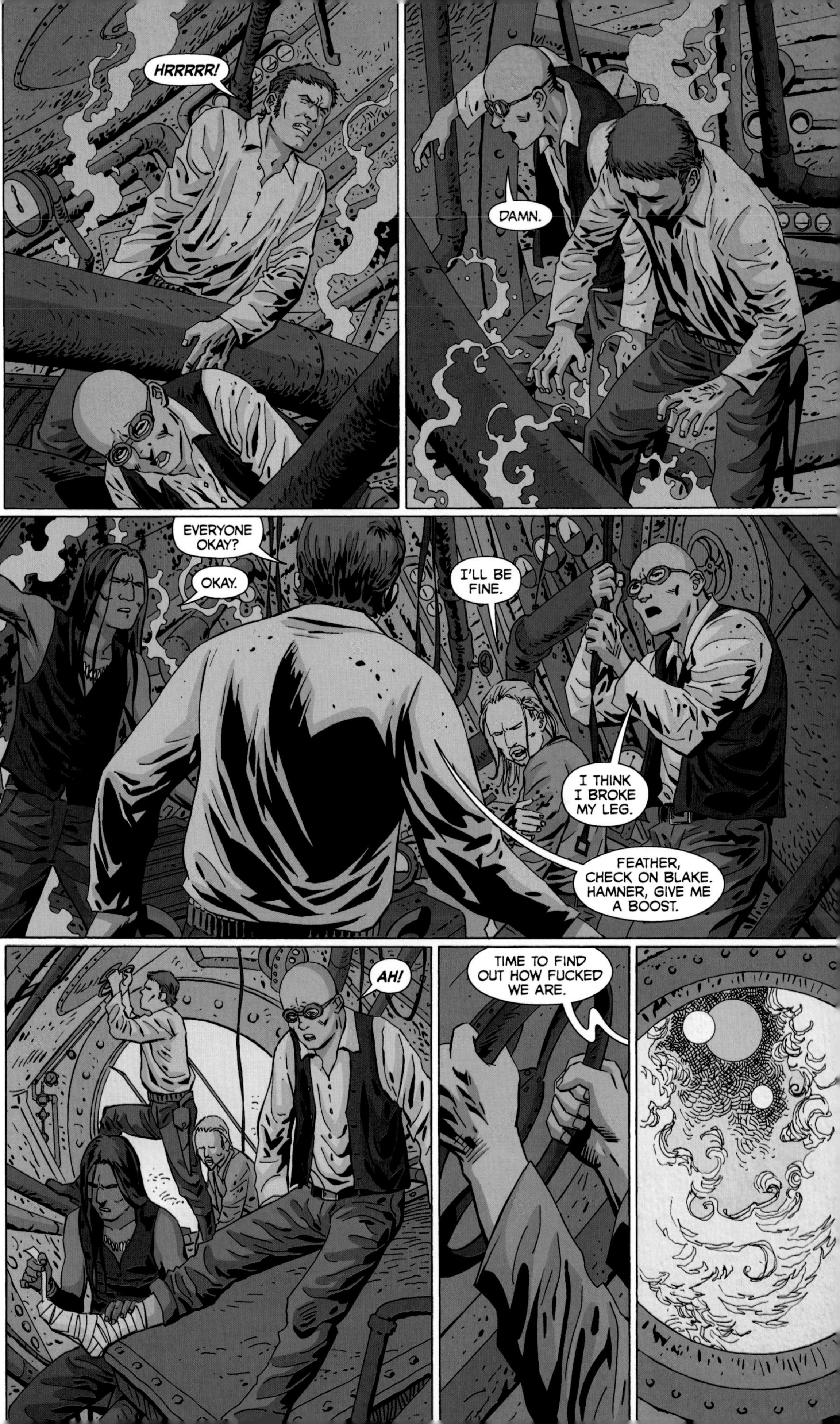
HRRRRR!
DAMN.
EVERYONE OKAY?
OKAY.
I'LL BE FINE.
I THINK I BROKE MY LEG.
FEATHER, CHECK ON BLAKE. HAMNER, GIVE ME A BOOST.
AH!
TIME TO FIND OUT HOW FUCKED WE ARE.

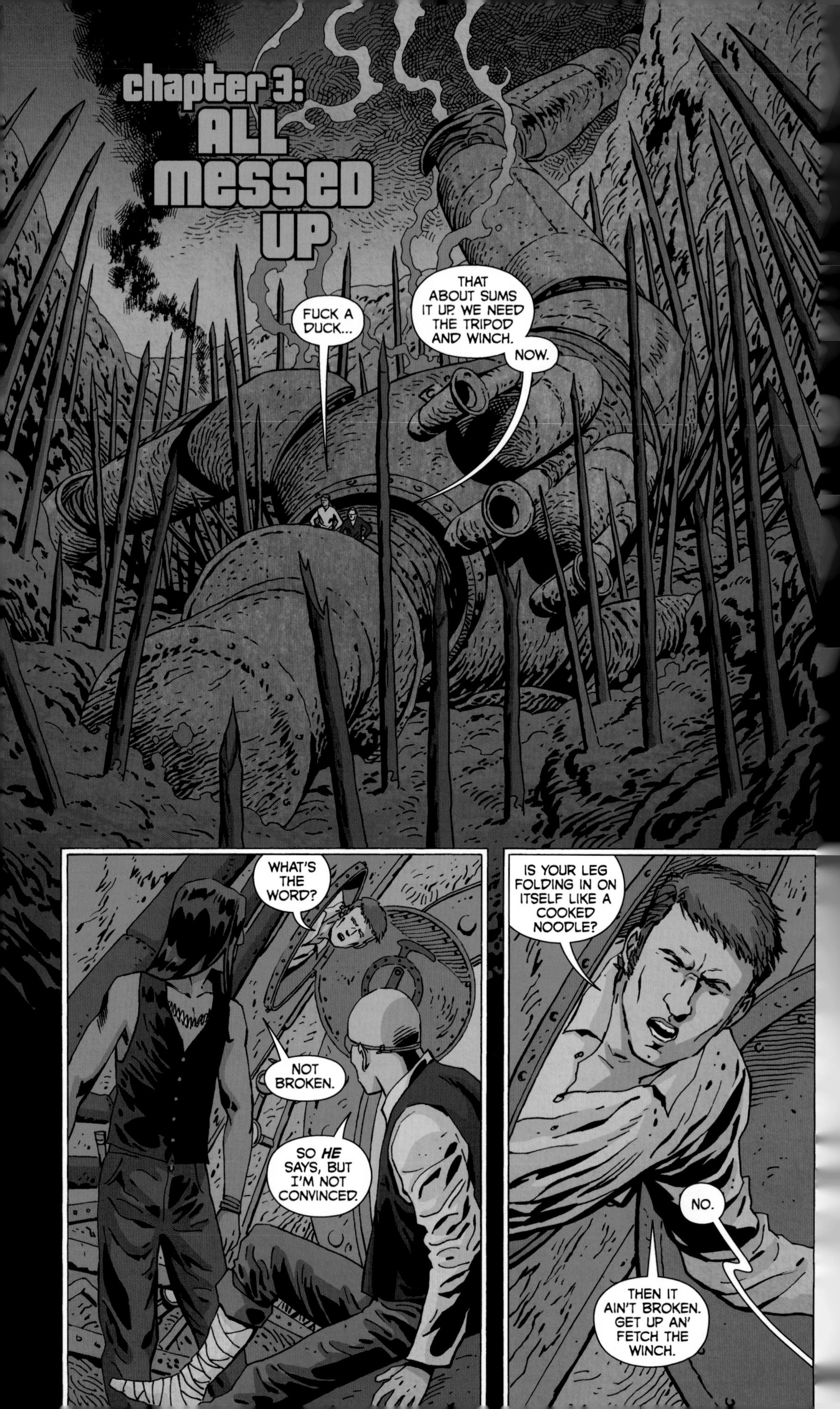
chapter 3:
ALL MESSED UP
FUCK A DUCK...
THAT ABOUT SUMS IT UP. WE NEED THE TRIPOD AND WINCH.
NOW.
WHAT'S THE WORD?
NOT BROKEN.
SO HE SAYS, BUT I'M NOT CONVINCED.
IS YOUR LEG FOLDING IN ON ITSELF LIKE A COOKED NOODLE?
NO.
THEN IT AIN'T BROKEN. GET UP AN' FETCH THE WINCH.

LAST ONE.

LET'S GET TO WORK.

PUSH!

PUSH!

ALMOST!

JUST. ONE. MORE--

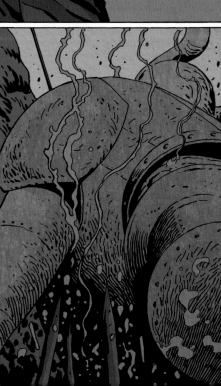

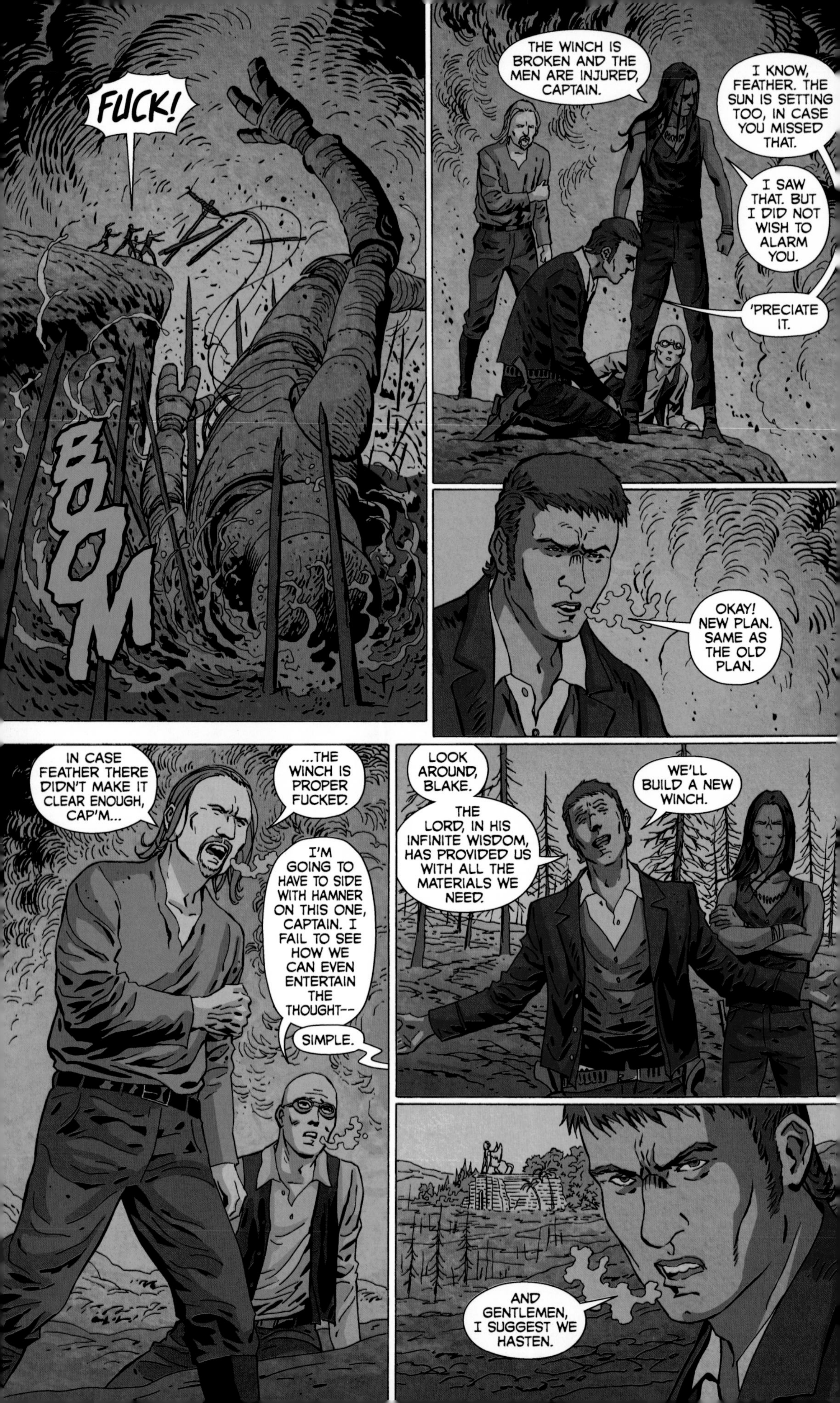
FUCK!
BOOM
THE WINCH IS BROKEN AND THE MEN ARE INJURED, CAPTAIN.
I KNOW, FEATHER. THE SUN IS SETTING TOO, IN CASE YOU MISSED THAT.
I SAW THAT. BUT I DID NOT WISH TO ALARM YOU.
'PRECIATE IT.
OKAY! NEW PLAN. SAME AS THE OLD PLAN.
IN CASE FEATHER THERE DIDN'T MAKE IT CLEAR ENOUGH, CAP'M...
...THE WINCH IS PROPER FUCKED.
I'M GOING TO HAVE TO SIDE WITH HAMNER ON THIS ONE, CAPTAIN. I FAIL TO SEE HOW WE CAN EVEN ENTERTAIN THE THOUGHT--
SIMPLE.
LOOK AROUND, BLAKE.
THE LORD, IN HIS INFINITE WISDOM, HAS PROVIDED US WITH ALL THE MATERIALS WE NEED.
WE'LL BUILD A NEW WINCH.
AND GENTLEMEN, I SUGGEST WE HASTEN.

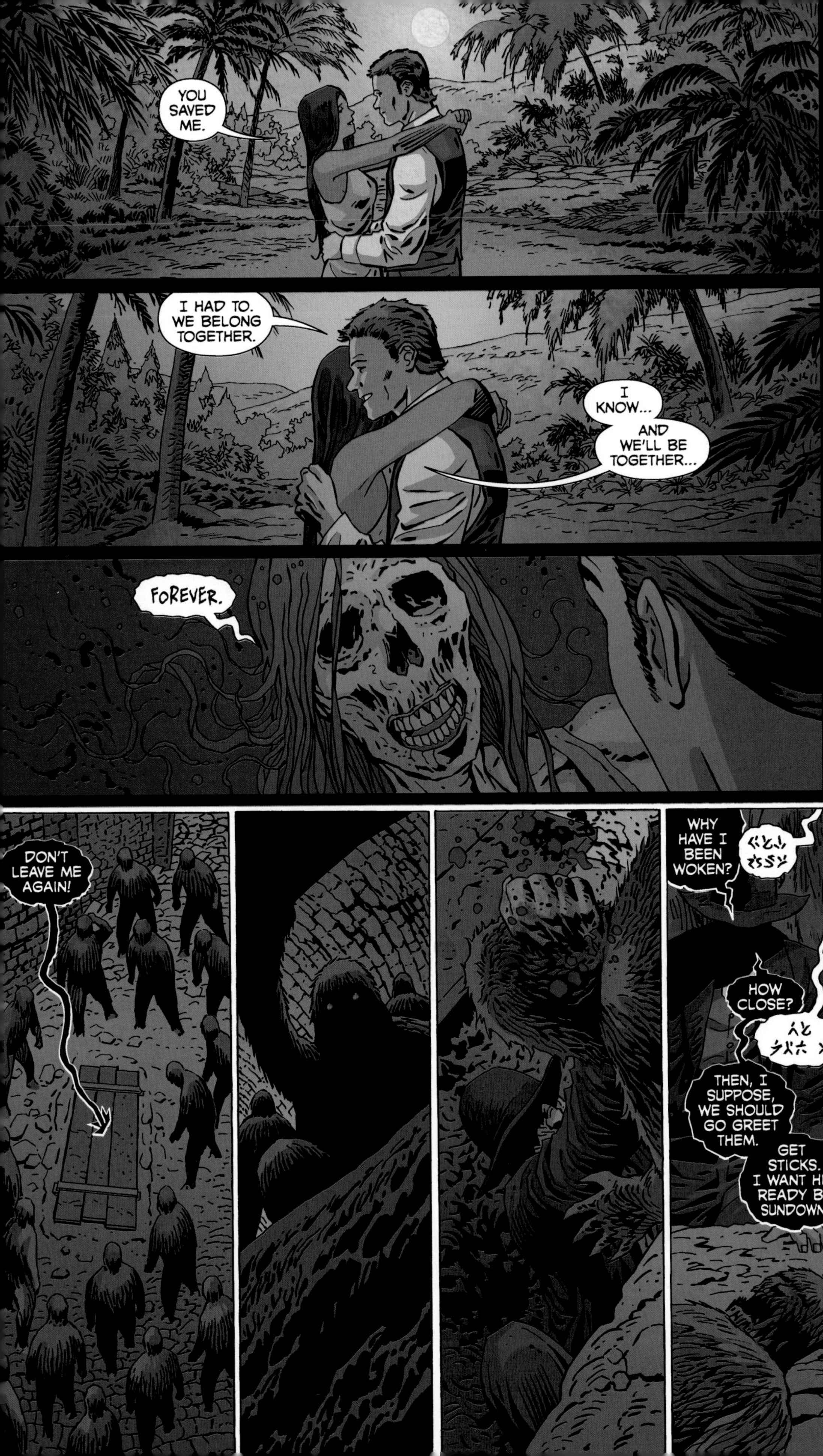
YOU SAVED ME.
I HAD TO. WE BELONG TOGETHER.
I KNOW...
AND WE'LL BE TOGETHER...
FOREVER.
DON'T LEAVE ME AGAIN!
WHY HAVE I BEEN WOKEN?
HOW CLOSE?
THEN, I SUPPOSE, WE SHOULD GO GREET THEM.
GET STICKS. I WANT HIM READY BY SUNDOWN.

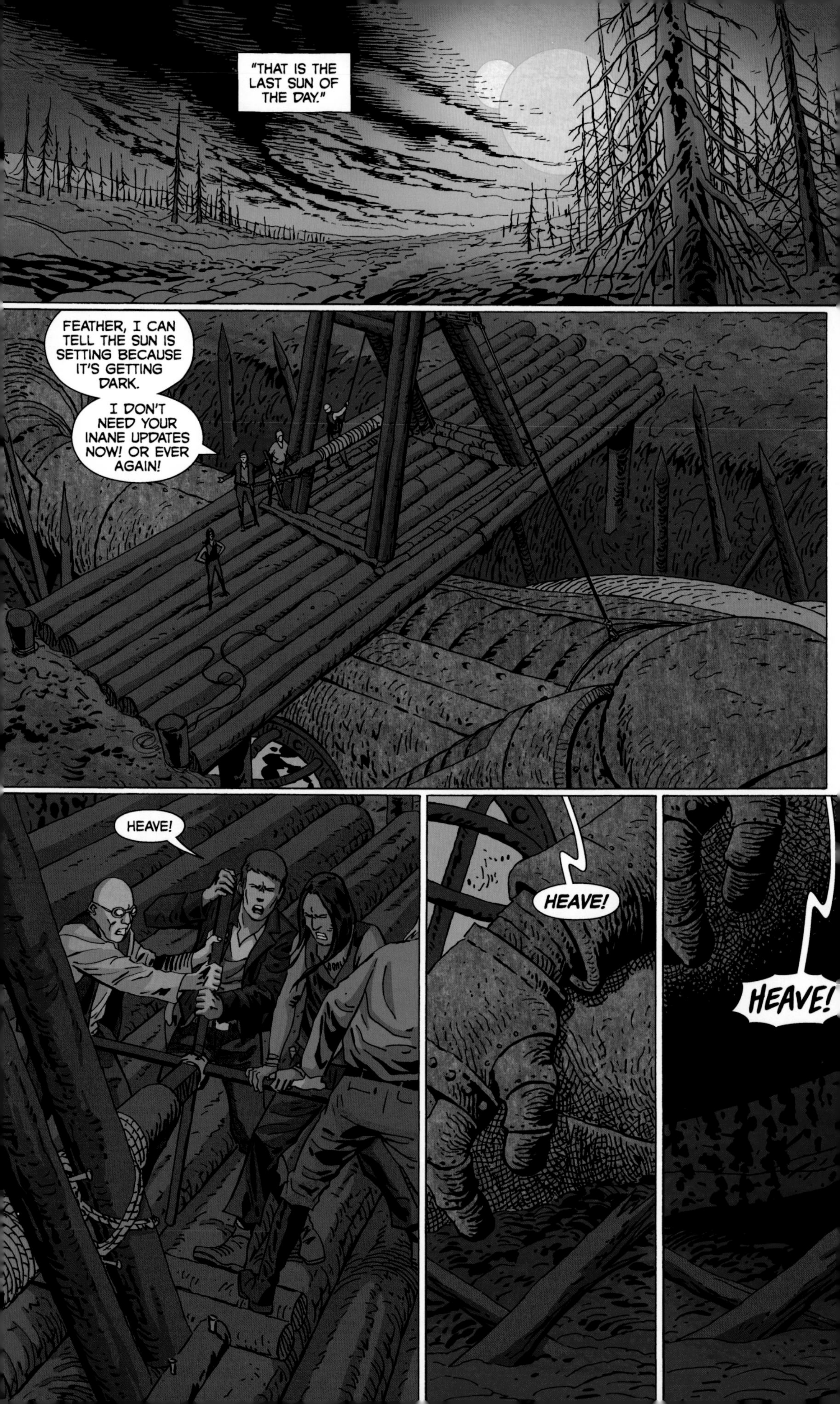
"THAT IS THE LAST SUN OF THE DAY."
FEATHER, I CAN TELL THE SUN IS SETTING BECAUSE IT'S GETTING DARK.
I DON'T NEED YOUR INANE UPDATES NOW! OR EVER AGAIN!
HEAVE!
HEAVE!
HEAVE!

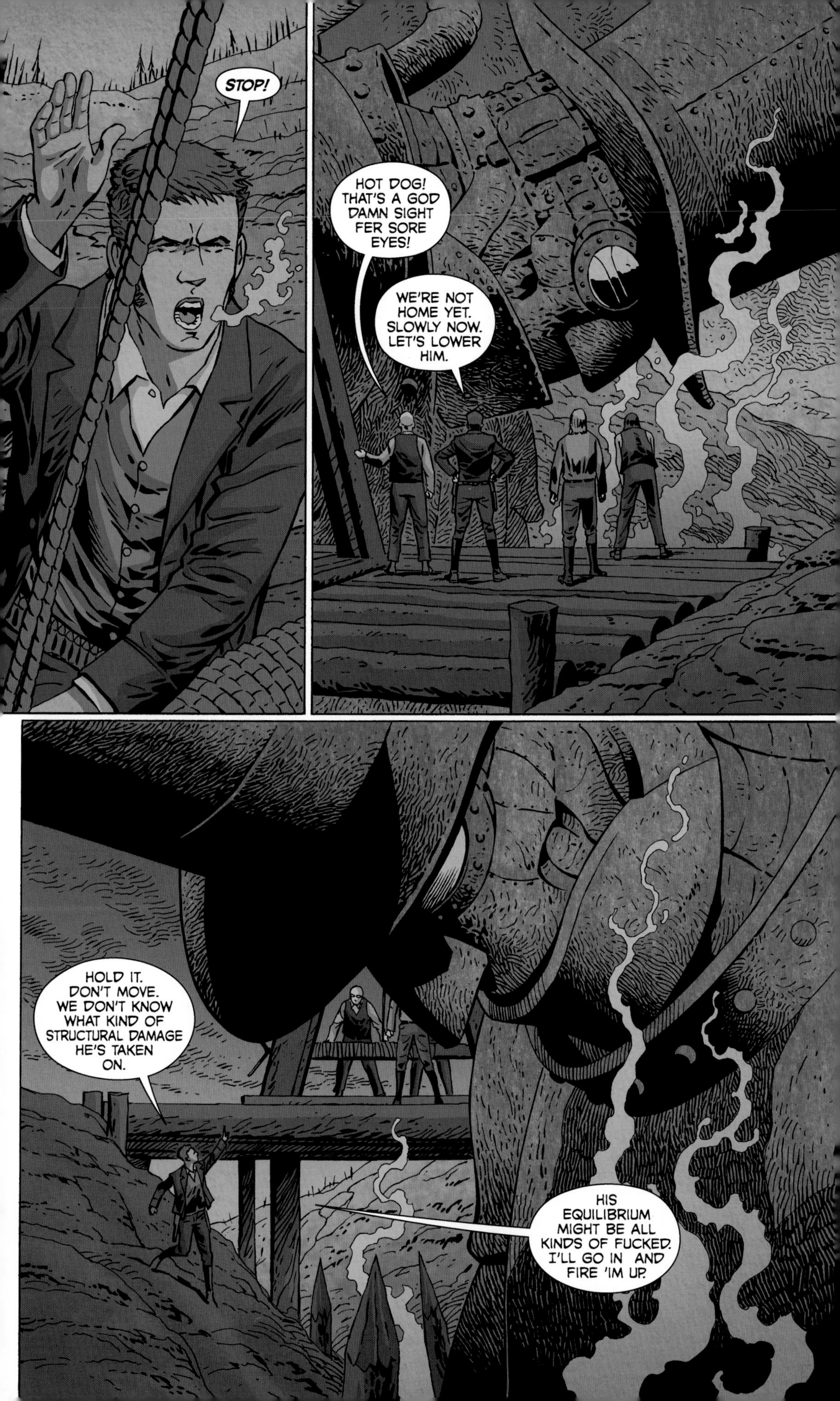
STOP!
HOT DOG! THAT'S A GOD DAMN SIGHT FER SORE EYES!
WE'RE NOT HOME YET. SLOWLY NOW. LET'S LOWER HIM.
HOLD IT. DON'T MOVE. WE DON'T KNOW WHAT KIND OF STRUCTURAL DAMAGE HE'S TAKEN ON.
HIS EQUILIBRIUM MIGHT BE ALL KINDS OF FUCKED. I'LL GO IN AND FIRE 'IM UP.

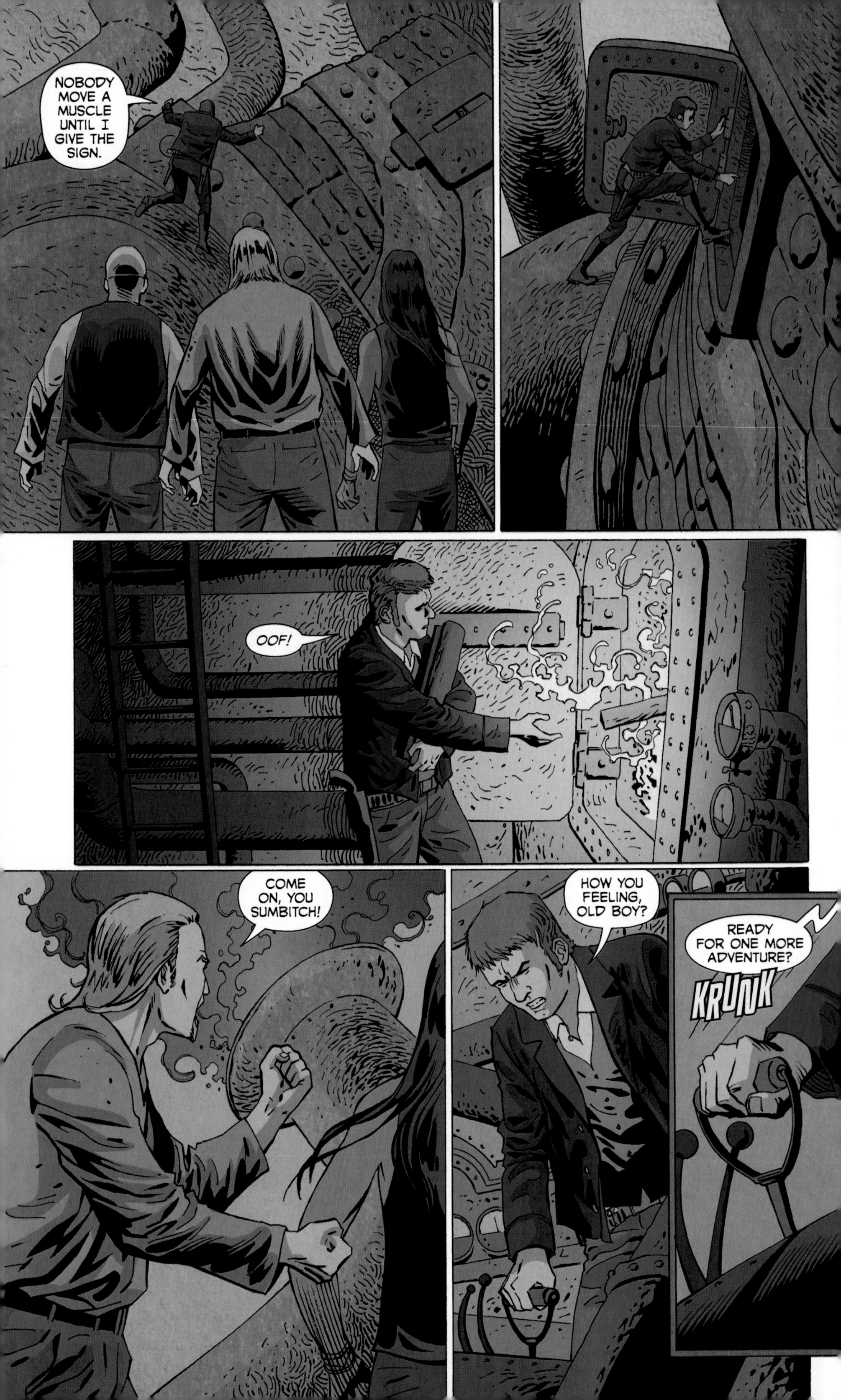
NOBODY MOVE A MUSCLE UNTIL I GIVE THE SIGN.
OOF!
COME ON, YOU SUMBITCH!
HOW YOU FEELING, OLD BOY?
READY FOR ONE MORE ADVENTURE?
KRUNK

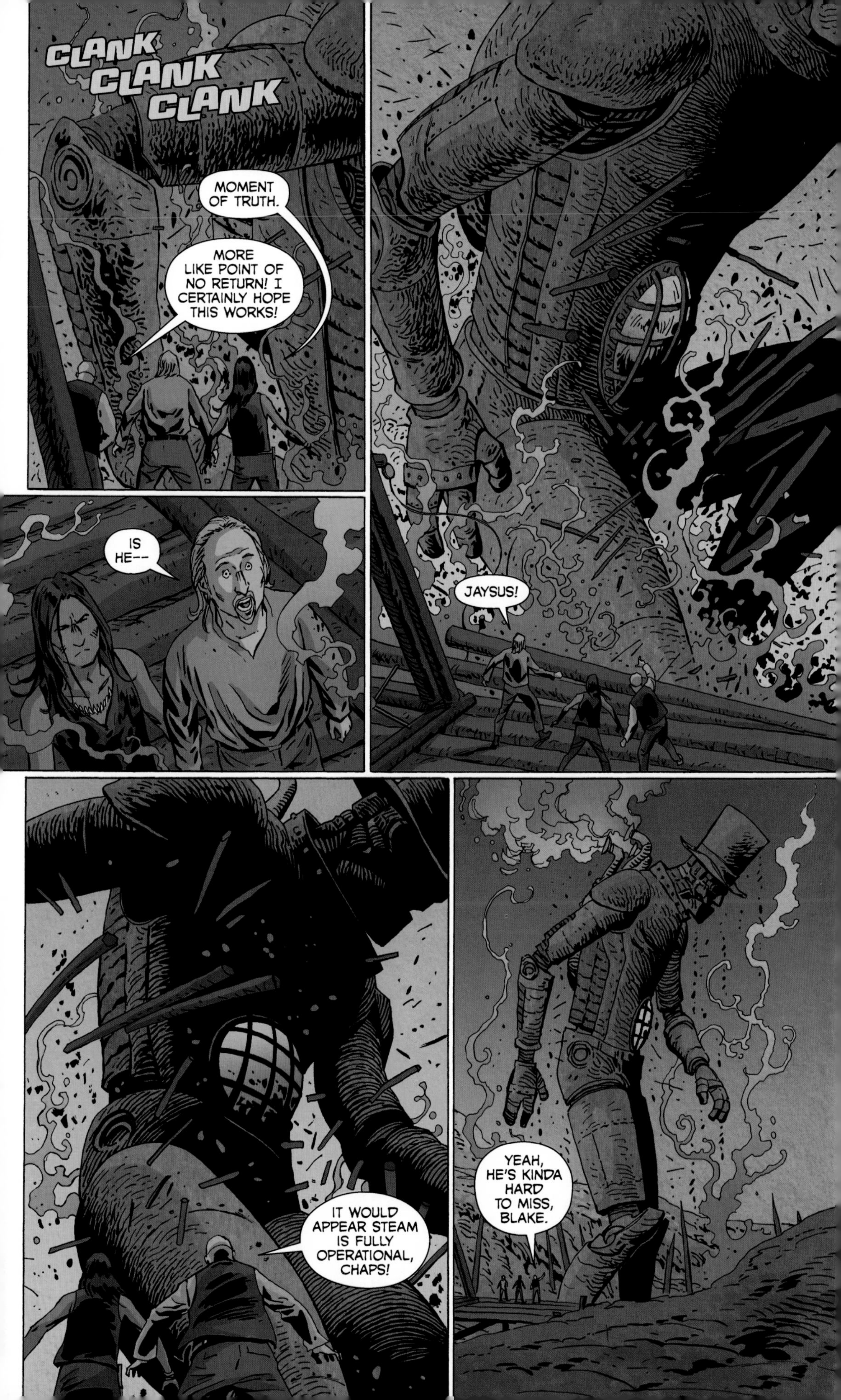
CLANK CLANK CLANK
MOMENT OF TRUTH.
MORE LIKE POINT OF NO RETURN! I CERTAINLY HOPE THIS WORKS!
IS HE--
JAYSUS!
IT WOULD APPEAR STEAM IS FULLY OPERATIONAL, CHAPS!
YEAH, HE'S KINDA HARD TO MISS, BLAKE.

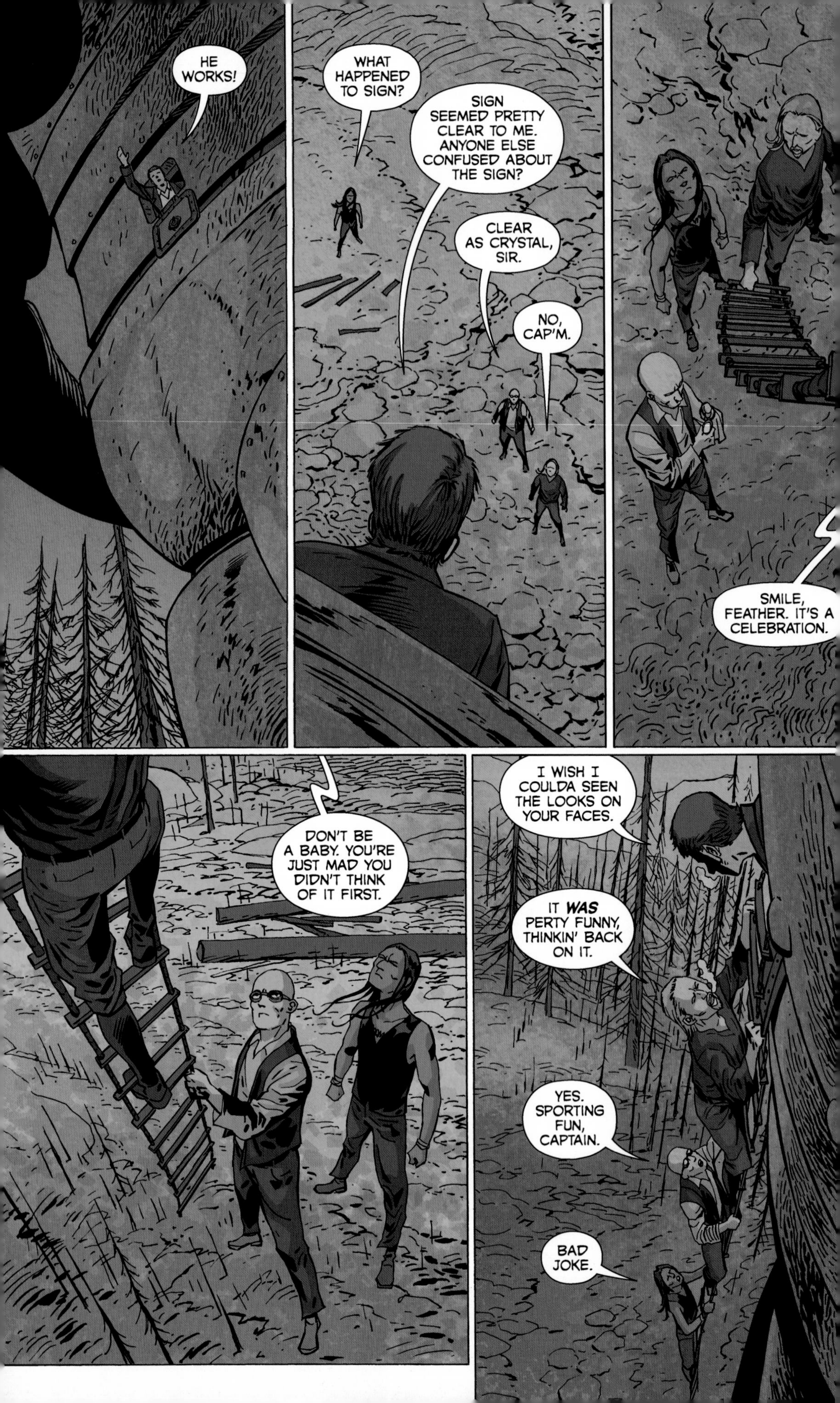
HE WORKS!
WHAT HAPPENED TO SIGN?
SIGN SEEMED PRETTY CLEAR TO ME. ANYONE ELSE CONFUSED ABOUT THE SIGN?
CLEAR AS CRYSTAL, SIR.
NO, CAP'M.
SMILE, FEATHER. IT'S A CELEBRATION.
DON'T BE A BABY. YOU'RE JUST MAD YOU DIDN'T THINK OF IT FIRST.
I WISH I COULDA SEEN THE LOOKS ON YOUR FACES.
IT ***WAS*** PERTY FUNNY, THINKIN' BACK ON IT.
YES. SPORTING FUN, CAPTAIN.
BAD JOKE.

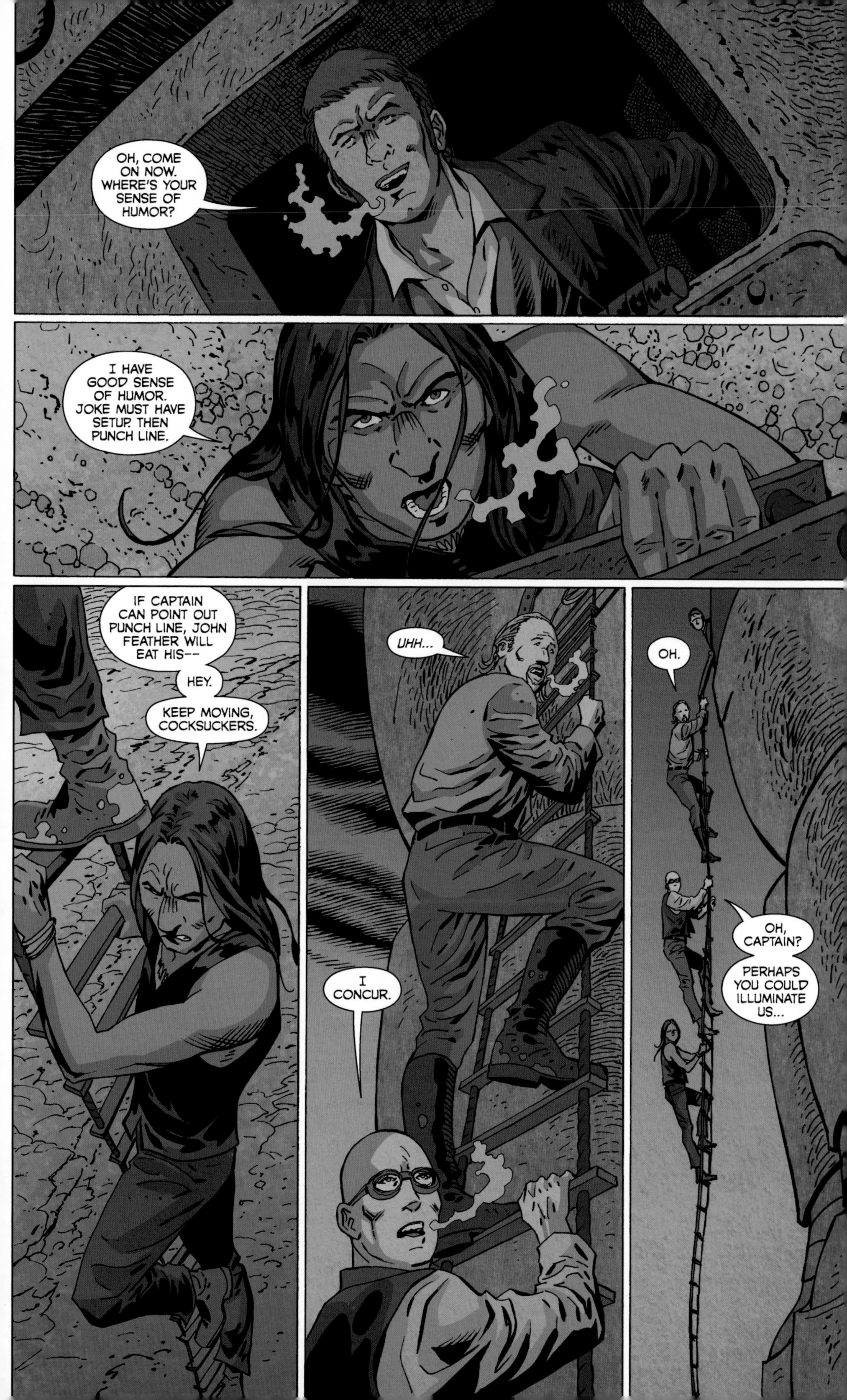
OH, COME ON NOW. WHERE'S YOUR SENSE OF HUMOR?
I HAVE GOOD SENSE OF HUMOR. JOKE MUST HAVE SETUP. THEN PUNCH LINE.
IF CAPTAIN CAN POINT OUT PUNCH LINE, JOHN FEATHER WILL EAT HIS--
HEY.
KEEP MOVING, COCKSUCKERS.
UHH...
I CONCUR.
OH.
OH, CAPTAIN?
PERHAPS YOU COULD ILLUMINATE US...

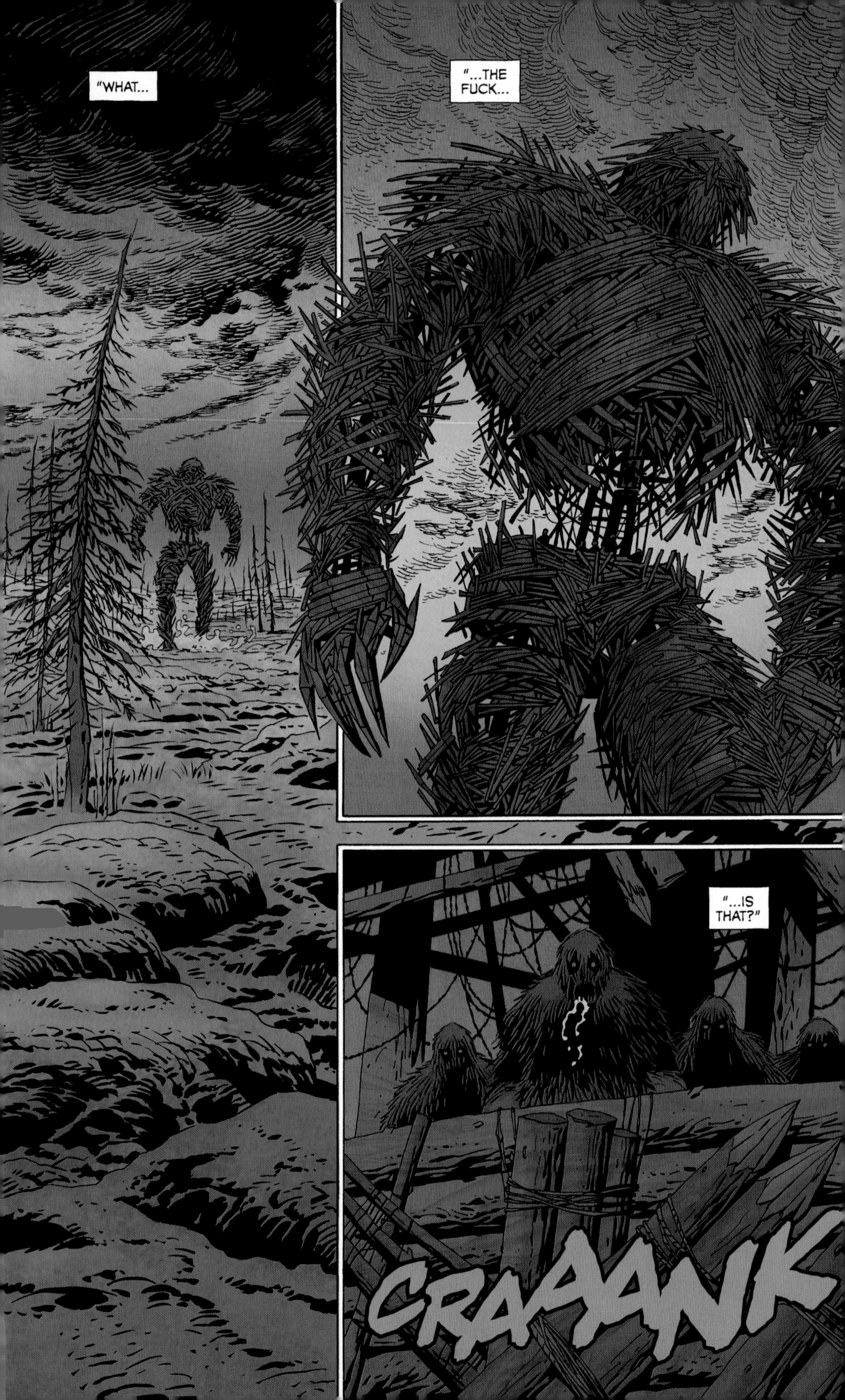
"WHAT...
"...THE FUCK...
"...IS THAT?"
CRAAANK

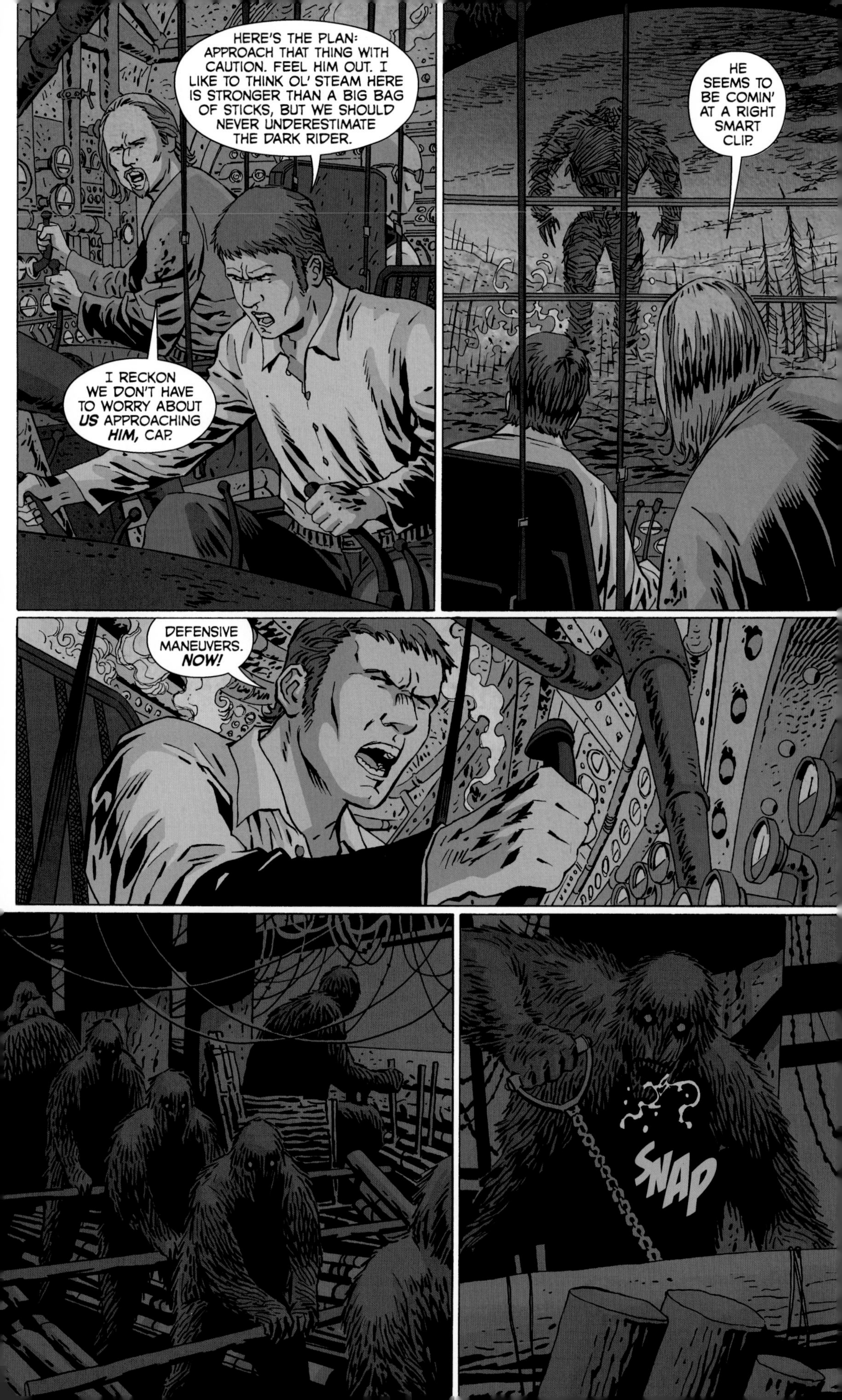
HERE'S THE PLAN: APPROACH THAT THING WITH CAUTION. FEEL HIM OUT. I LIKE TO THINK OL' STEAM HERE IS STRONGER THAN A BIG BAG OF STICKS, BUT WE SHOULD NEVER UNDERESTIMATE THE DARK RIDER.
I RECKON WE DON'T HAVE TO WORRY ABOUT *US* APPROACHING *HIM,* CAP.
HE SEEMS TO BE COMIN' AT A RIGHT SMART CLIP.
DEFENSIVE MANEUVERS. *NOW!*
SNAP

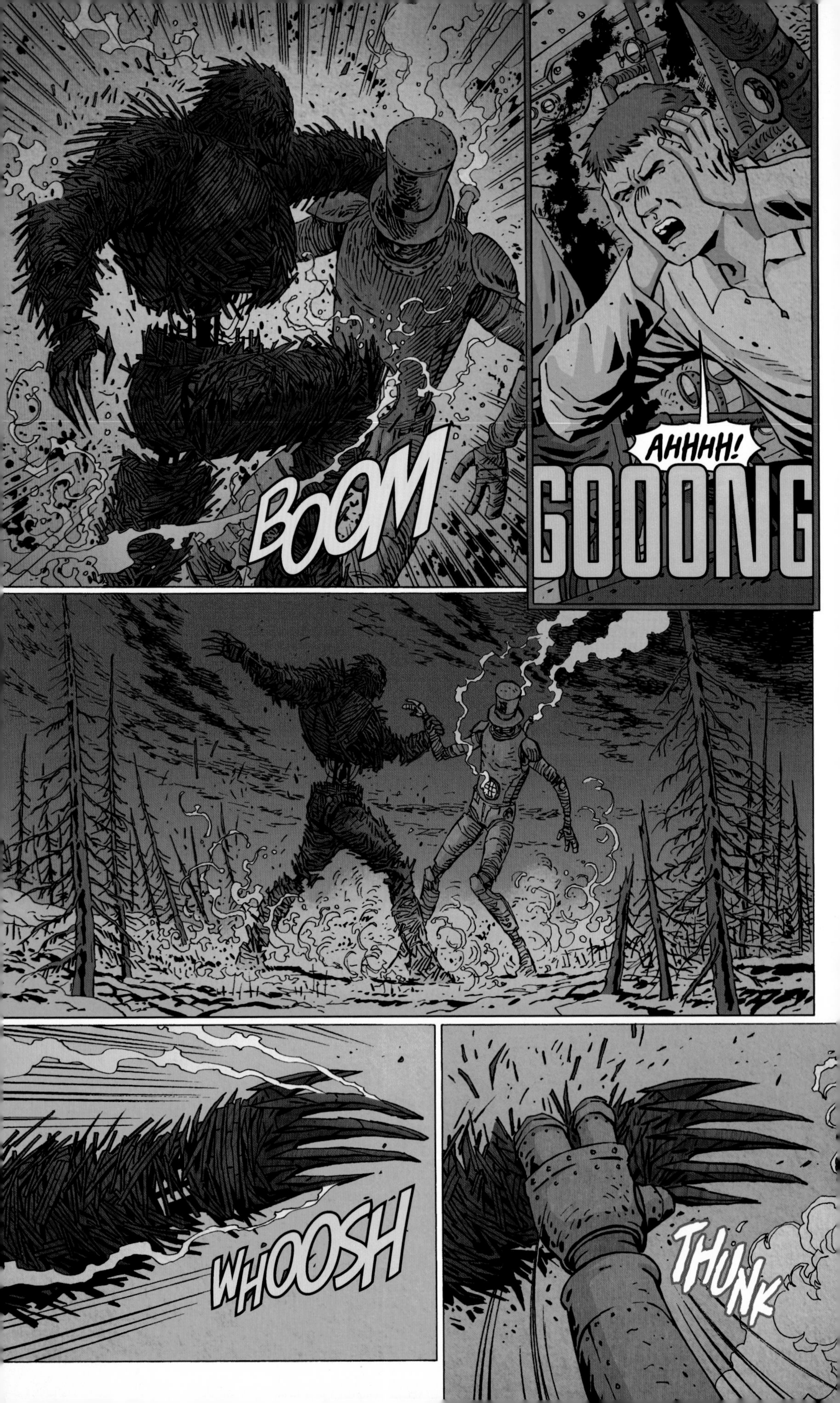
BOOM
AHHHH!
GOOONG
WHOOSH
THUNK

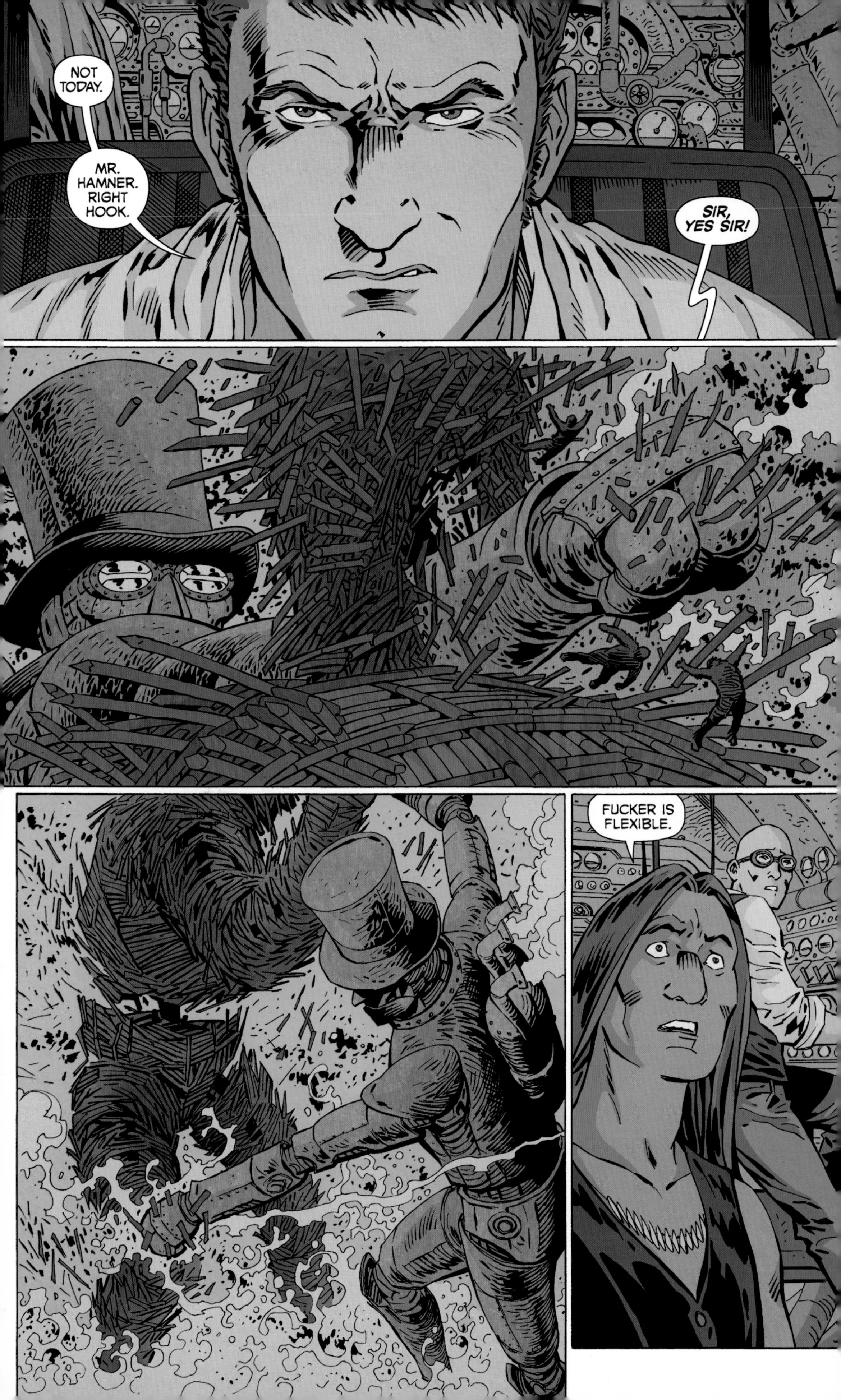
NOT TODAY.
MR. HAMNER. RIGHT HOOK.
SIR, YES SIR!
FUCKER IS FLEXIBLE.

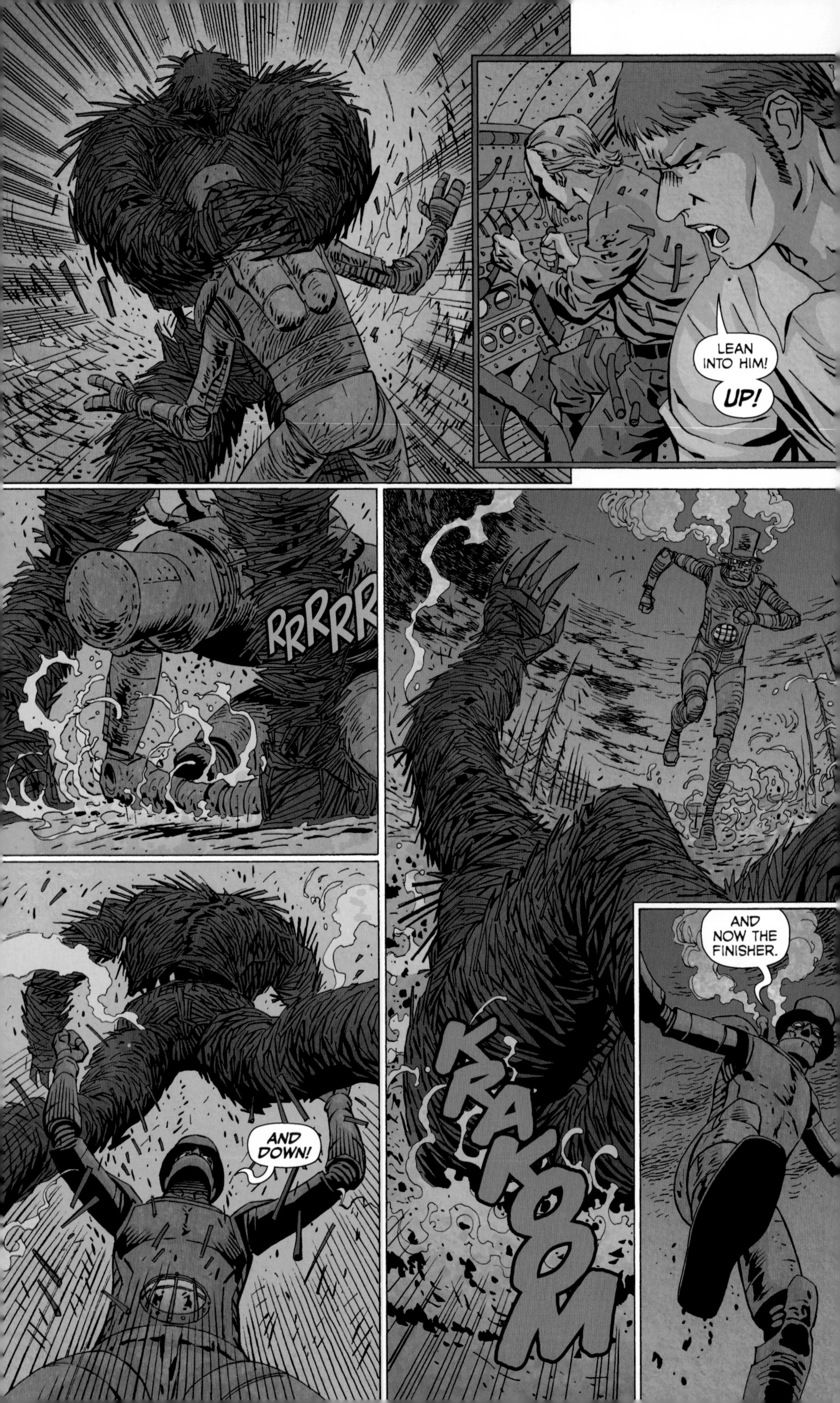
LEAN INTO HIM!
UP!
RRRRR
AND DOWN!
KRAKOOM
AND NOW THE FINISHER.

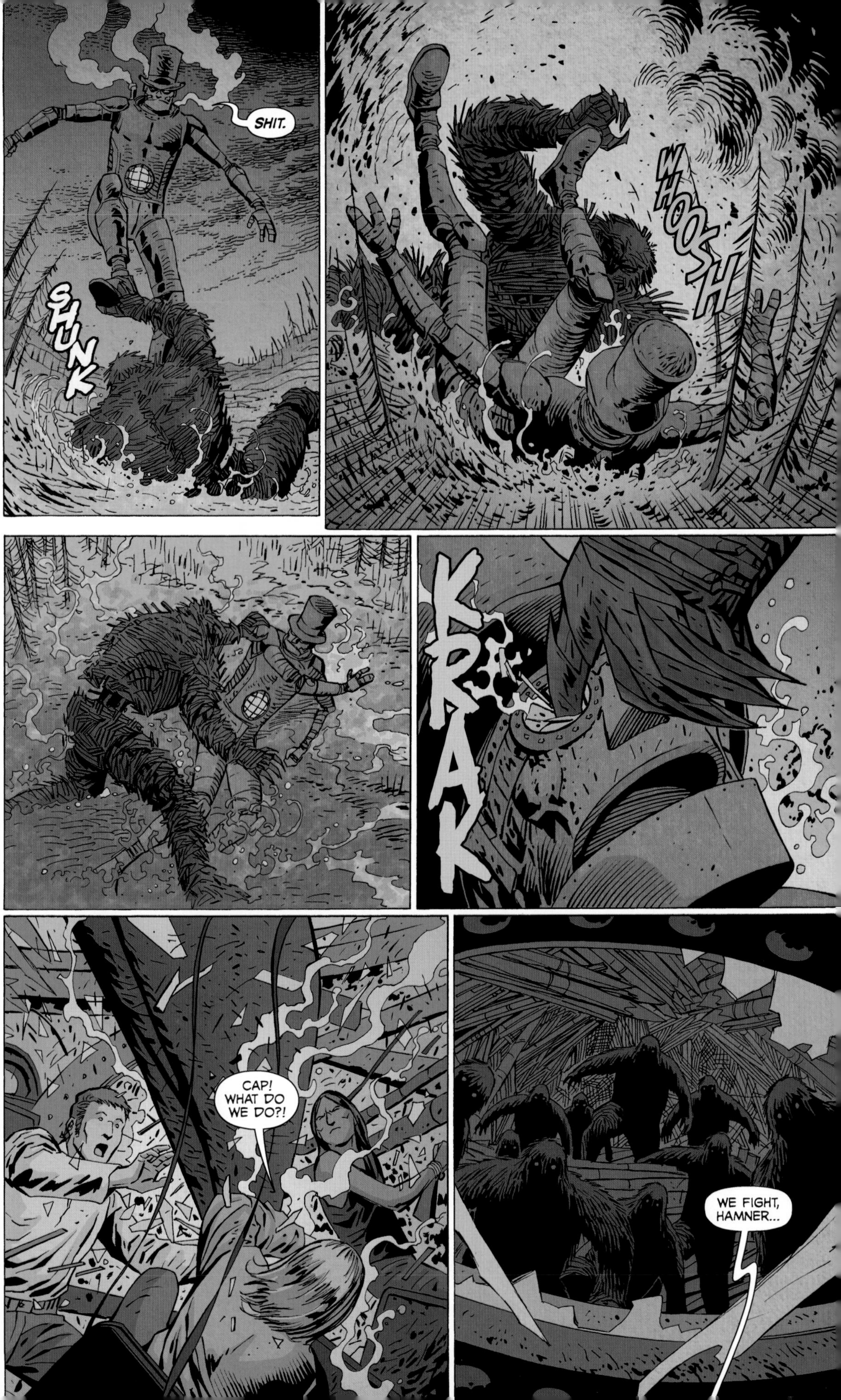
SHIT.
SHUNK
WHOOSH
KRAK
CAP! WHAT DO WE DO?!
WE FIGHT, HAMNER...

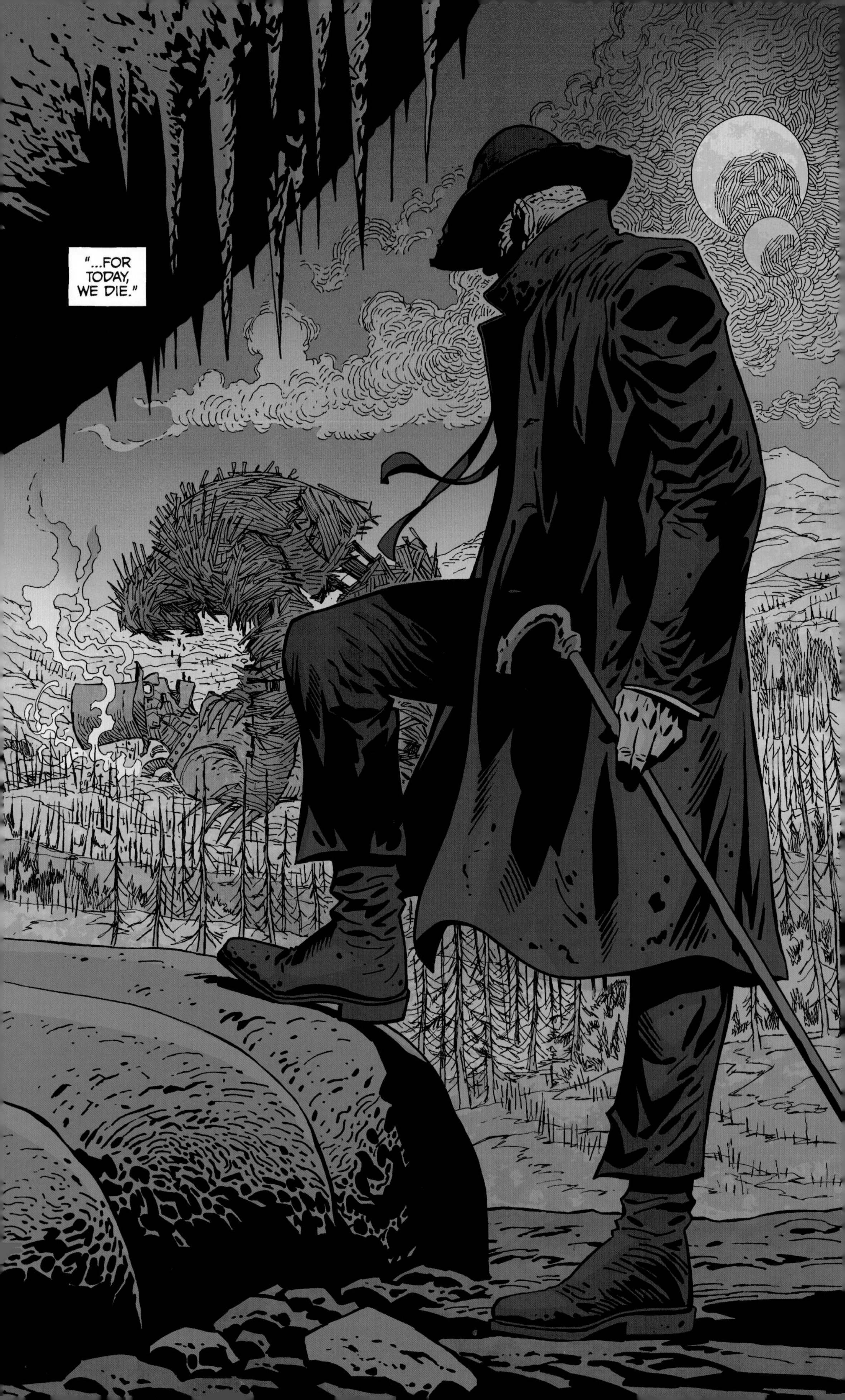
"...FOR TODAY, WE DIE."

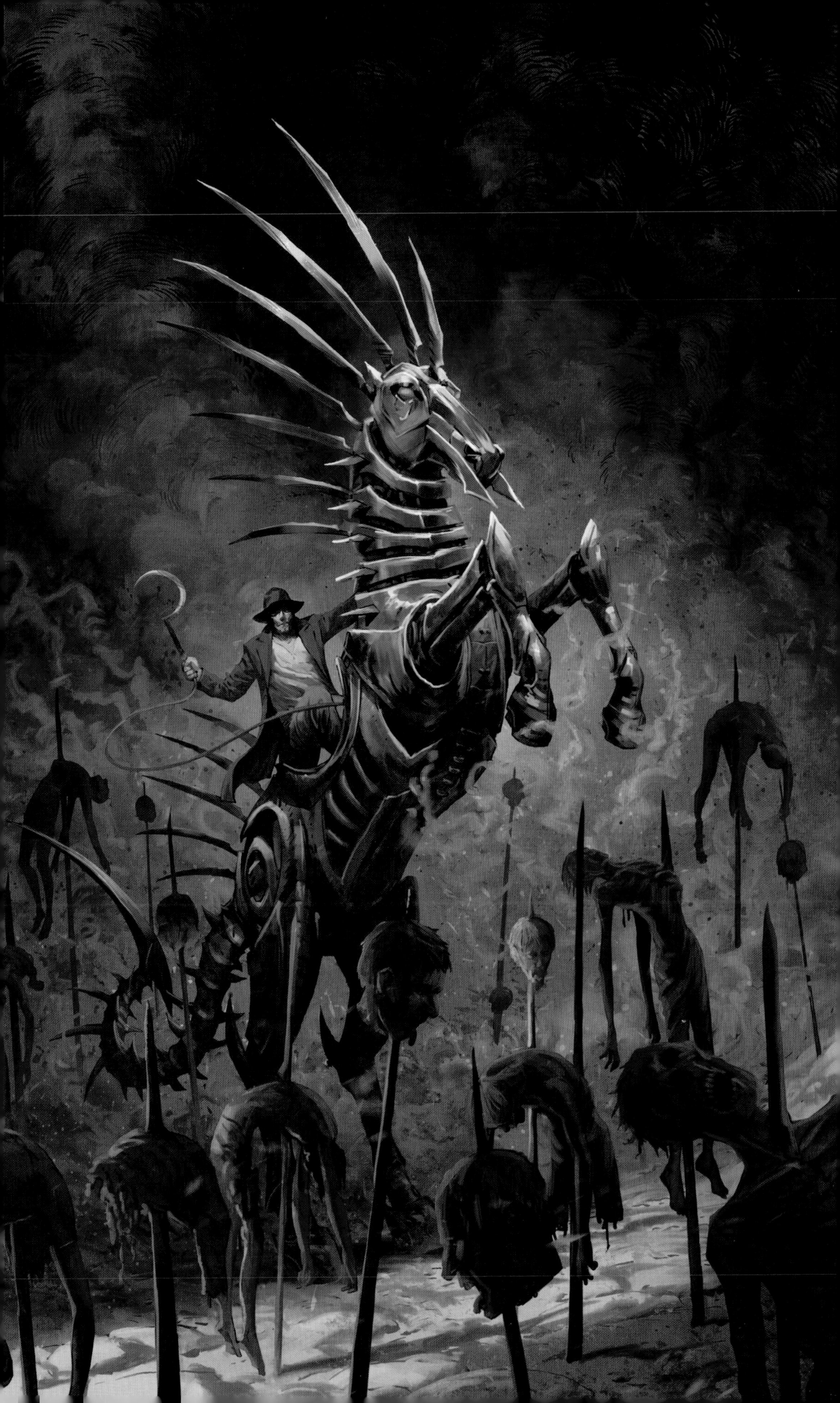

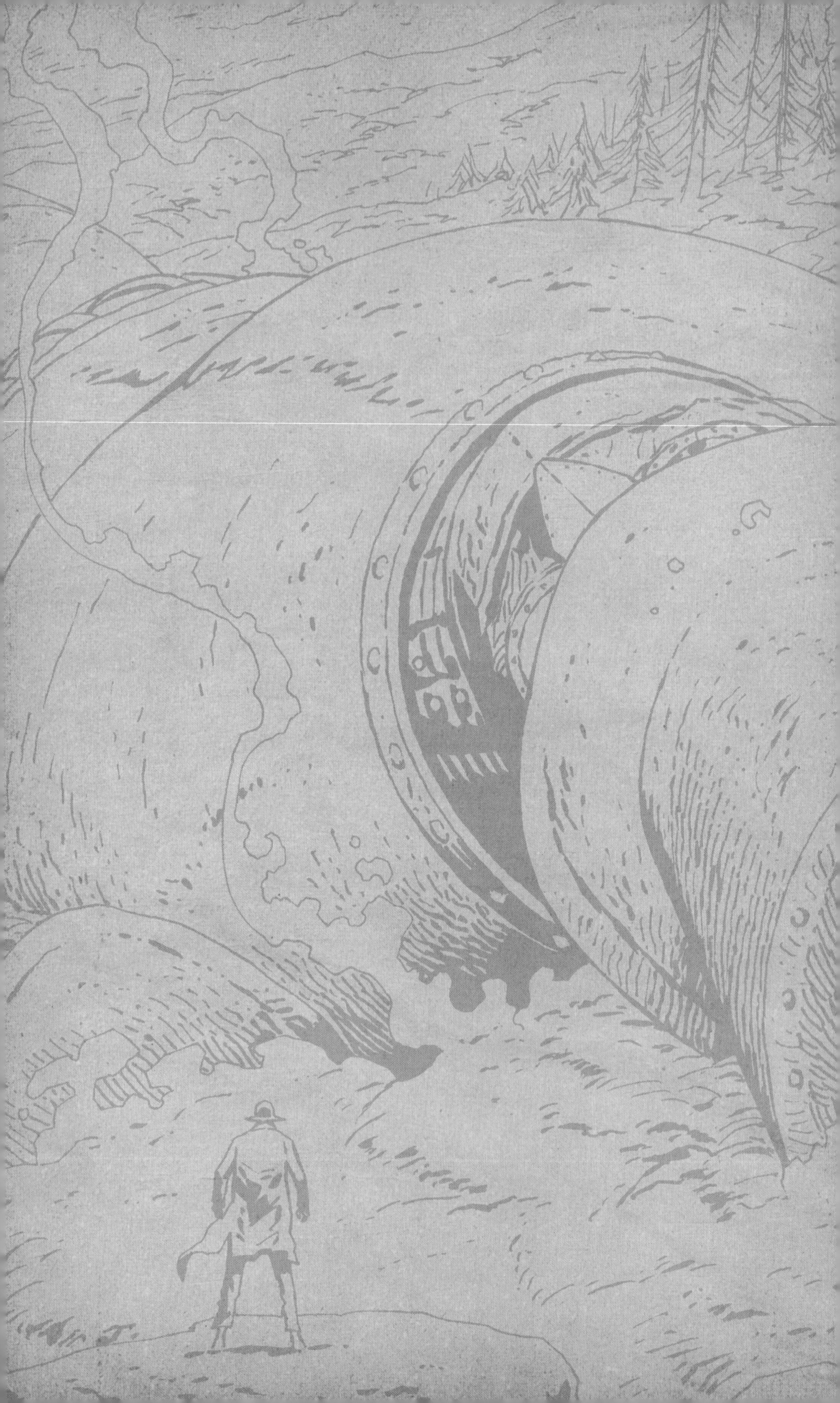

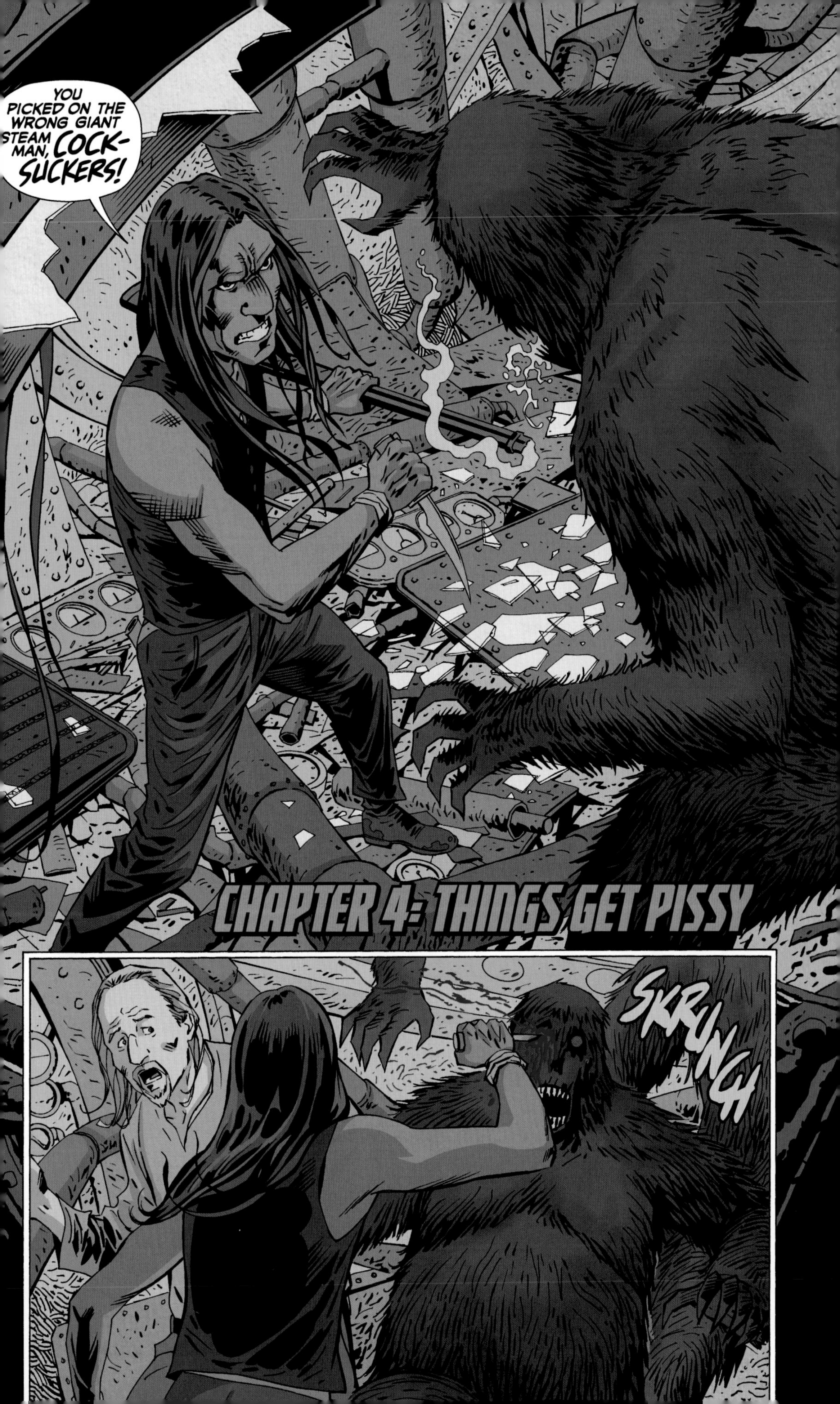

YOU PICKED ON THE WRONG GIANT STEAM MAN, COCK-SUCKERS!
CHAPTER 4: THINGS GET PISSY
SKRUNCH

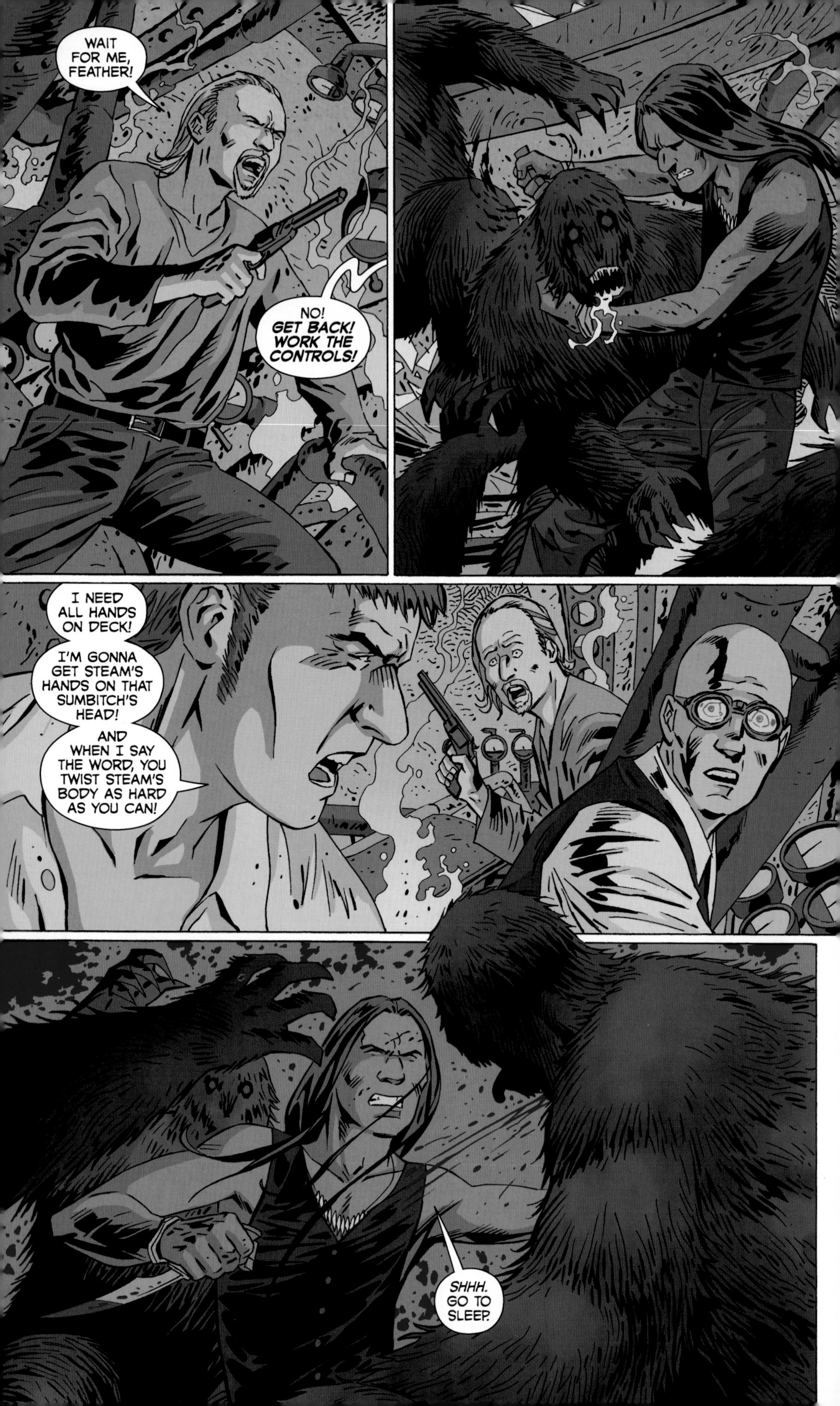
WAIT FOR ME, FEATHER!
NO! GET BACK! WORK THE CONTROLS!
I NEED ALL HANDS ON DECK!
I'M GONNA GET STEAM'S HANDS ON THAT SUMBITCH'S HEAD!
AND WHEN I SAY THE WORD, YOU TWIST STEAM'S BODY AS HARD AS YOU CAN!
SHHH. GO TO SLEEP.

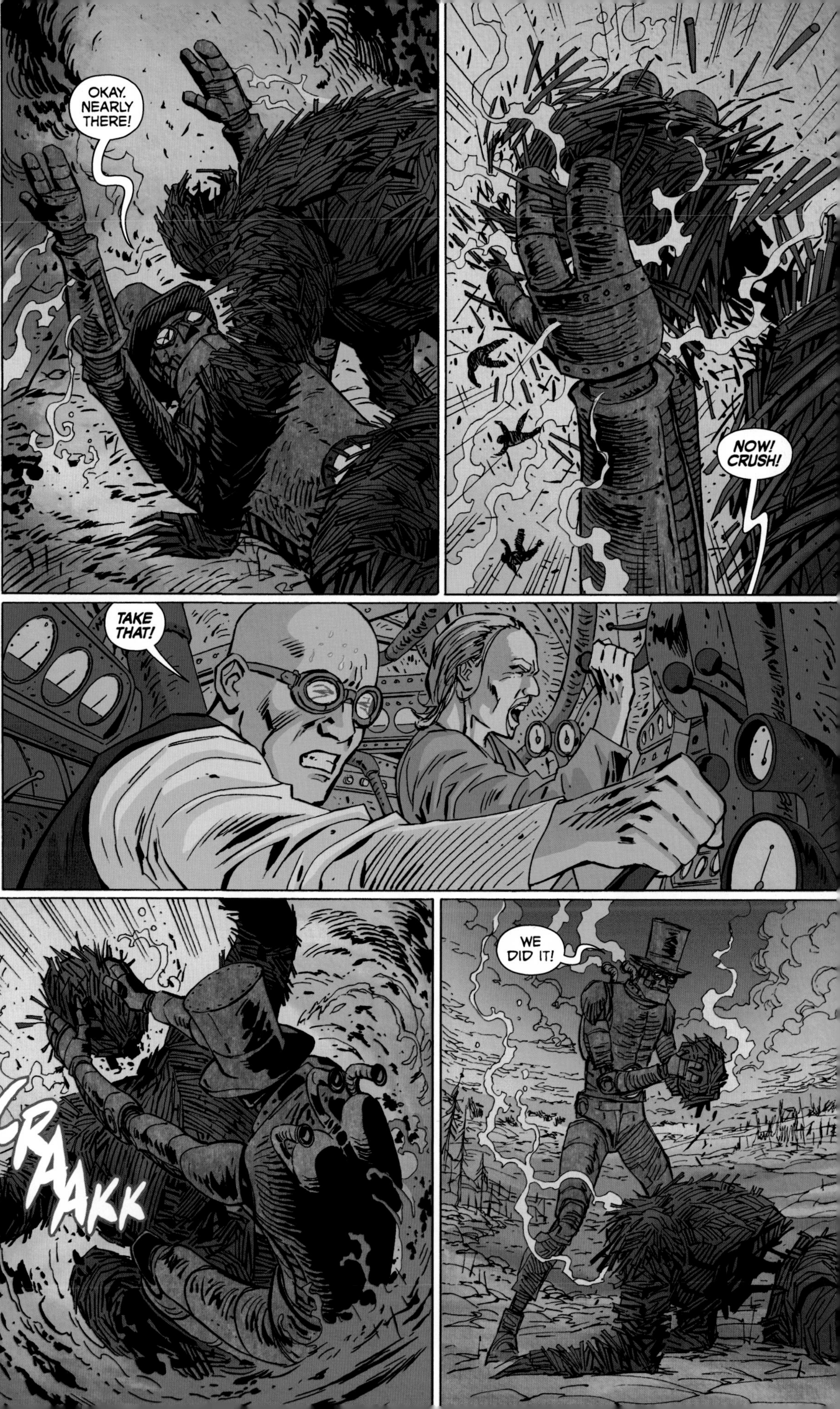
OKAY. NEARLY THERE!
NOW! CRUSH!
TAKE THAT!
CRAAKK
WE DID IT!

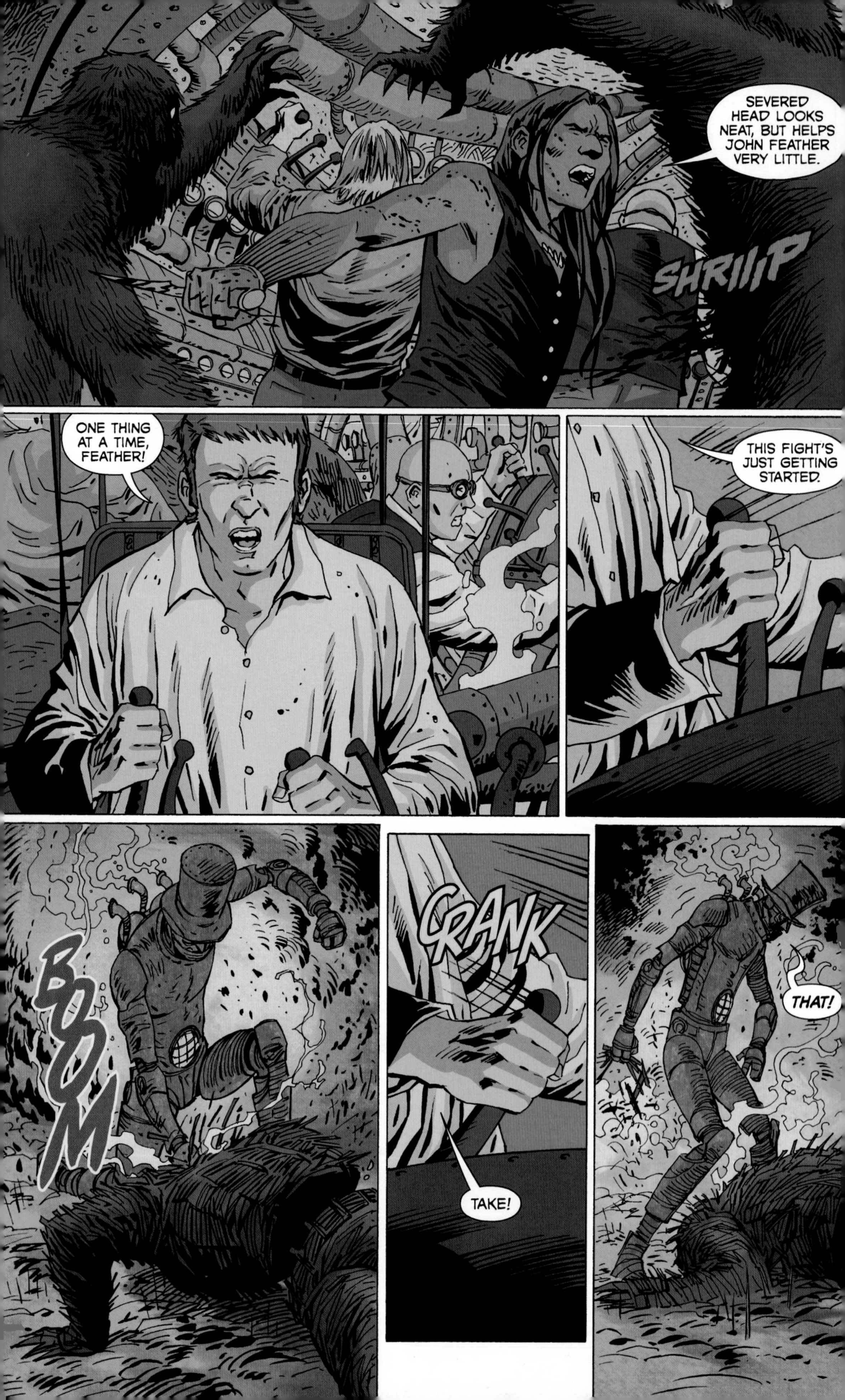
SEVERED HEAD LOOKS NEAT, BUT HELPS JOHN FEATHER VERY LITTLE.
SHRIIIP
ONE THING AT A TIME, FEATHER!
THIS FIGHT'S JUST GETTING STARTED.
BOOM
CRANK
TAKE!
THAT!

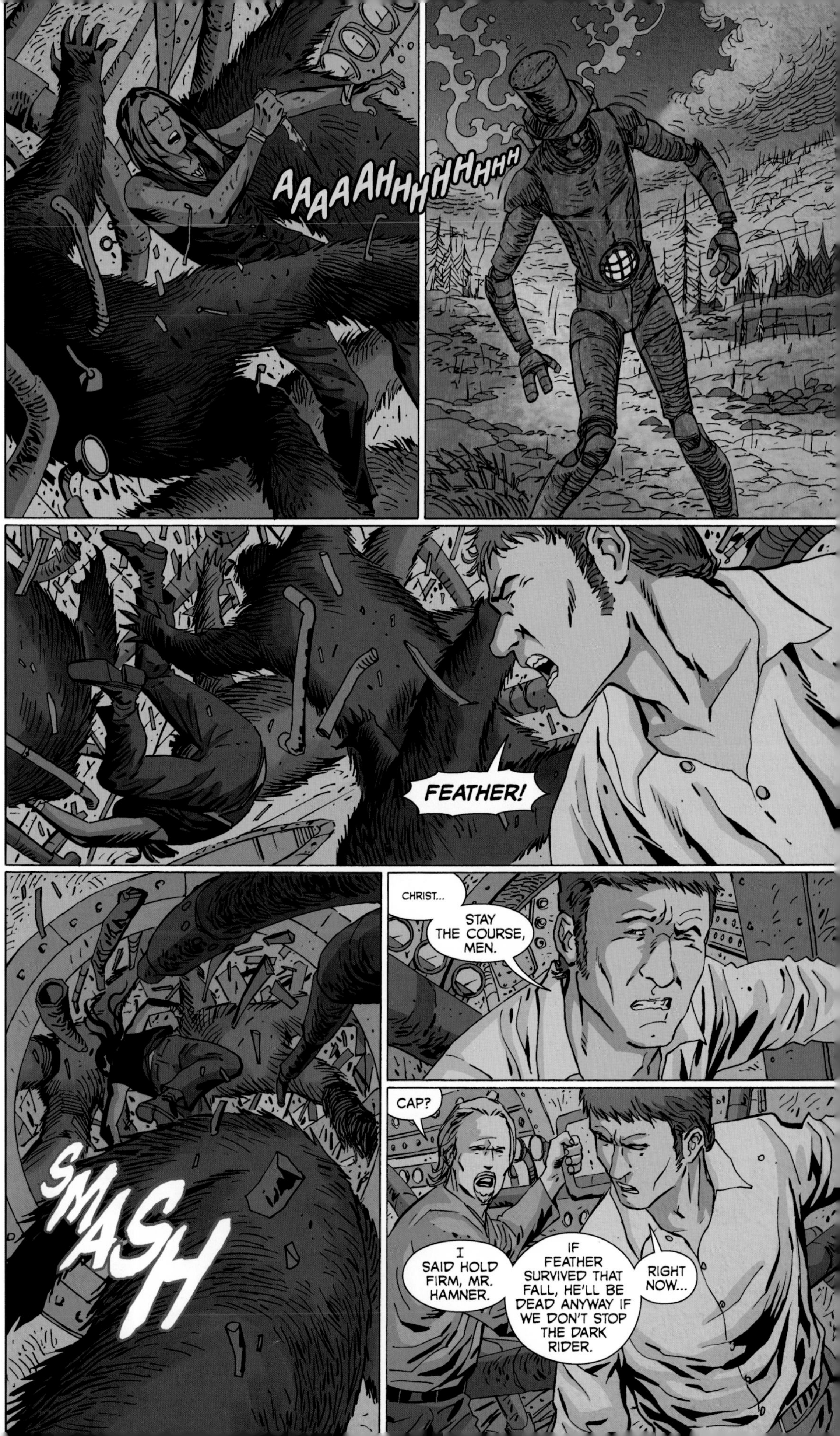
AAAAAHHHHHHHH
FEATHER!
CHRIST...
STAY THE COURSE, MEN.
SMASH
CAP?
I SAID HOLD FIRM, MR. HAMNER.
IF FEATHER SURVIVED THAT FALL, HE'LL BE DEAD ANYWAY IF WE DON'T STOP THE DARK RIDER.
RIGHT NOW...

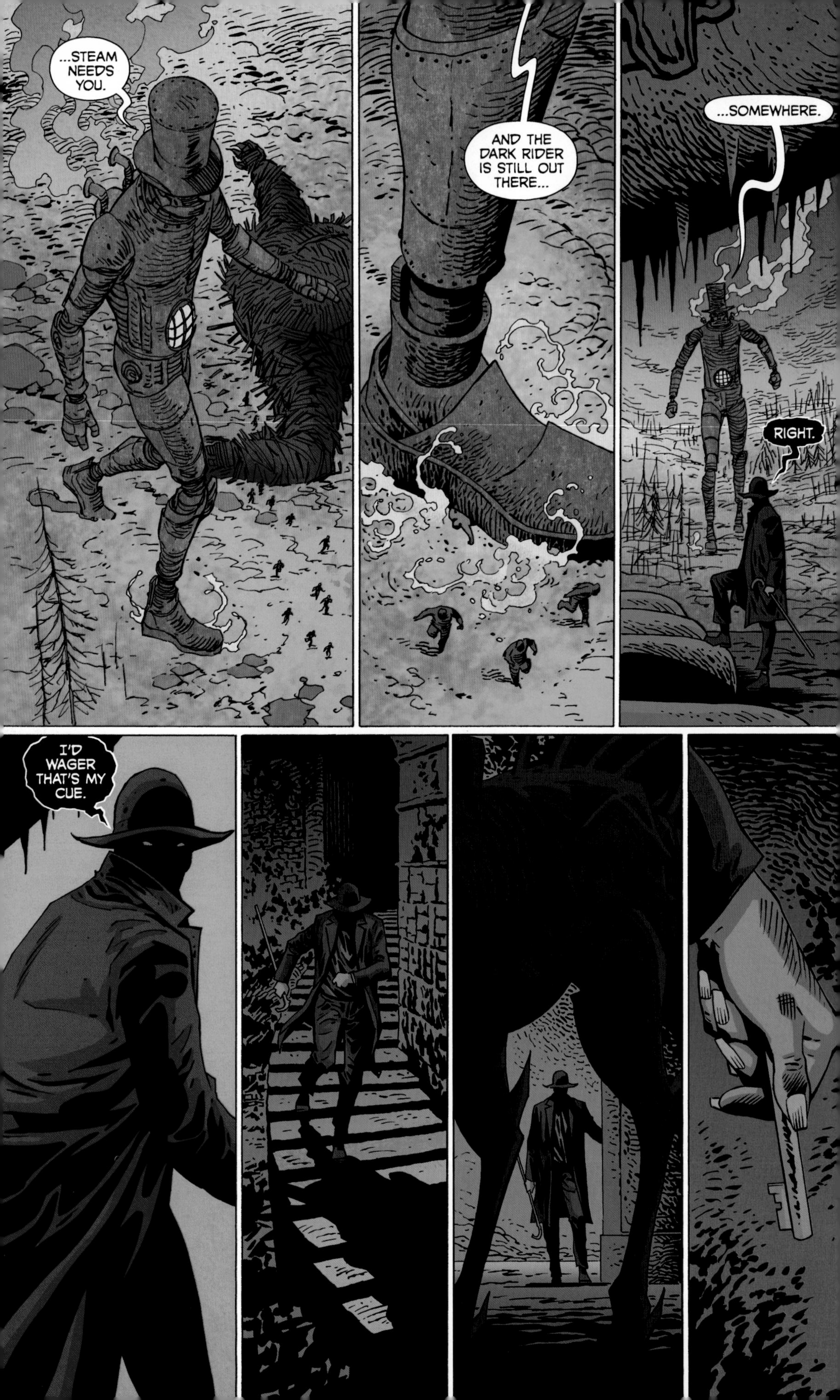
...STEAM NEEDS YOU.
AND THE DARK RIDER IS STILL OUT THERE...
...SOMEWHERE.
RIGHT.
I'D WAGER THAT'S MY CUE.

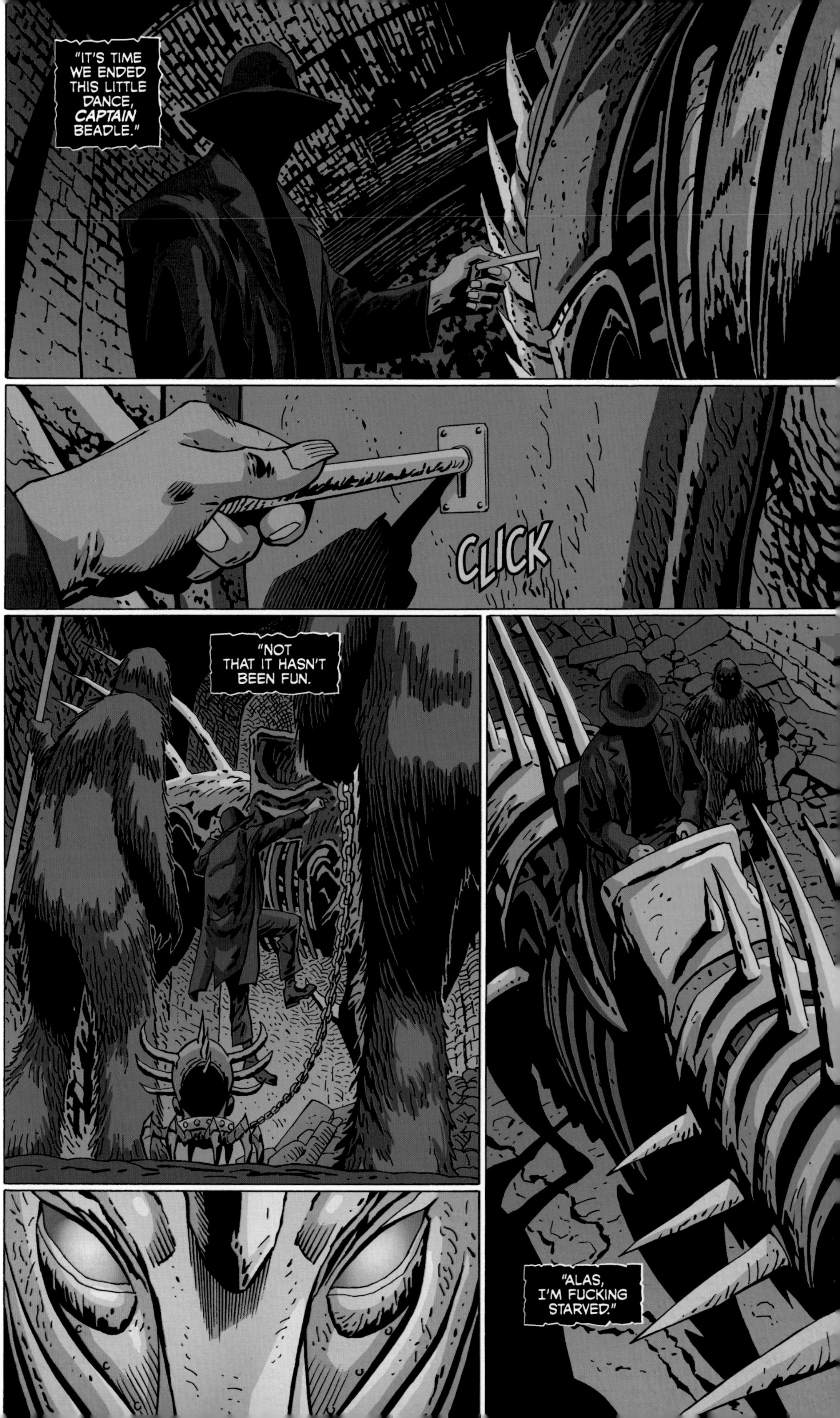

"IT'S TIME WE ENDED THIS LITTLE DANCE, CAPTAIN BEADLE."
CLICK
"NOT THAT IT HASN'T BEEN FUN.
"ALAS, I'M FUCKING STARVED."

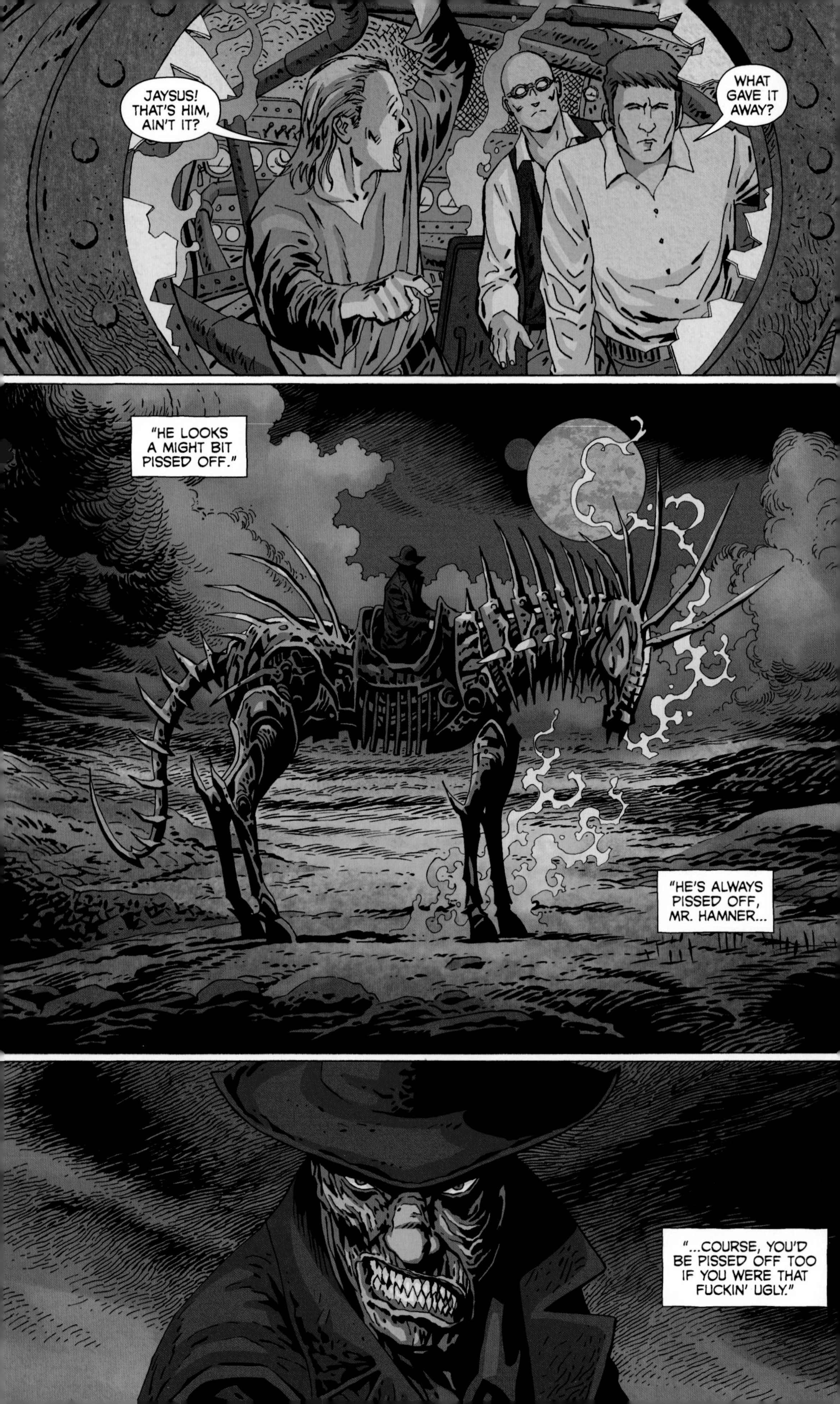
JAYSUS! THAT'S HIM, AIN'T IT?
WHAT GAVE IT AWAY?
"HE LOOKS A MIGHT BIT PISSED OFF."
"HE'S ALWAYS PISSED OFF, MR. HAMNER...
"...COURSE, YOU'D BE PISSED OFF TOO IF YOU WERE THAT FUCKIN' UGLY."

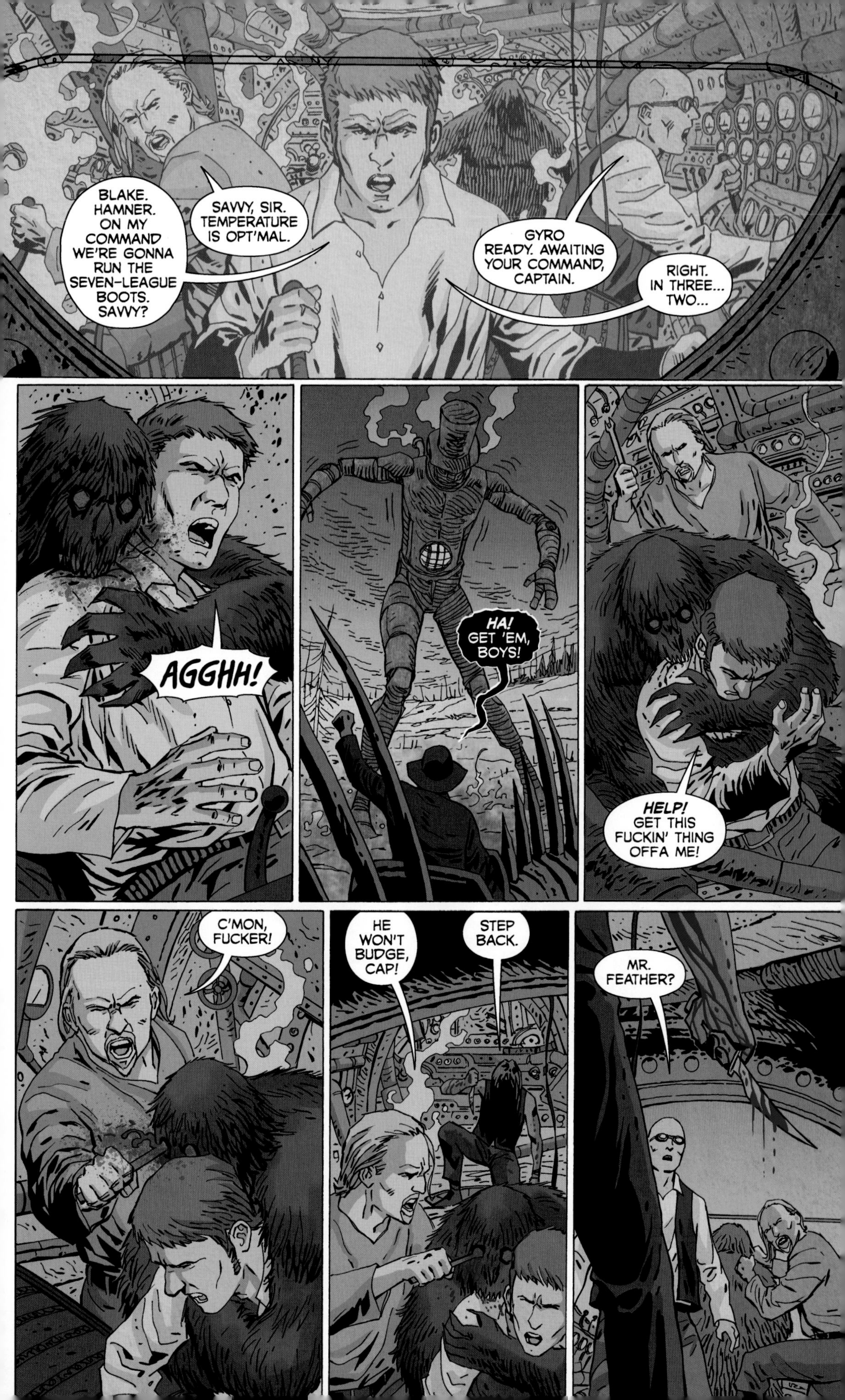
BLAKE. HAMNER. ON MY COMMAND WE'RE GONNA RUN THE SEVEN-LEAGUE BOOTS. SAVVY?
SAVVY, SIR. TEMPERATURE IS OPT'MAL.
GYRO READY. AWAITING YOUR COMMAND, CAPTAIN.
RIGHT. IN THREE... TWO...
AGGHH!
HA! GET 'EM, BOYS!
HELP! GET THIS FUCKIN' THING OFFA ME!
C'MON, FUCKER!
HE WON'T BUDGE, CAP!
STEP BACK.
MR. FEATHER?

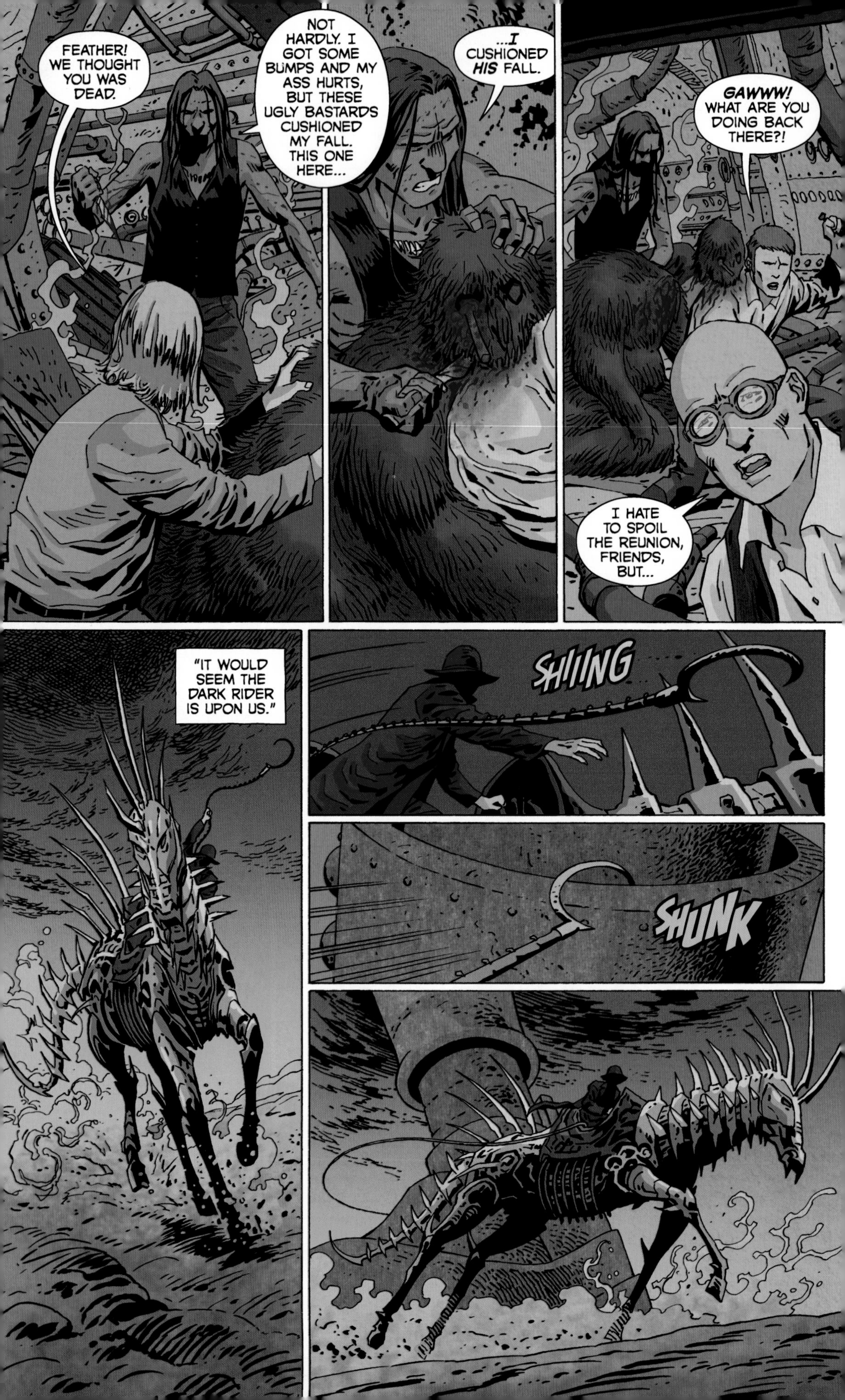
FEATHER! WE THOUGHT YOU WAS DEAD.
NOT HARDLY. I GOT SOME BUMPS AND MY ASS HURTS, BUT THESE UGLY BASTARDS CUSHIONED MY FALL. THIS ONE HERE...
...I CUSHIONED HIS FALL.
GAWWW! WHAT ARE YOU DOING BACK THERE?!
I HATE TO SPOIL THE REUNION, FRIENDS, BUT...
"IT WOULD SEEM THE DARK RIDER IS UPON US."
SHIIING
SHUNK

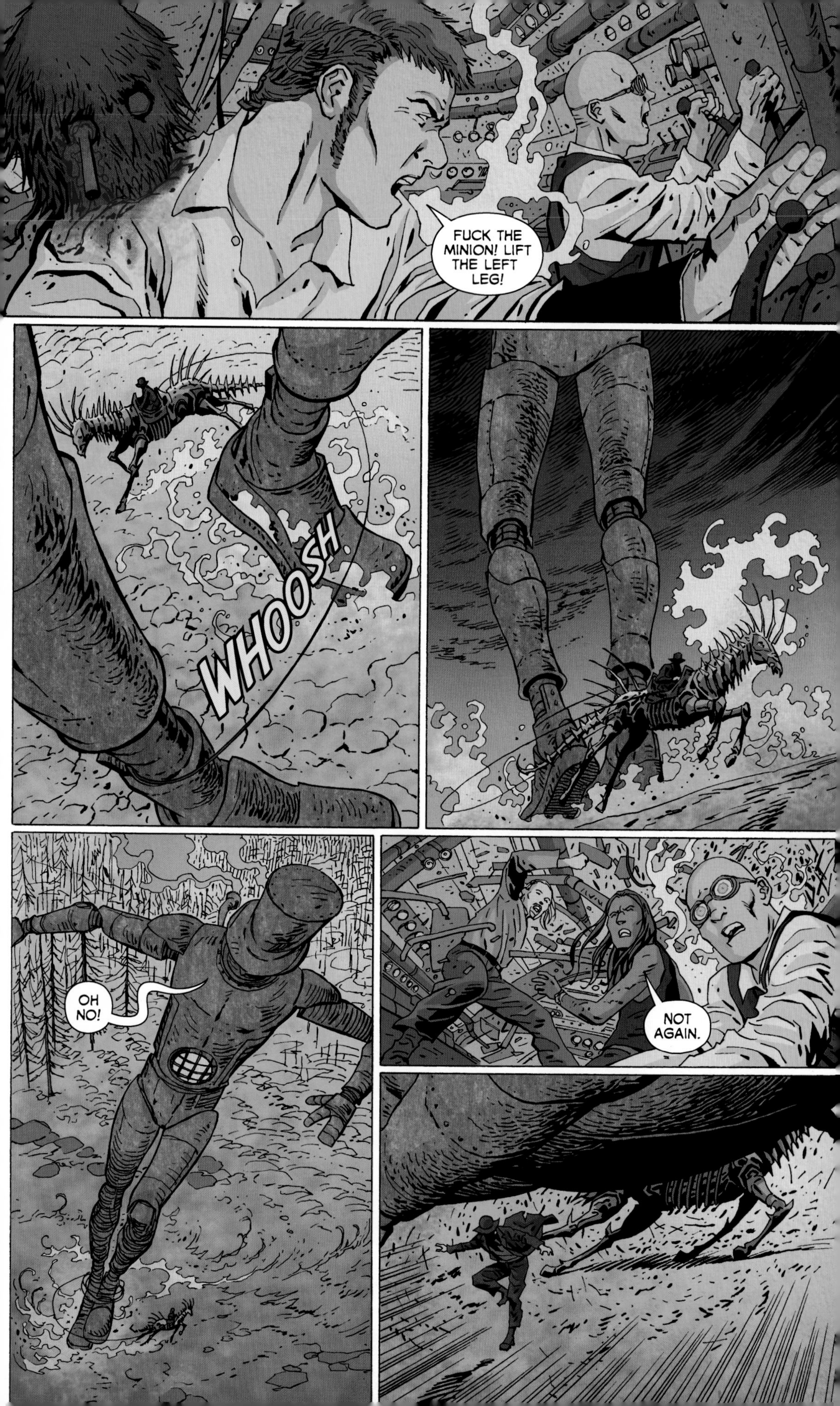
FUCK THE MINION! LIFT THE LEFT LEG!
WHOOSH
OH NO!
NOT AGAIN.

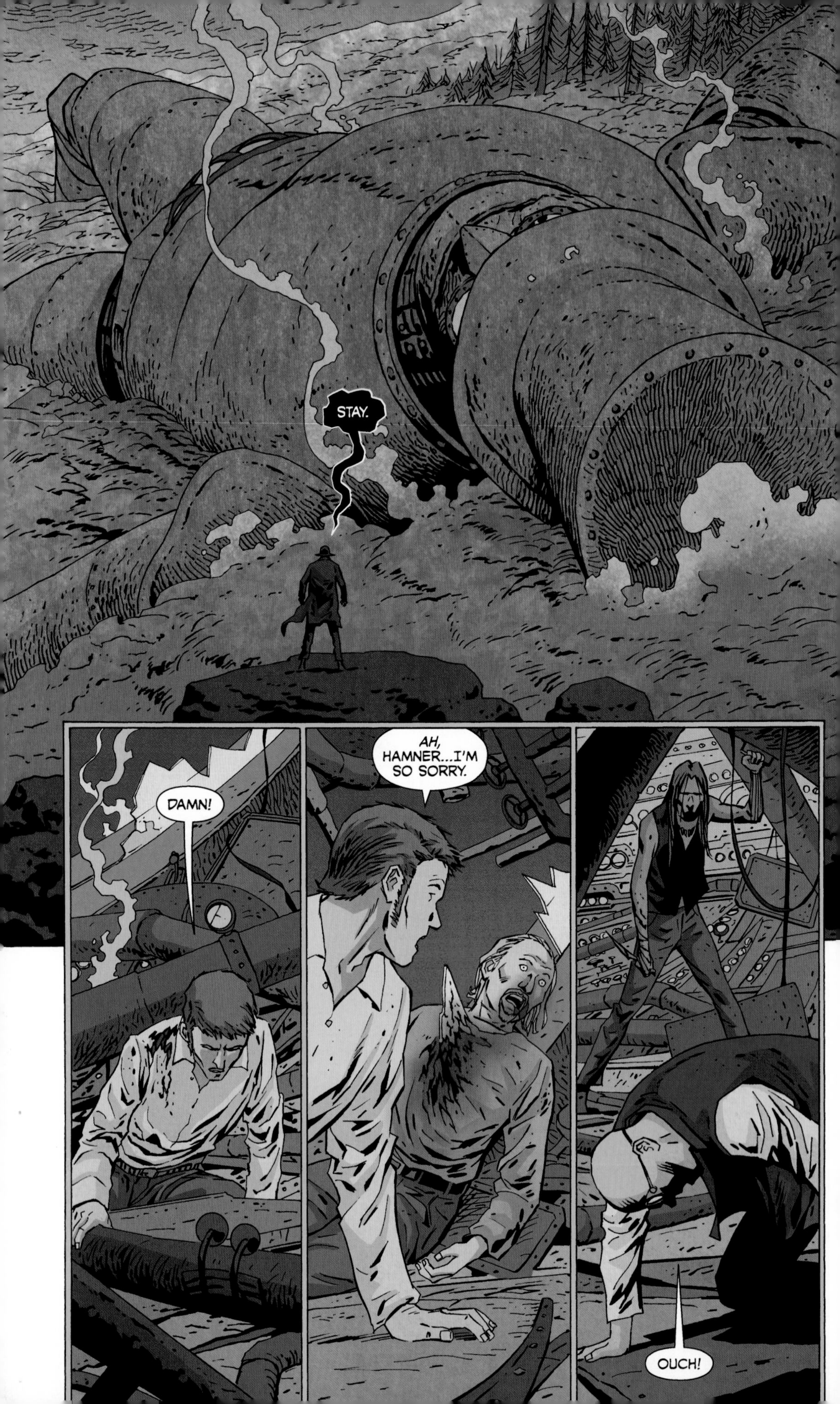
STAY.
DAMN!
AH, HAMNER...I'M SO SORRY.
OUCH!

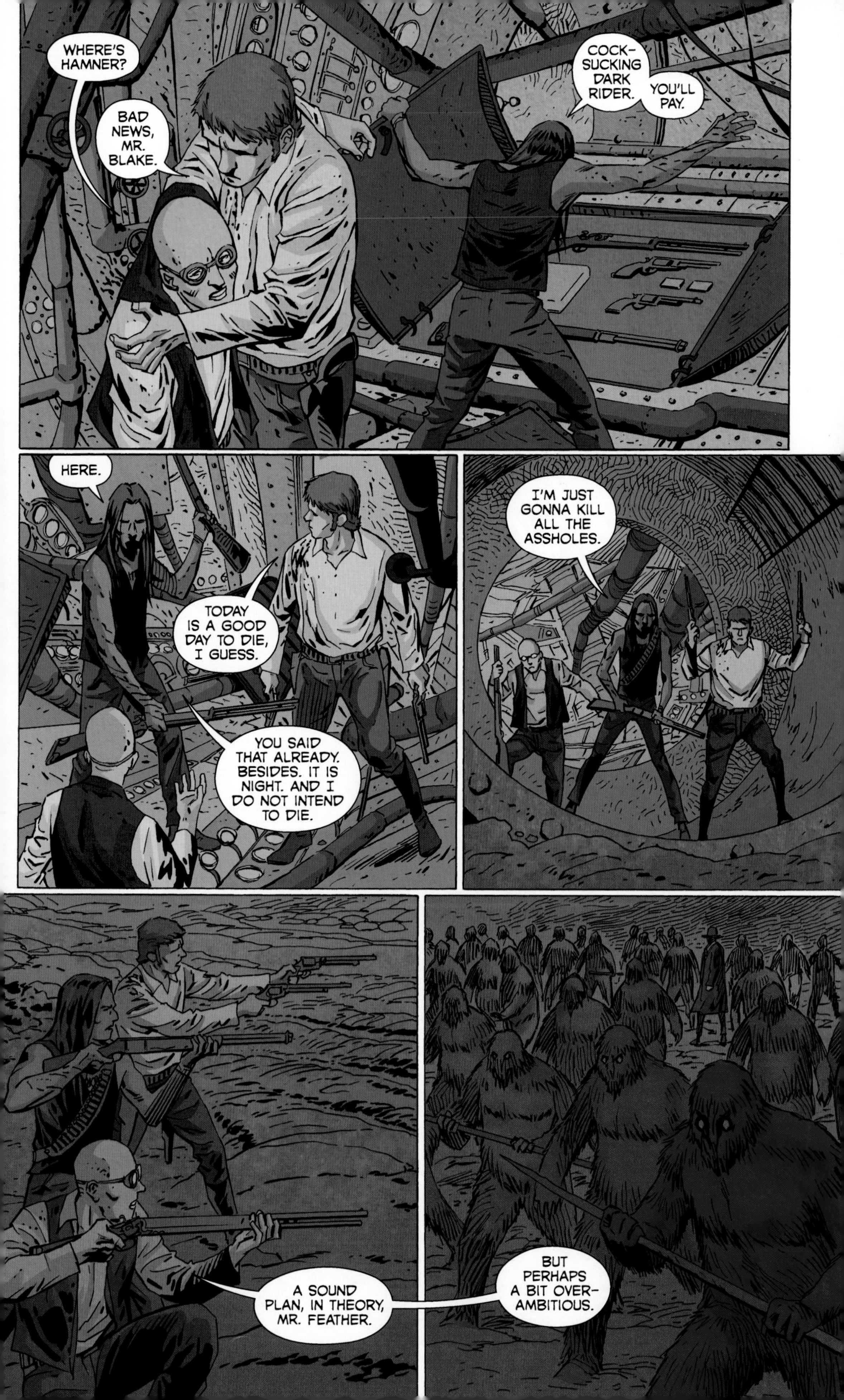
WHERE'S HAMNER?
BAD NEWS, MR. BLAKE.
COCK-SUCKING DARK RIDER.
YOU'LL PAY.
HERE.
TODAY IS A GOOD DAY TO DIE, I GUESS.
YOU SAID THAT ALREADY. BESIDES. IT IS NIGHT. AND I DO NOT INTEND TO DIE.
I'M JUST GONNA KILL ALL THE ASSHOLES.
A SOUND PLAN, IN THEORY, MR. FEATHER.
BUT PERHAPS A BIT OVER-AMBITIOUS.

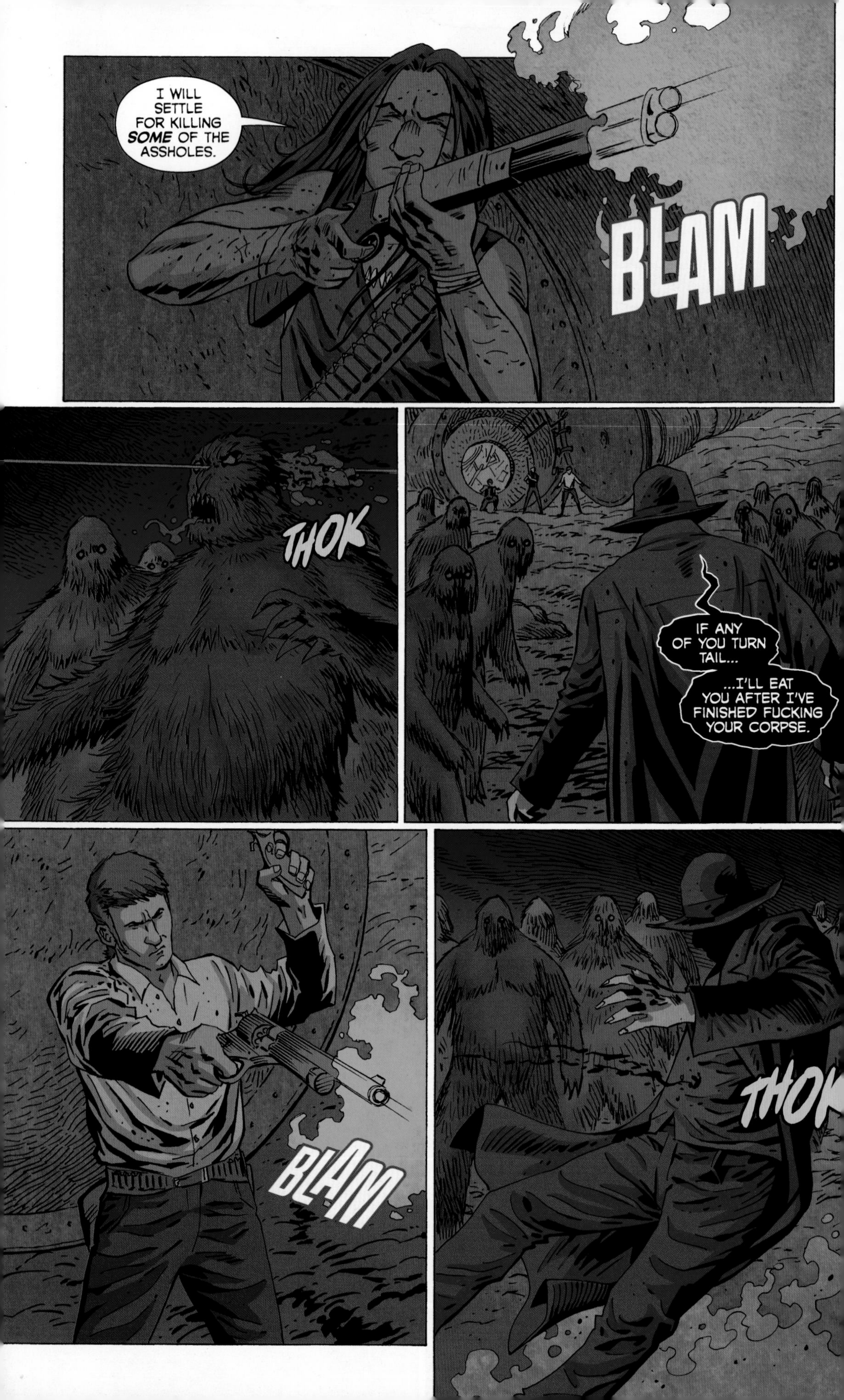
I WILL SETTLE FOR KILLING *SOME* OF THE ASSHOLES.
BLAM
THOK
IF ANY OF YOU TURN TAIL...
...I'LL EAT YOU AFTER I'VE FINISHED FUCKING YOUR CORPSE.
BLAM
THOK

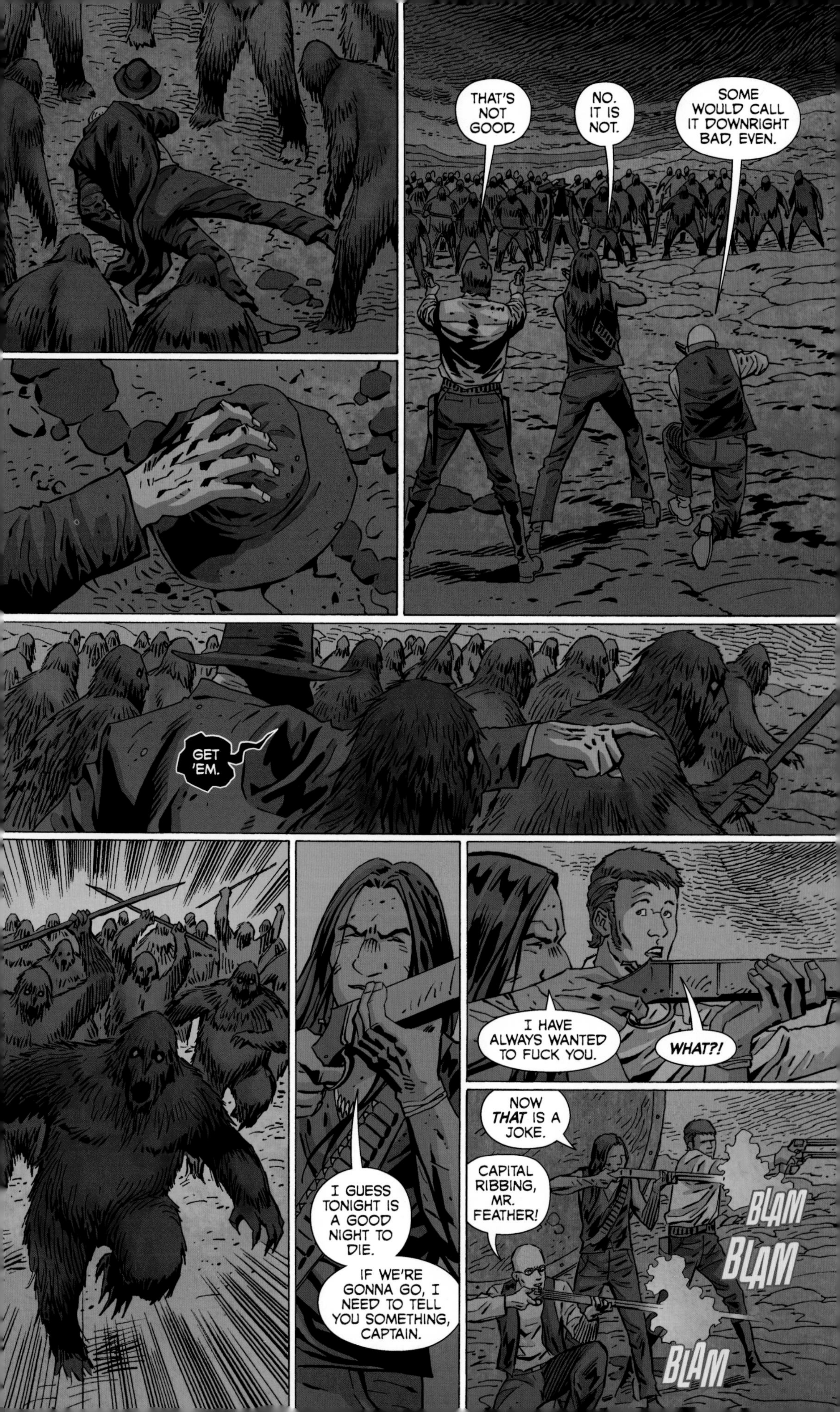
THAT'S NOT GOOD.
NO. IT IS NOT.
SOME WOULD CALL IT DOWNRIGHT BAD, EVEN.
GET 'EM.
I GUESS TONIGHT IS A GOOD NIGHT TO DIE.
IF WE'RE GONNA GO, I NEED TO TELL YOU SOMETHING, CAPTAIN.
I HAVE ALWAYS WANTED TO FUCK YOU.
WHAT?!
NOW THAT IS A JOKE.
CAPITAL RIBBING, MR. FEATHER!
BLAM
BLAM
BLAM

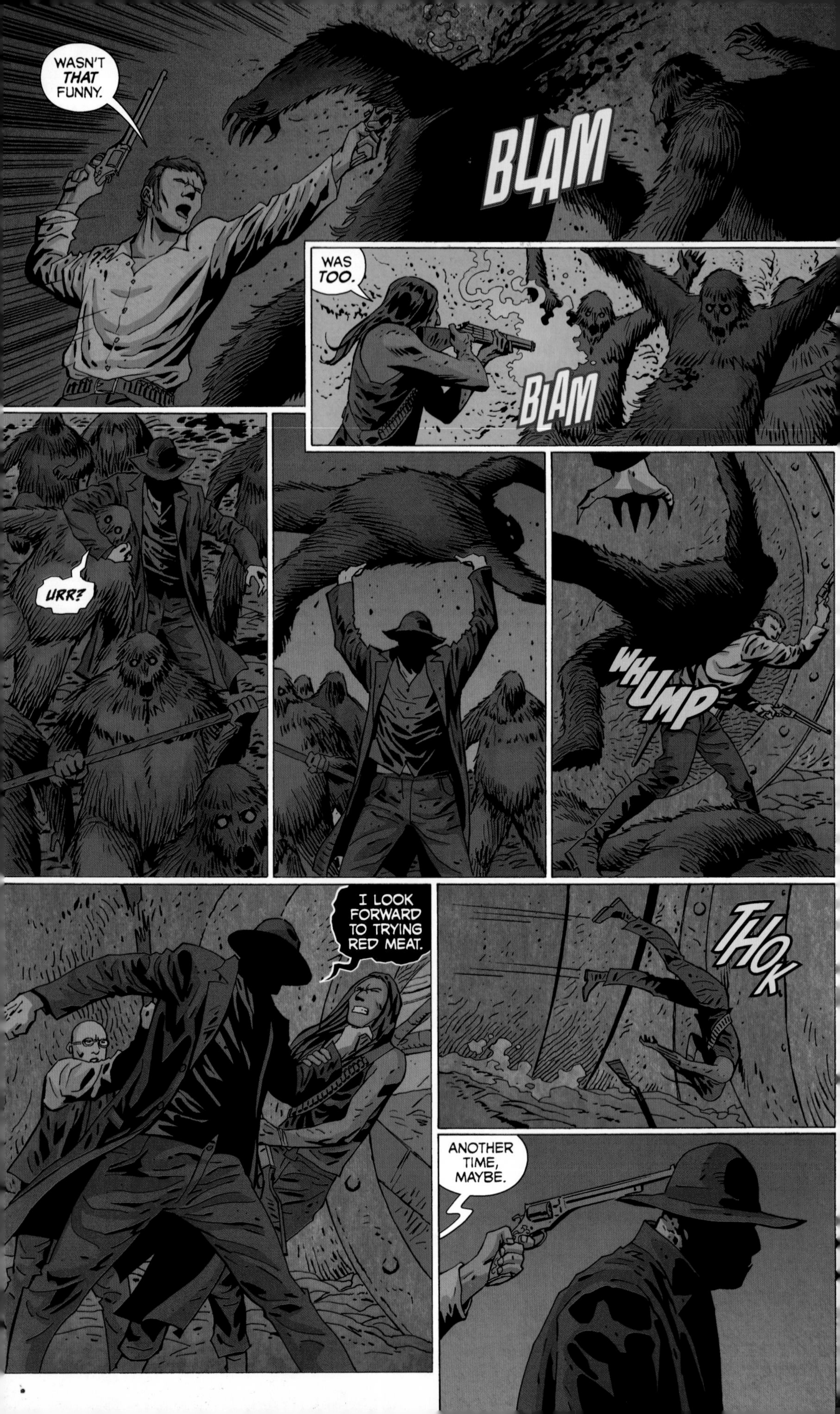

WASN'T *THAT* FUNNY.
BLAM
WAS *TOO*.
BLAM
URR?
WHUMP
I LOOK FORWARD TO TRYING RED MEAT.
THOK
ANOTHER TIME, MAYBE.

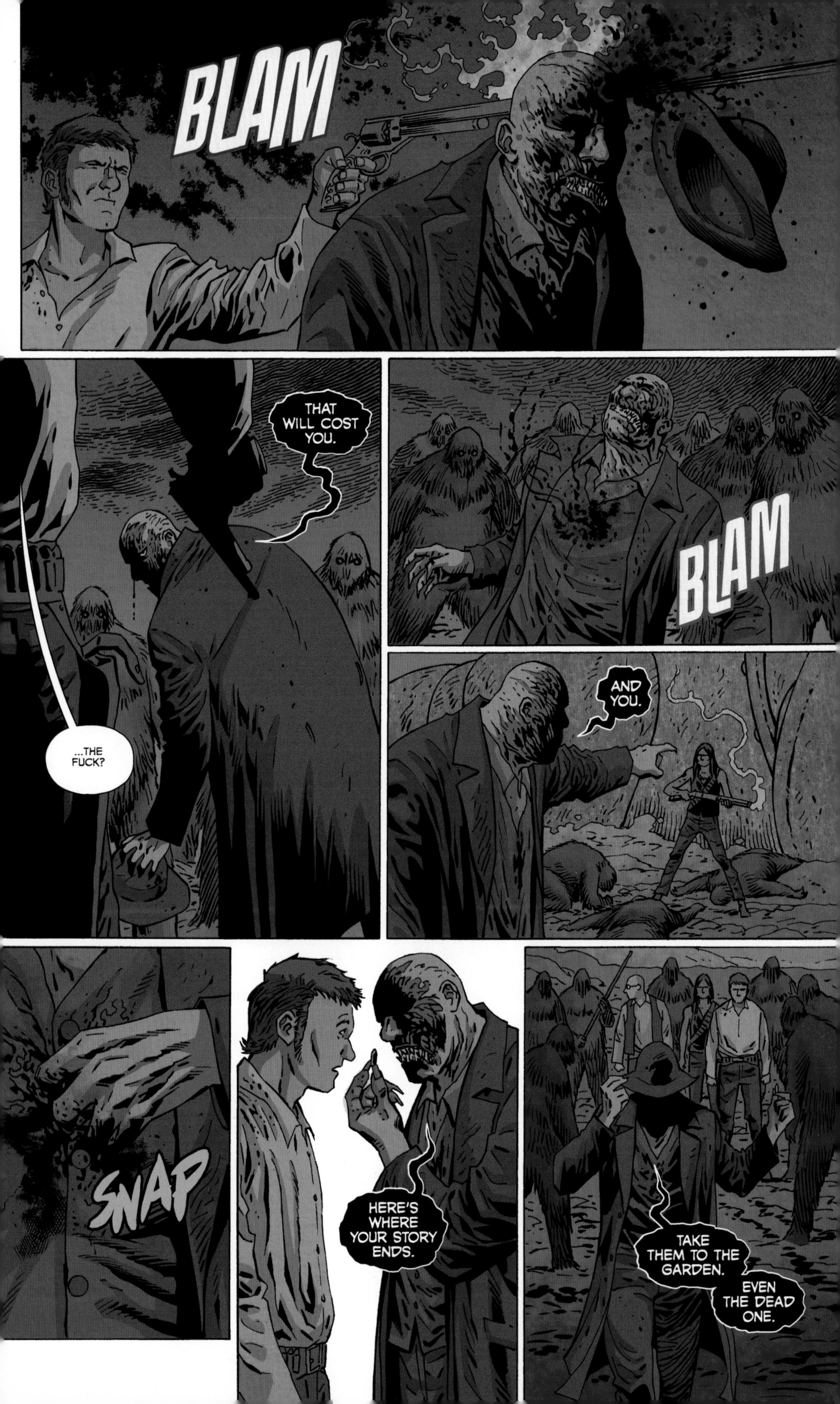
BLAM
THAT WILL COST YOU.
...THE FUCK?
BLAM
AND YOU.
SNAP
HERE'S WHERE YOUR STORY ENDS.
TAKE THEM TO THE GARDEN.
EVEN THE DEAD ONE.

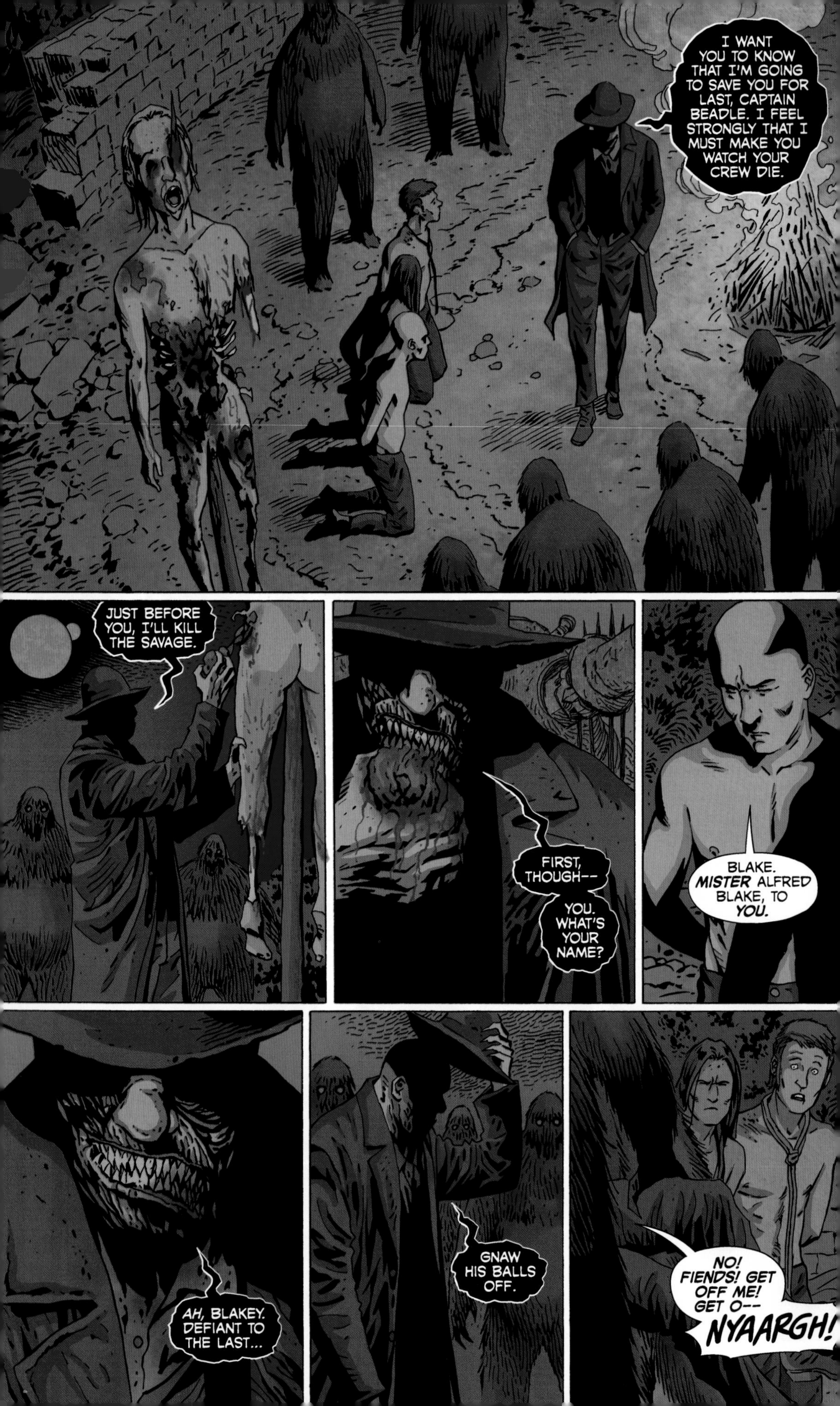
I WANT YOU TO KNOW THAT I'M GOING TO SAVE YOU FOR LAST, CAPTAIN BEADLE. I FEEL STRONGLY THAT I MUST MAKE YOU WATCH YOUR CREW DIE.
JUST BEFORE YOU, I'LL KILL THE SAVAGE.
FIRST, THOUGH--
YOU. WHAT'S YOUR NAME?
BLAKE. *MISTER* ALFRED BLAKE, TO *YOU.*
AH, BLAKEY. DEFIANT TO THE LAST...
GNAW HIS BALLS OFF.
NO! FIENDS! GET OFF ME! GET O--
NYAARGH!

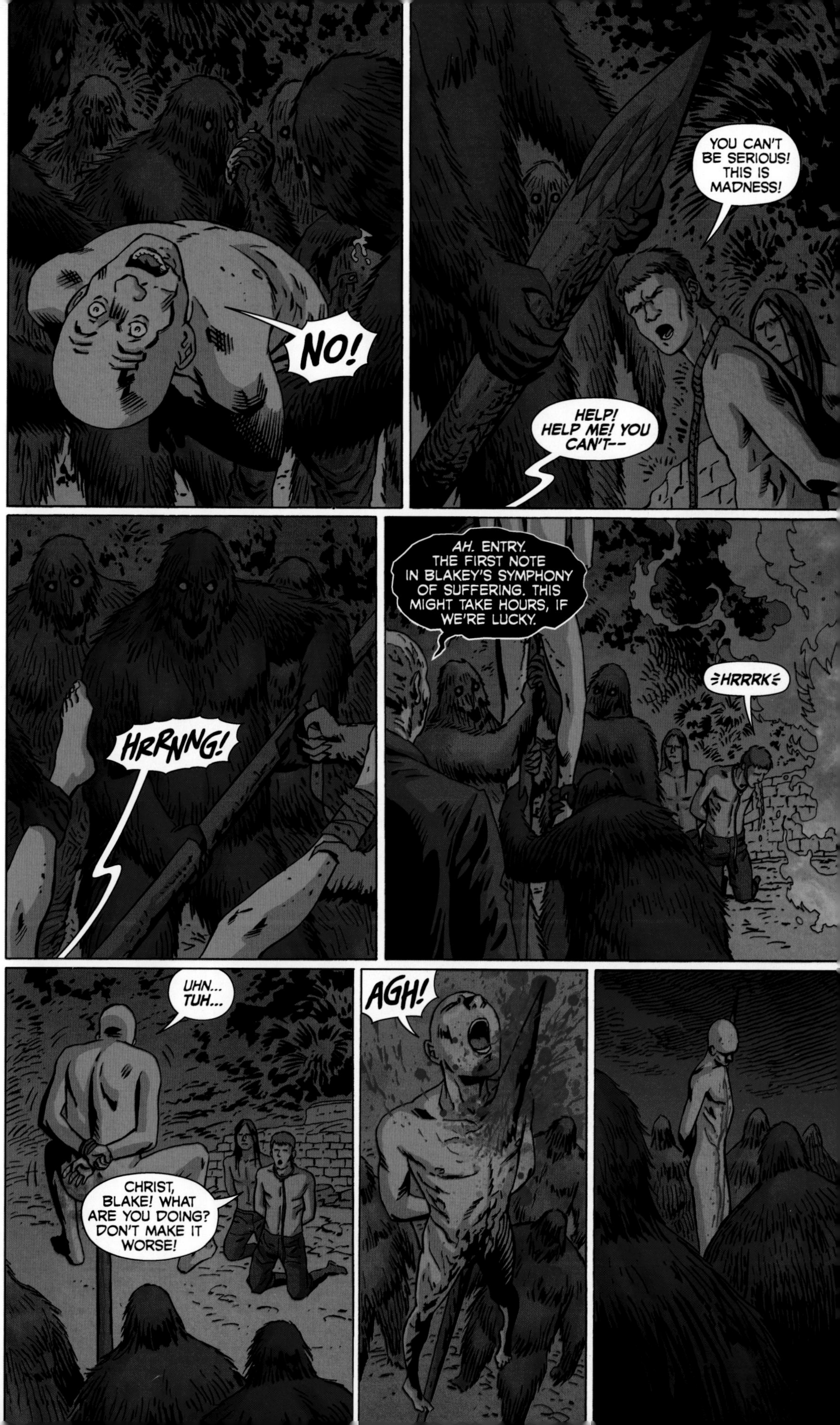
NO!
YOU CAN'T BE SERIOUS! THIS IS MADNESS!
HELP! HELP ME! YOU CAN'T--
HRRNNG!
AH. ENTRY. THE FIRST NOTE IN BLAKEY'S SYMPHONY OF SUFFERING. THIS MIGHT TAKE HOURS, IF WE'RE LUCKY.
HRRRK
UHN... TUH...
CHRIST, BLAKE! WHAT ARE YOU DOING? DON'T MAKE IT WORSE!
AGH!

THAT WAS SMART. IT WILL BE THE WAY WE SHOULD DO IT. FORCE IT TO BE QUICKER.

THAT'S A FIRST. MY, HE WAS BRAVE.

QUITE UNLIKE YOU. TAKES A REAL NO-DICKED PIECE OF SHIT TO PREY ON WOMEN AND CHILDREN HOW ABOUT FIGHTING A GROWN MAN? NO WEAPONS. NO SOLDIERS NOTHING TO HIDE BEHIND.

OH, HERE IT IS. THE PART WHERE YOU PLAY TO MY EGO. I DON'T MUCH CARE HOW I'M THOUGHT OF, MR. BEADLE.

SINCE VERY LITTLE CAUSES ME DAMAGE, AND I HAVE THE STRENGTH OF TEN MEN, IT'S SORT OF HARD TO BE CONCERNED ABOUT SUCH A THREAT.

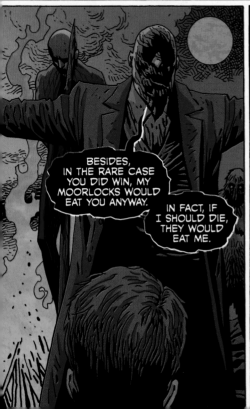

BESIDES, IN THE RARE CASE YOU DID WIN, MY MOORLOCKS WOULD EAT YOU ANYWAY.

IN FACT, IF I SHOULD DIE, THEY WOULD EAT ME.

ISN'T THAT RIGHT, BOYS?

I'M NOT GOING TO FIGHT YOU, CAPTAIN BEADLE. THIS ISN'T THAT KIND OF STORY.

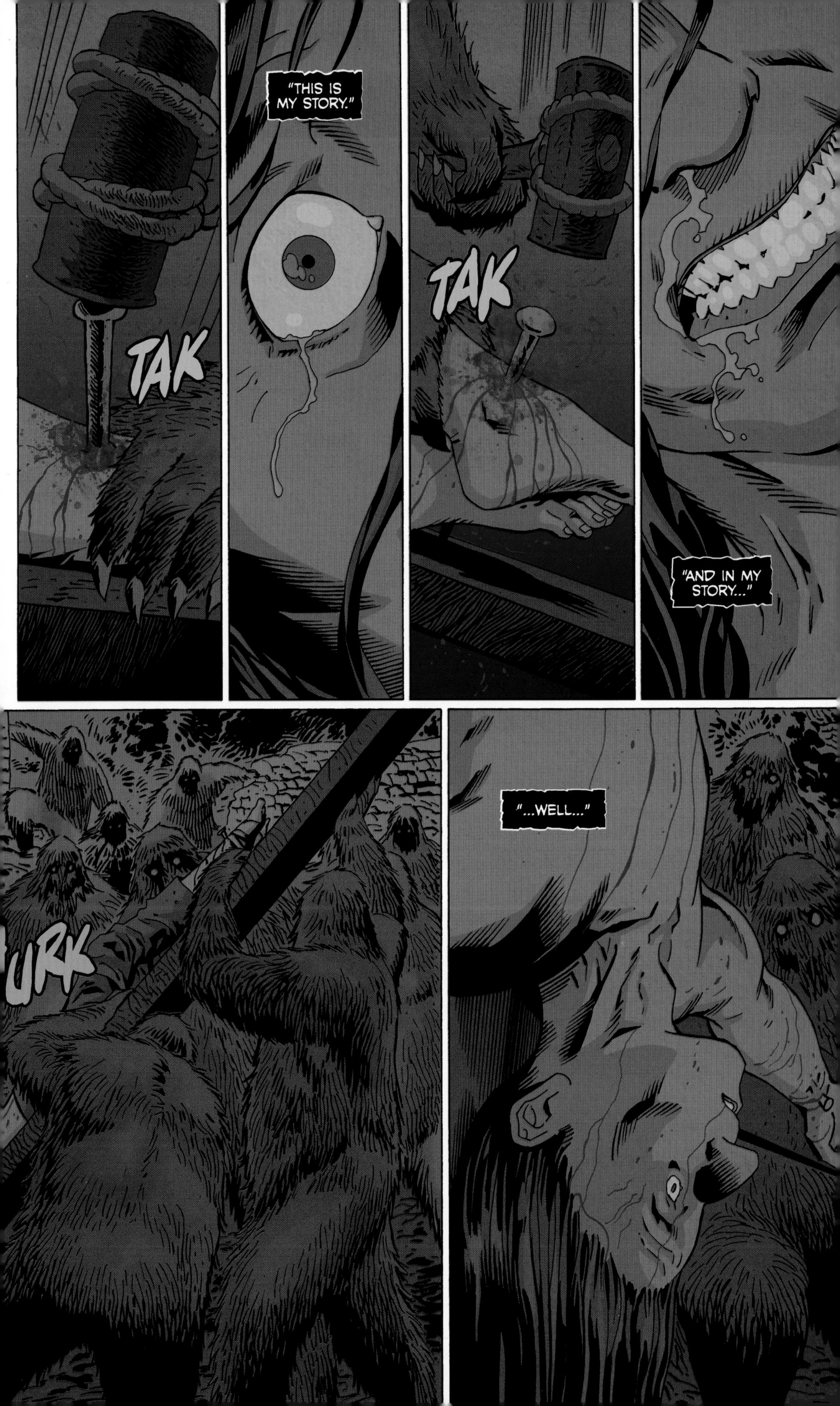
TAK
"THIS IS MY STORY."
TAK
"AND IN MY STORY..."
URK
"...WELL..."

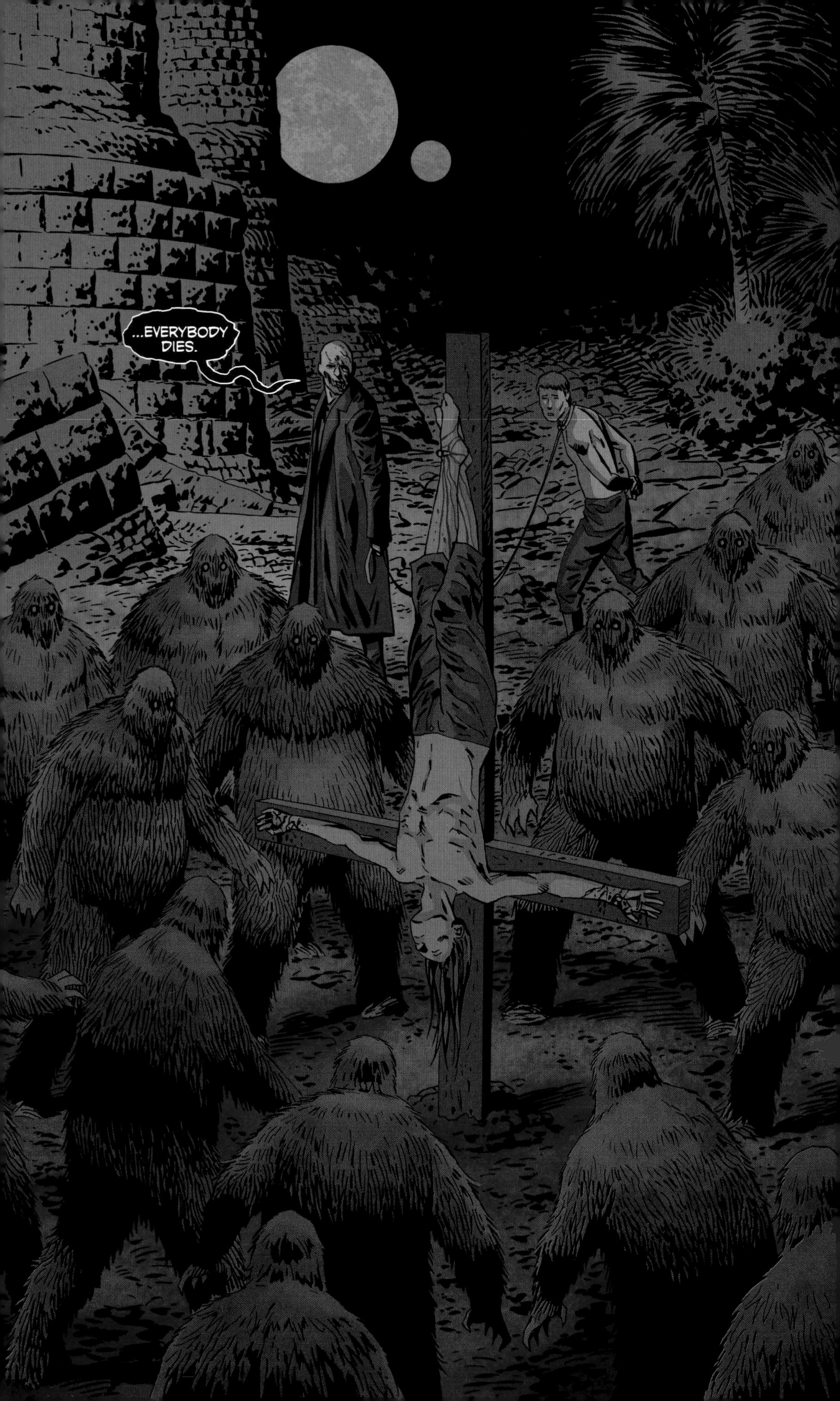
...EVERYBODY DIES.

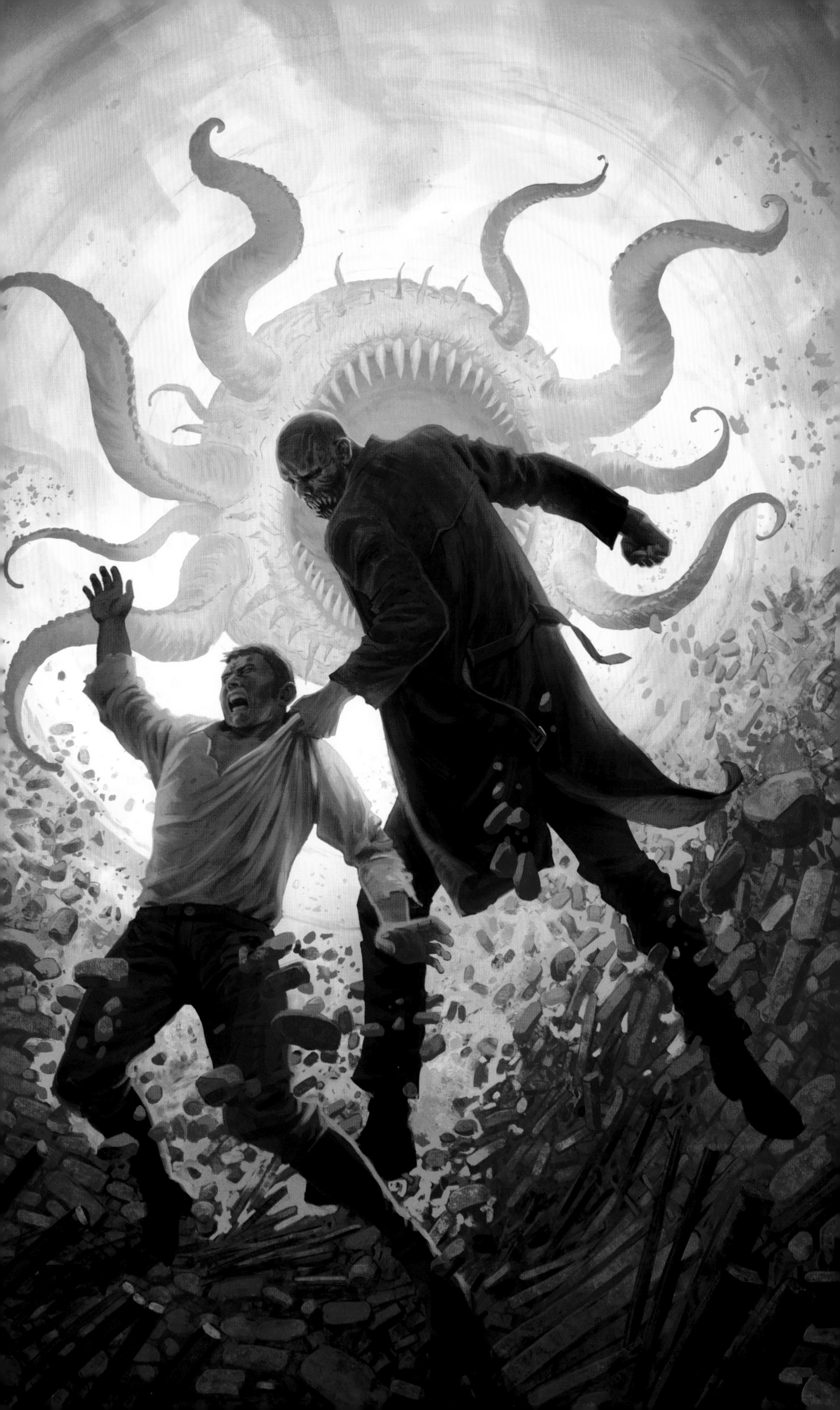

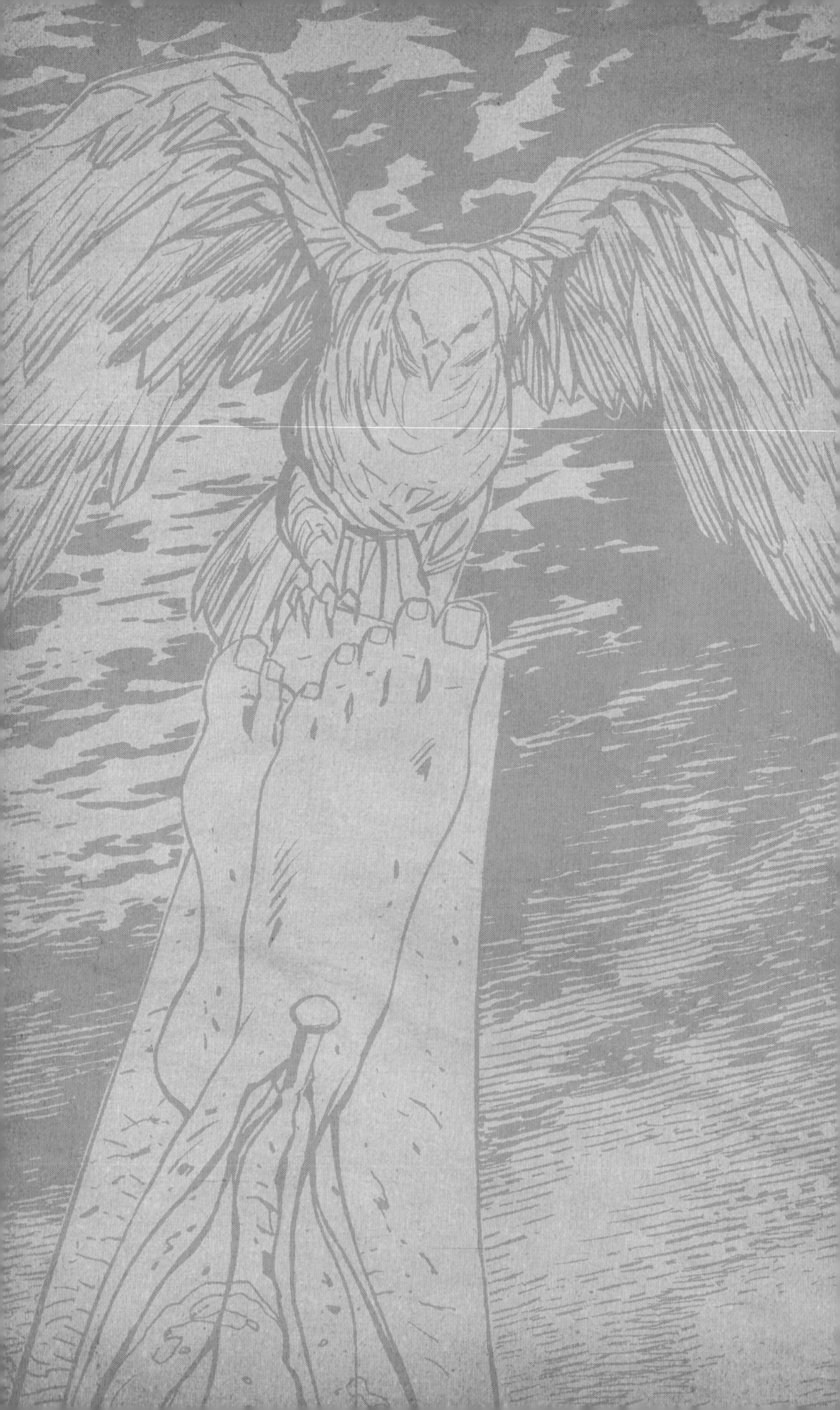

I BLACKED OUT AGAIN.

HOW LONG THIS TIME?

LONG ENOUGH, I SEE.

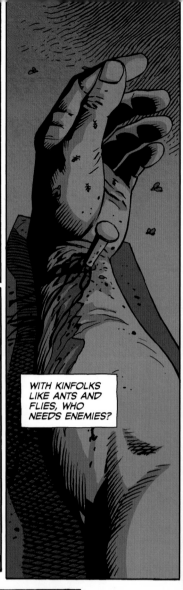

WITH KINFOLKS LIKE ANTS AND FLIES, WHO NEEDS ENEMIES?

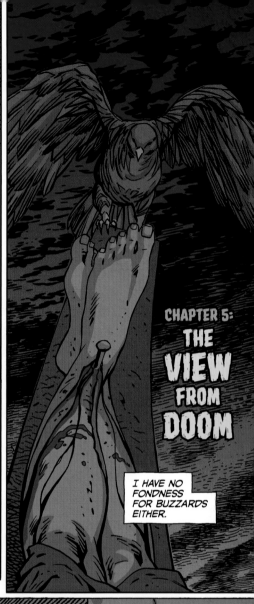

CHAPTER 5:
THE VIEW FROM DOOM

I HAVE NO FONDNESS FOR BUZZARDS EITHER.

I DON'T LIKE COYOTES MUCH. BUT WITH THE WAY MY LUCK IS GOING--

--PRETTY SOON THEY WILL SHOW UP TOO.

I HAVE TO DO SOMETHING ABOUT THIS.

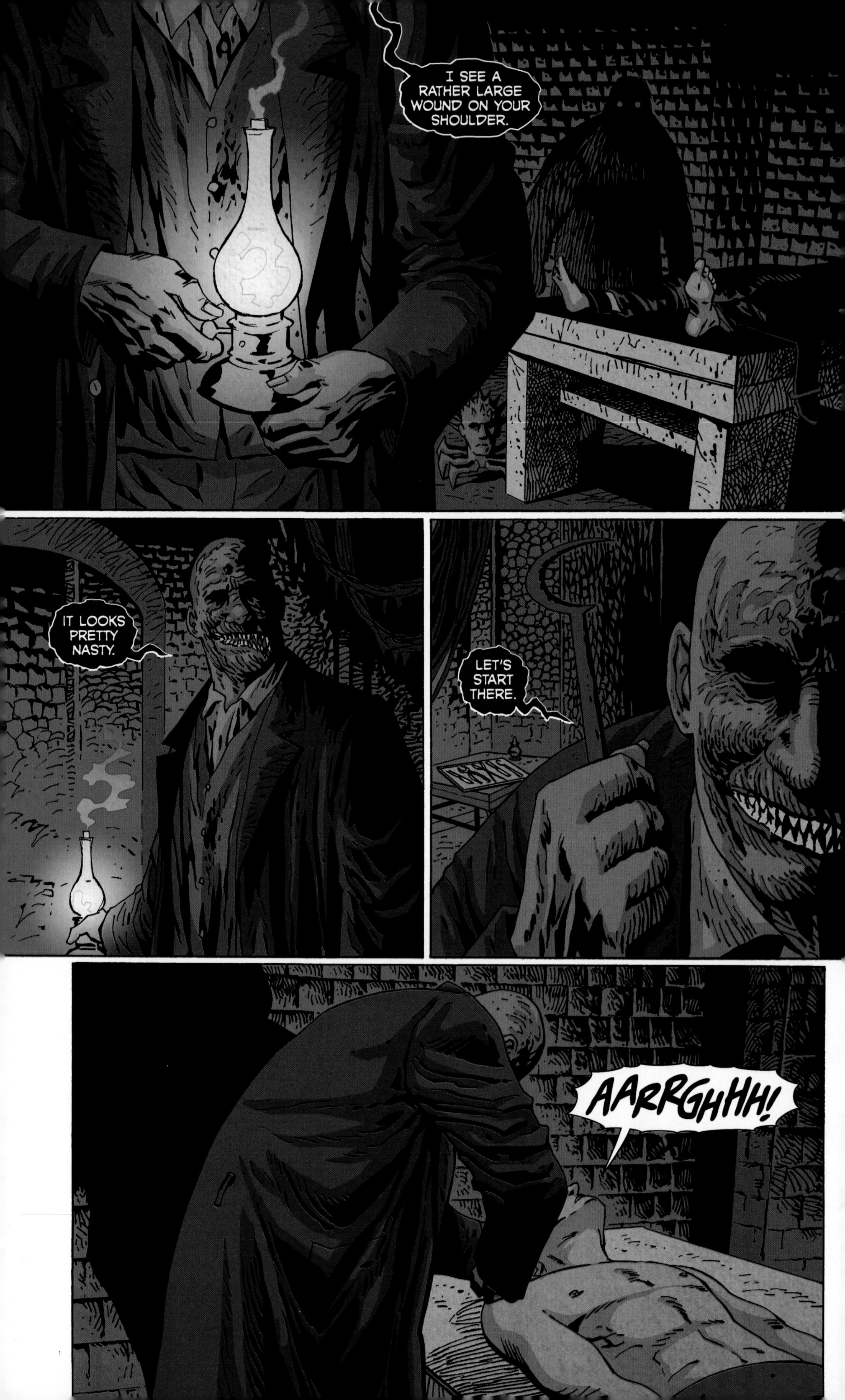
I SEE A RATHER LARGE WOUND ON YOUR SHOULDER.
IT LOOKS PRETTY NASTY.
LET'S START THERE.
AARRGHHH!

JUMPIN'--

--JESUS!

I THINK YOUR MEN WOULD BE DISAPPOINTED IN YOUR CATERWAULING, CAPTAIN BEADLE.

I, ON THE OTHER HAND...

...COULDN'T BE MORE PLEASED.

THERE WE ARE. AFTER THIS...

HNNNGGG!

...WE SHALL BEGIN WORK ON YOUR TOENAILS.

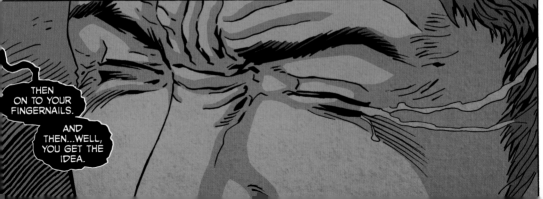

THEN ON TO YOUR FINGERNAILS.

AND THEN...WELL, YOU GET THE IDEA.

YOU CAN DO THIS.

THE FLESH IS NOT THAT STRONG.

IT WILL GIVE EASILY ENOUGH.

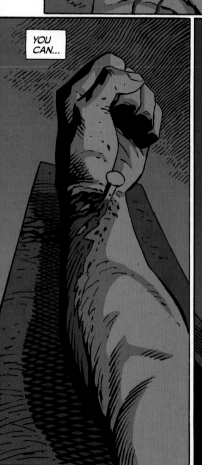

YOU CAN...

...DO THIS!

YYAAAAAAA

UURGGHHH!

ONE DOWN.

TWO TO GO.

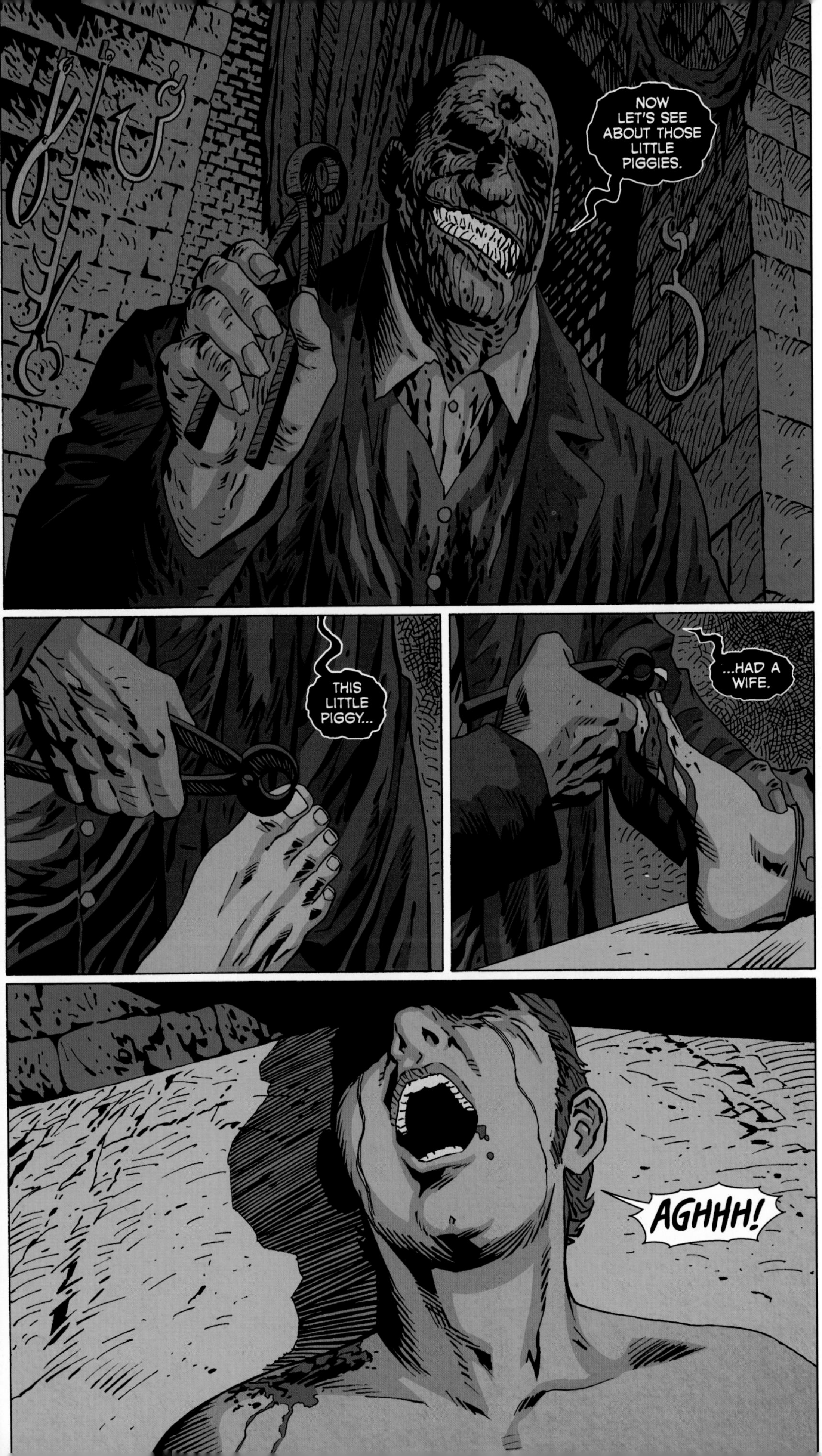
NOW LET'S SEE ABOUT THOSE LITTLE PIGGIES.
THIS LITTLE PIGGY...
...HAD A WIFE.
AGHHH!

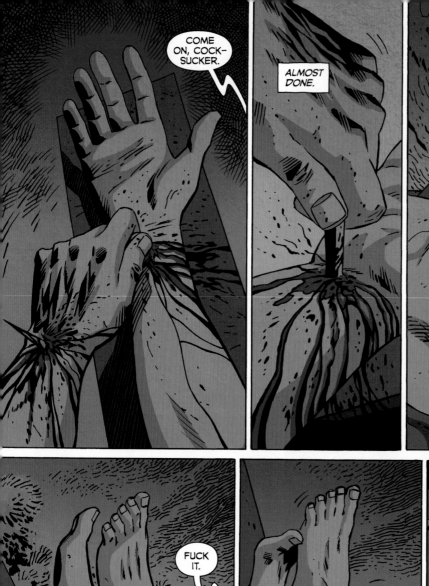

COME ON, COCK-SUCKER.

ALMOST DONE.

ONE...

TWO...

FUCK IT.

FFFFF--

FESTERING! FOX BALLS!

THIS FUCKING HURTS.

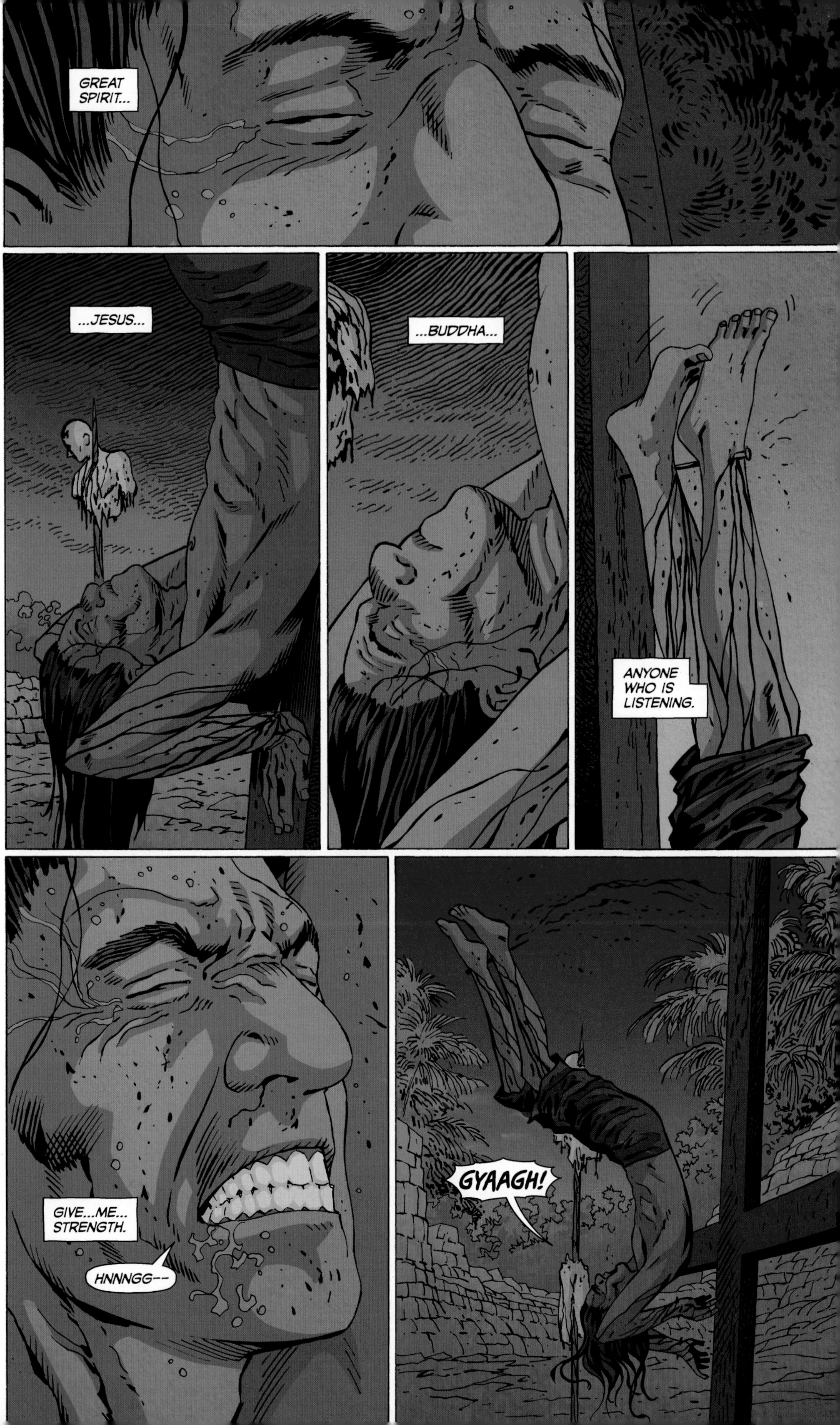
GREAT SPIRIT...
...JESUS...
...BUDDHA...
ANYONE WHO IS LISTENING.
GIVE...ME... STRENGTH.
HNNNGG--
GYAAGH!

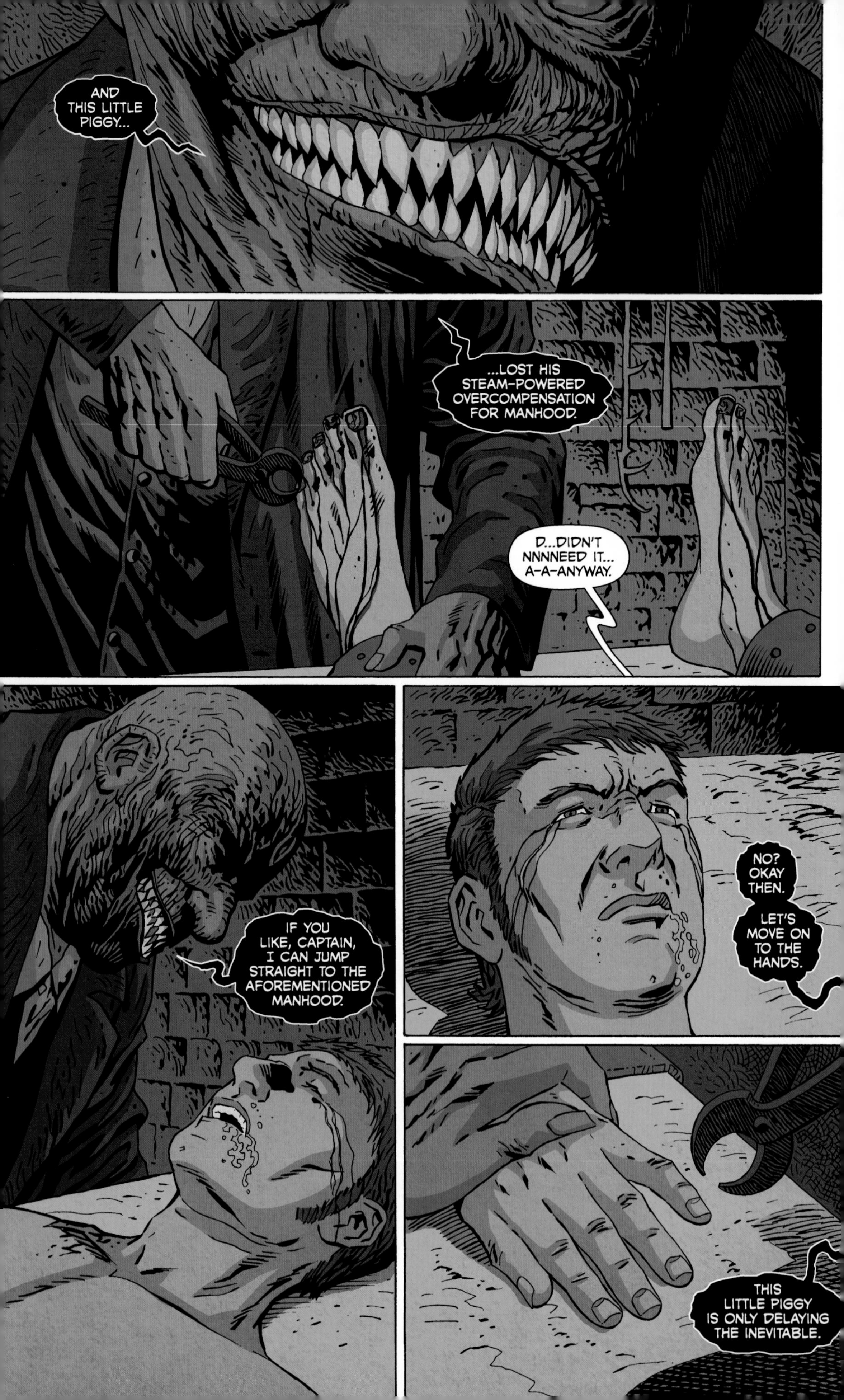
AND THIS LITTLE PIGGY...
...LOST HIS STEAM-POWERED OVERCOMPENSATION FOR MANHOOD.
D...DIDN'T NNNNEED IT... A-A-ANYWAY.
IF YOU LIKE, CAPTAIN, I CAN JUMP STRAIGHT TO THE AFOREMENTIONED MANHOOD.
NO? OKAY THEN.
LET'S MOVE ON TO THE HANDS.
THIS LITTLE PIGGY IS ONLY DELAYING THE INEVITABLE.

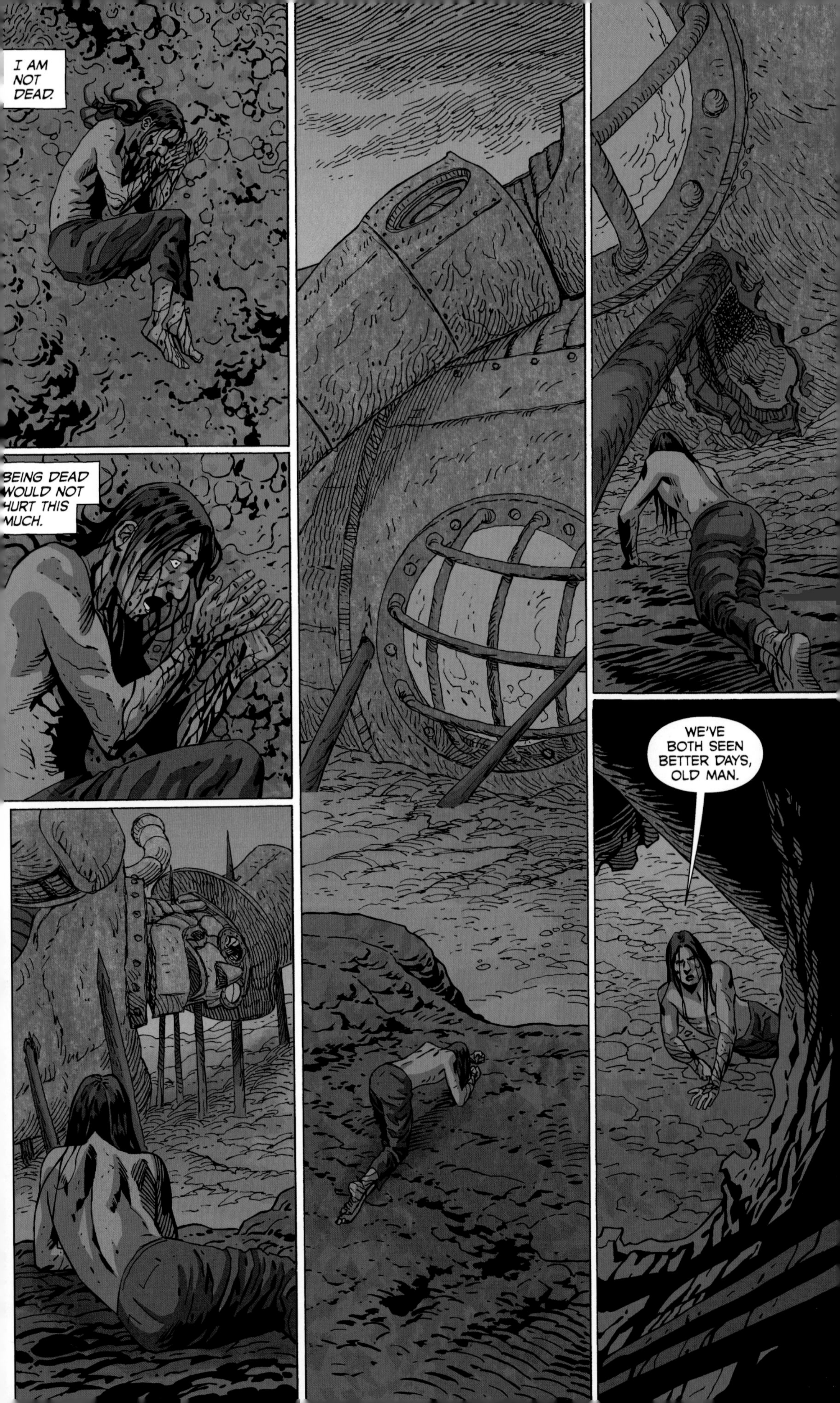

I AM NOT DEAD.
BEING DEAD WOULD NOT HURT THIS MUCH.
WE'VE BOTH SEEN BETTER DAYS, OLD MAN.

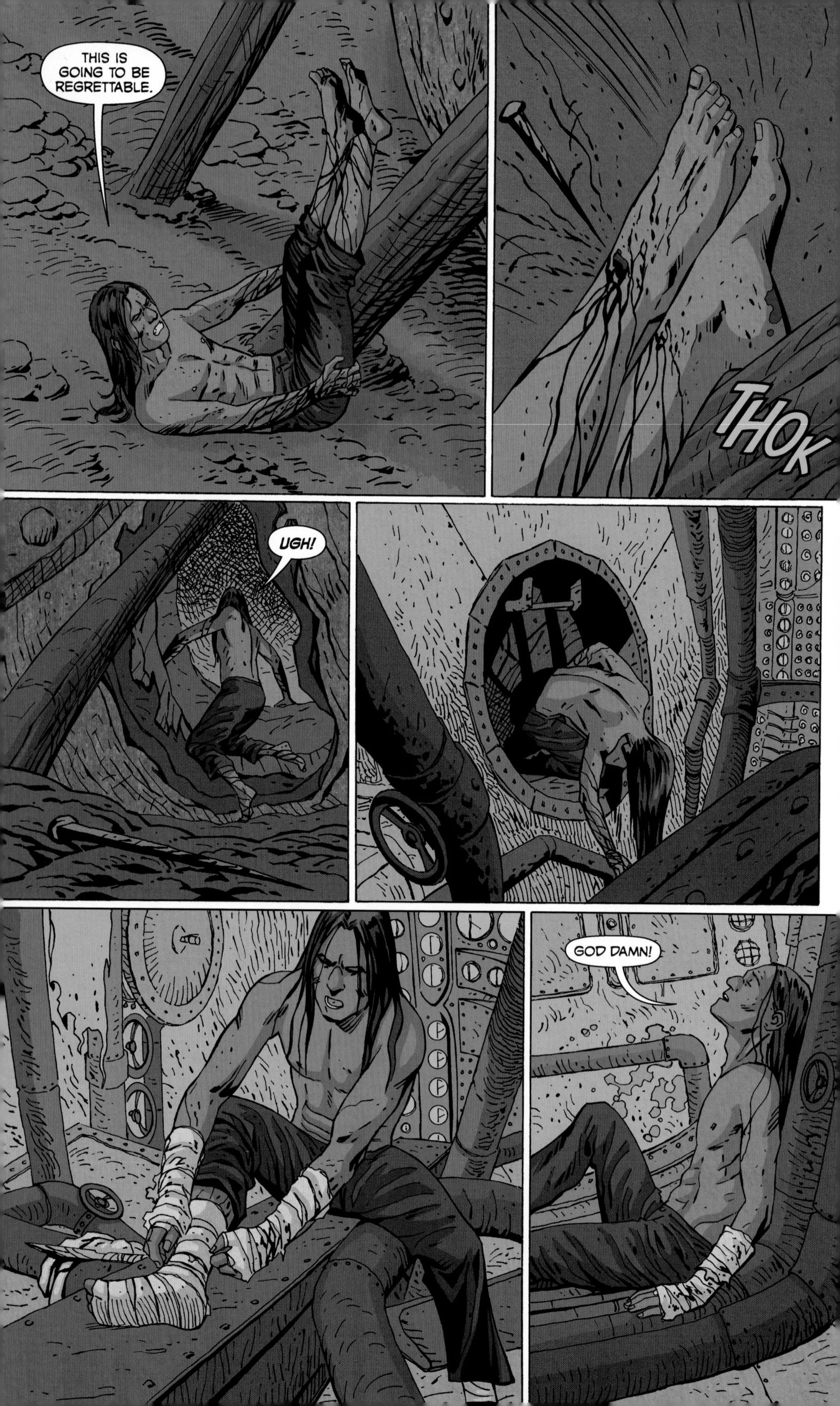
THIS IS GOING TO BE REGRETTABLE.
THOK
UGH!
GOD DAMN!

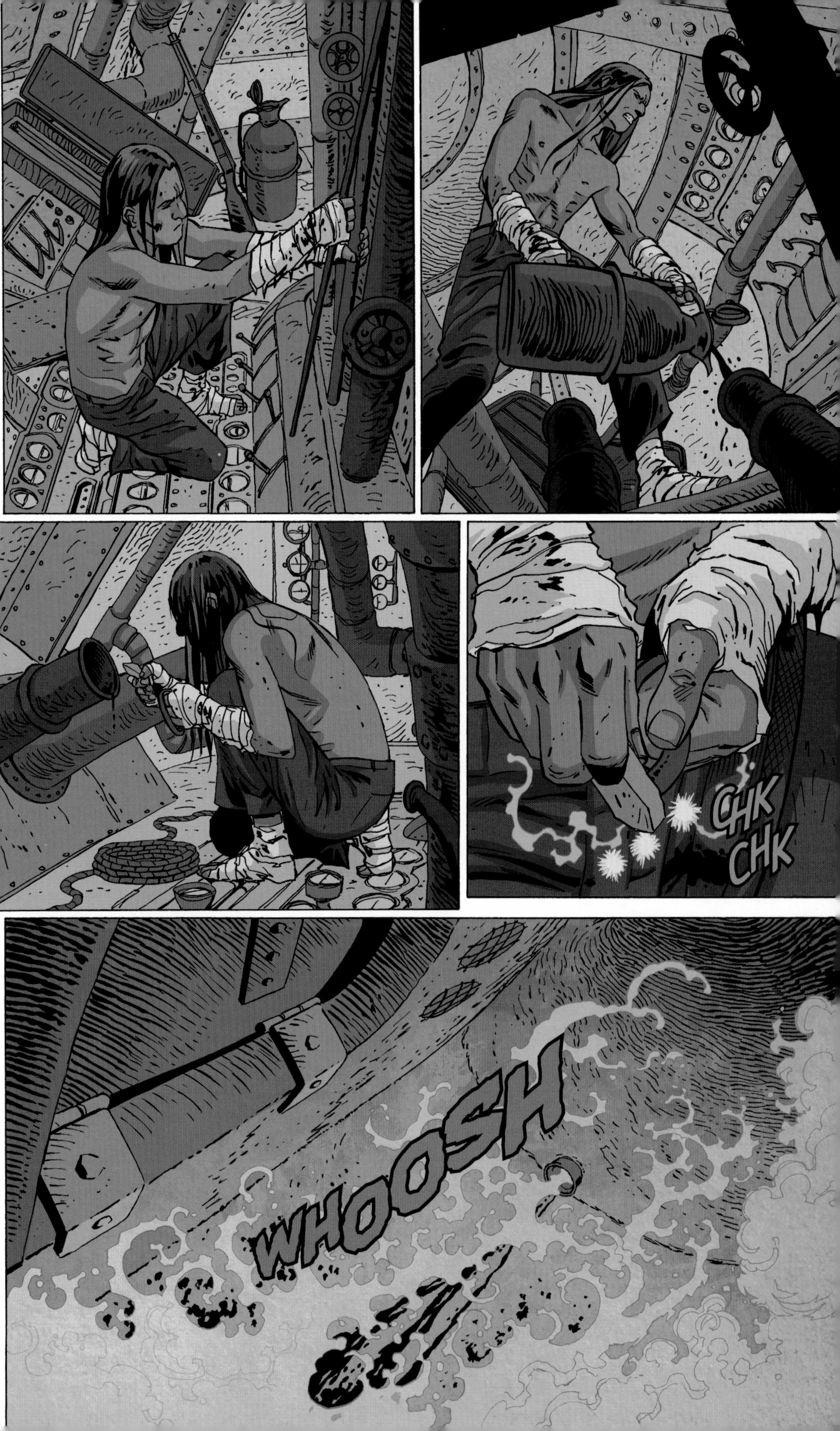
CHK
CHK
WHOOSH

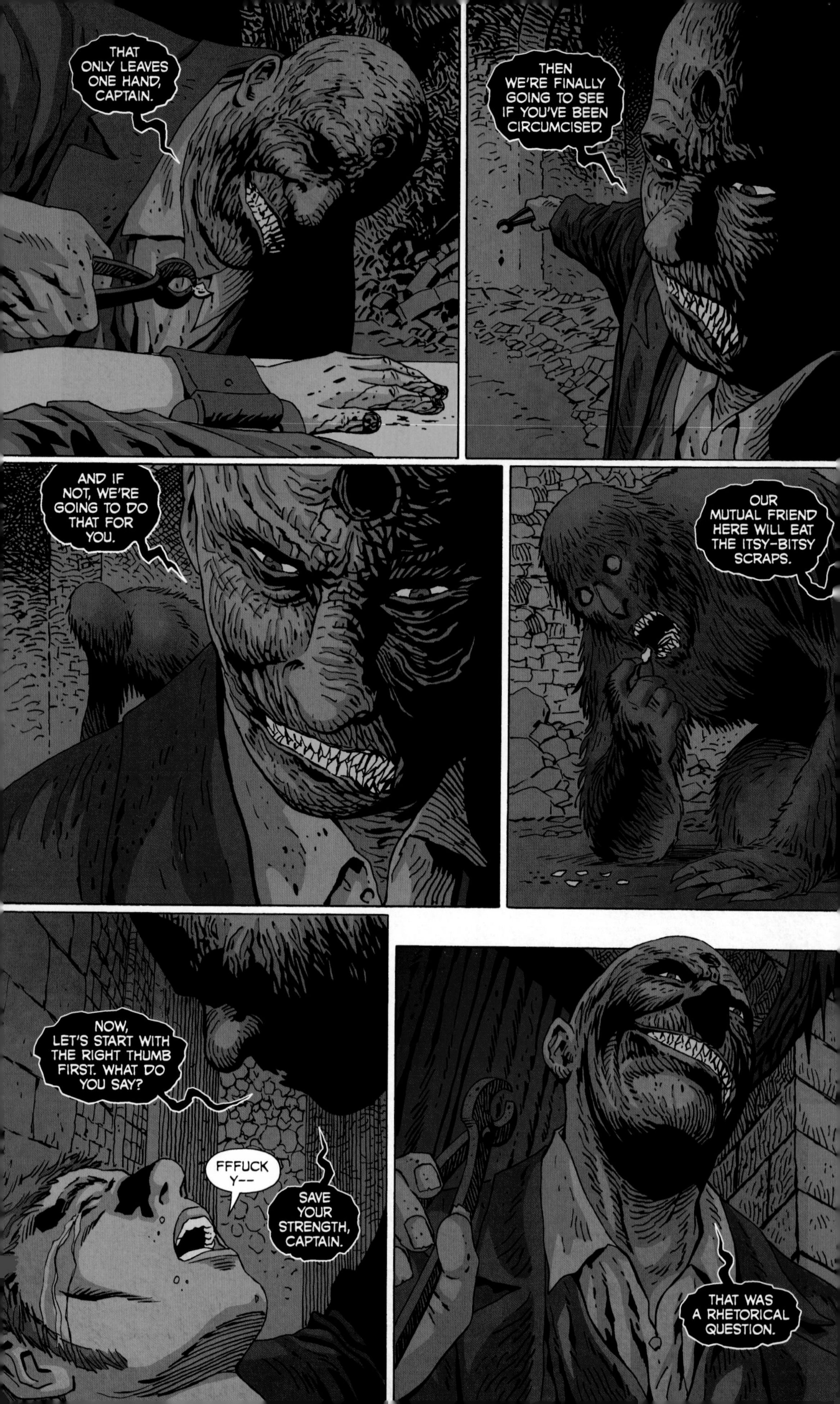
THAT ONLY LEAVES ONE HAND, CAPTAIN.
THEN WE'RE FINALLY GOING TO SEE IF YOU'VE BEEN CIRCUMCISED.
AND IF NOT, WE'RE GOING TO DO THAT FOR YOU.
OUR MUTUAL FRIEND HERE WILL EAT THE ITSY-BITSY SCRAPS.
NOW, LET'S START WITH THE RIGHT THUMB FIRST. WHAT DO YOU SAY?
FFFUCK Y--
SAVE YOUR STRENGTH, CAPTAIN.
THAT WAS A RHETORICAL QUESTION.

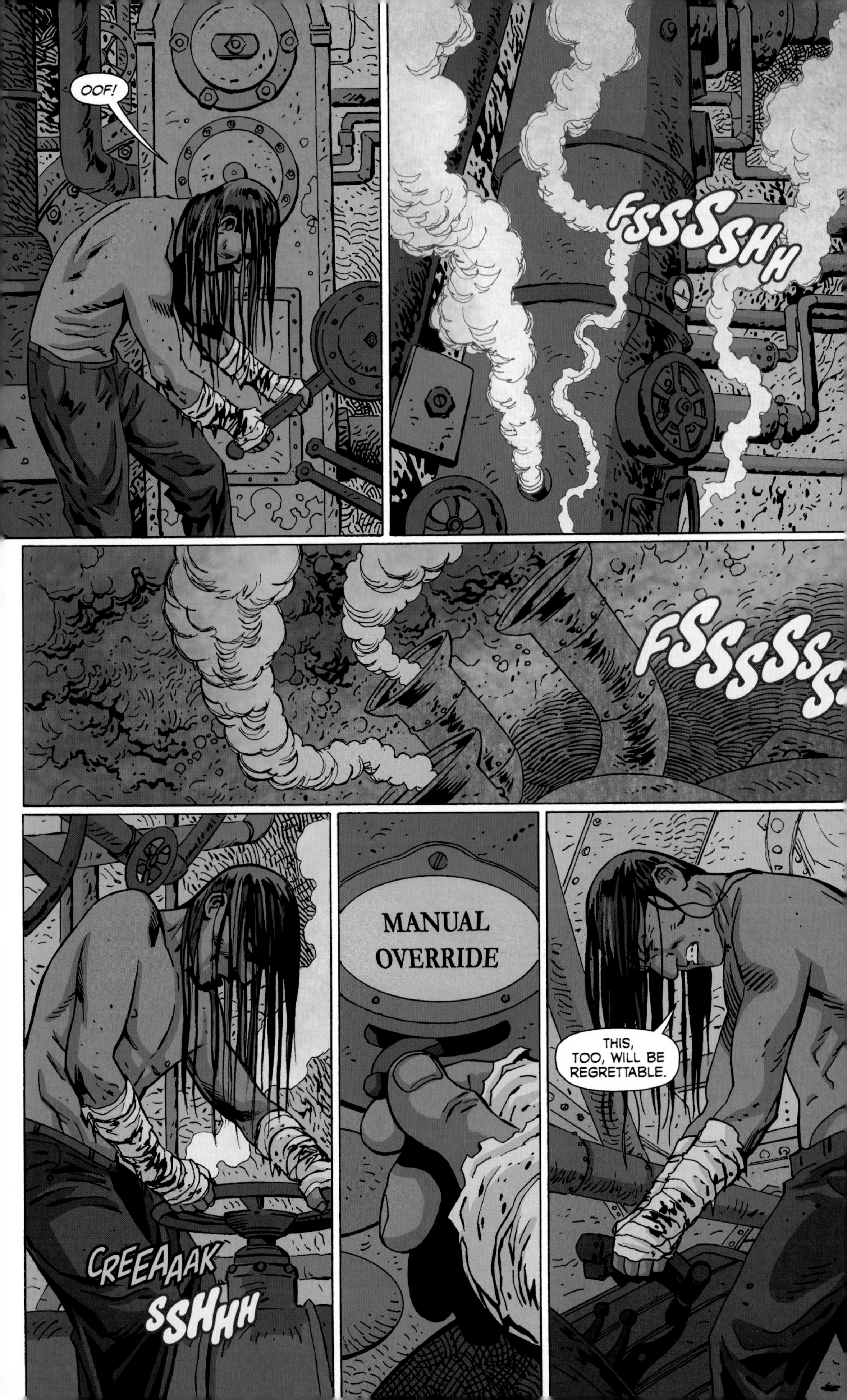
OOF!
FSSSSHH
FSSSSSS
CREEAAAK
SSHHH
MANUAL OVERRIDE
THIS, TOO, WILL BE REGRETTABLE.

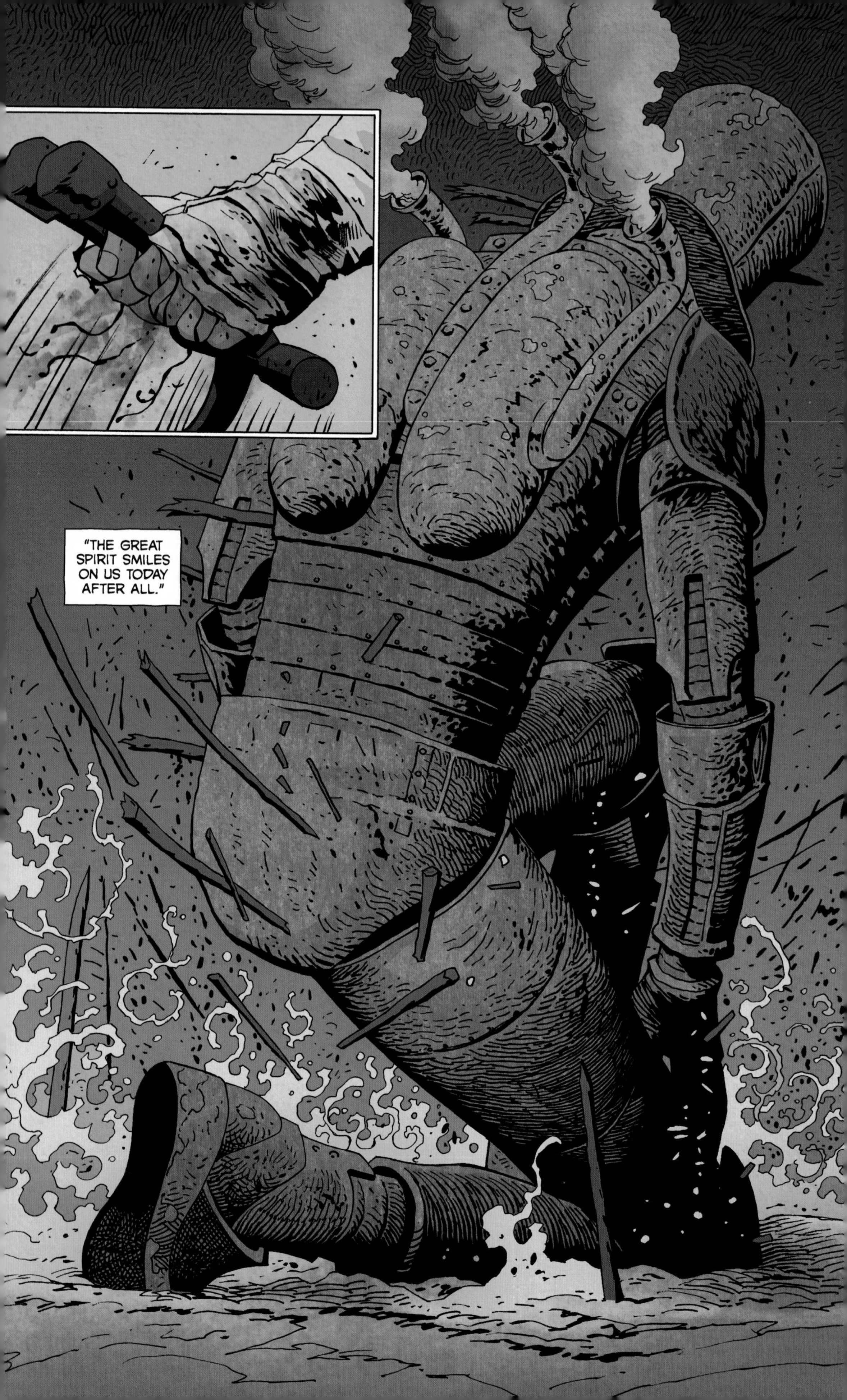
"THE GREAT SPIRIT SMILES ON US TODAY AFTER ALL."

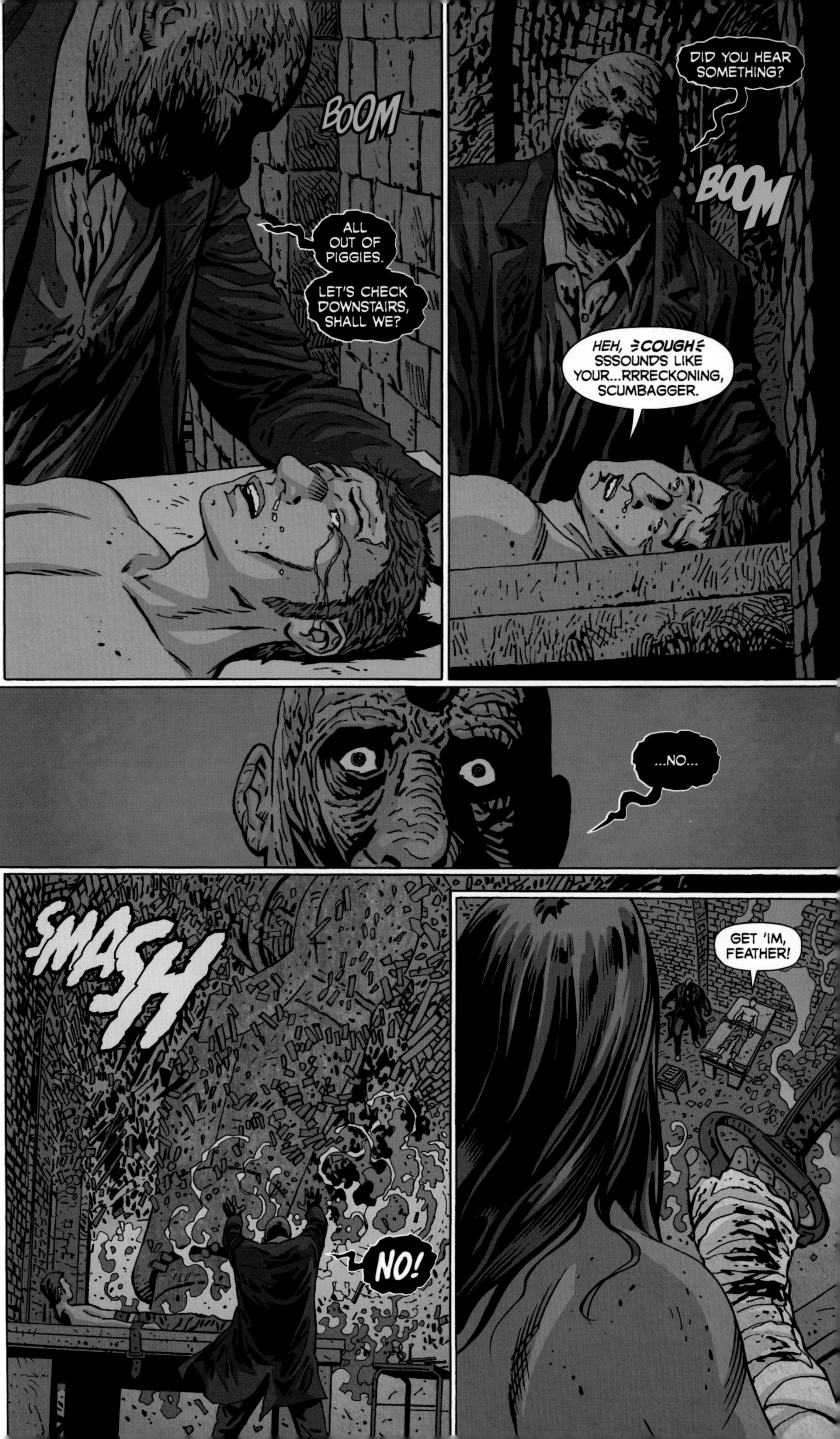
BOOM
ALL OUT OF PIGGIES.
LET'S CHECK DOWNSTAIRS, SHALL WE?
DID YOU HEAR SOMETHING?
BOOM
HEH, *COUGH* SSSOUNDS LIKE YOUR...RRRECKONING, SCUMBAGGER.
...NO...
SMASH
NO!
GET 'IM, FEATHER!

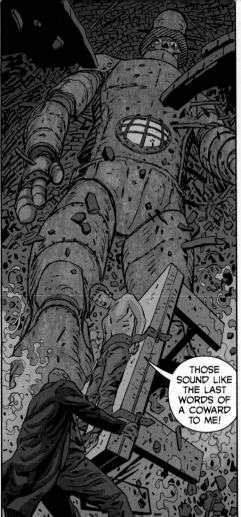

NNGH!

THOSE SOUND LIKE THE LAST WORDS OF A COWARD TO ME!

I SWORE WHAT I'D DO TO YOU, BEADLE. AND I AIM TO DO IT.

GUESS WE GO UP, THEN.

GHHRRR

RUN ALL YOU WANT, ASSHO--

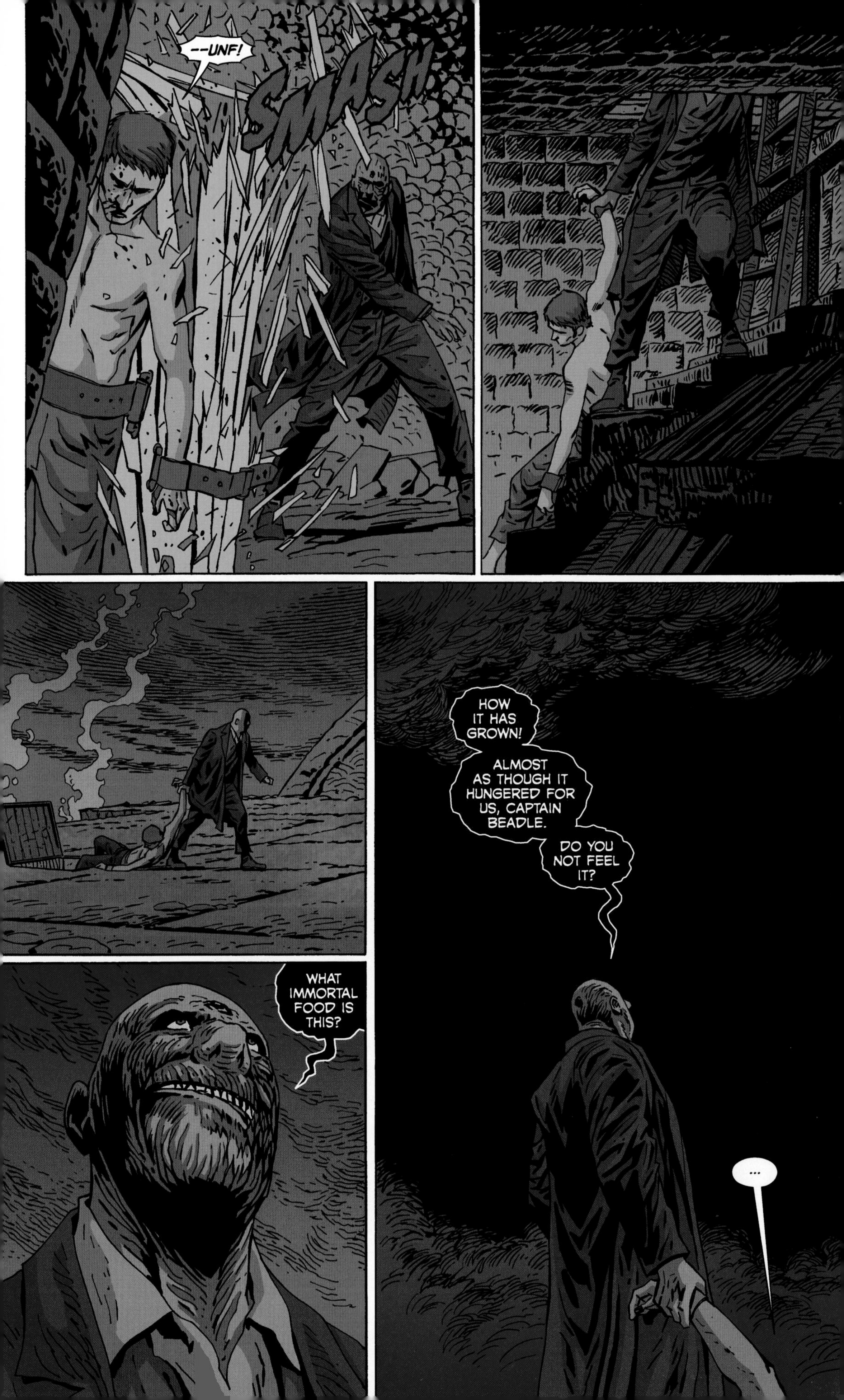
--UNF!
SMASH
HOW IT HAS GROWN!
ALMOST AS THOUGH IT HUNGERED FOR US, CAPTAIN BEADLE.
DO YOU NOT FEEL IT?
WHAT IMMORTAL FOOD IS THIS?
...

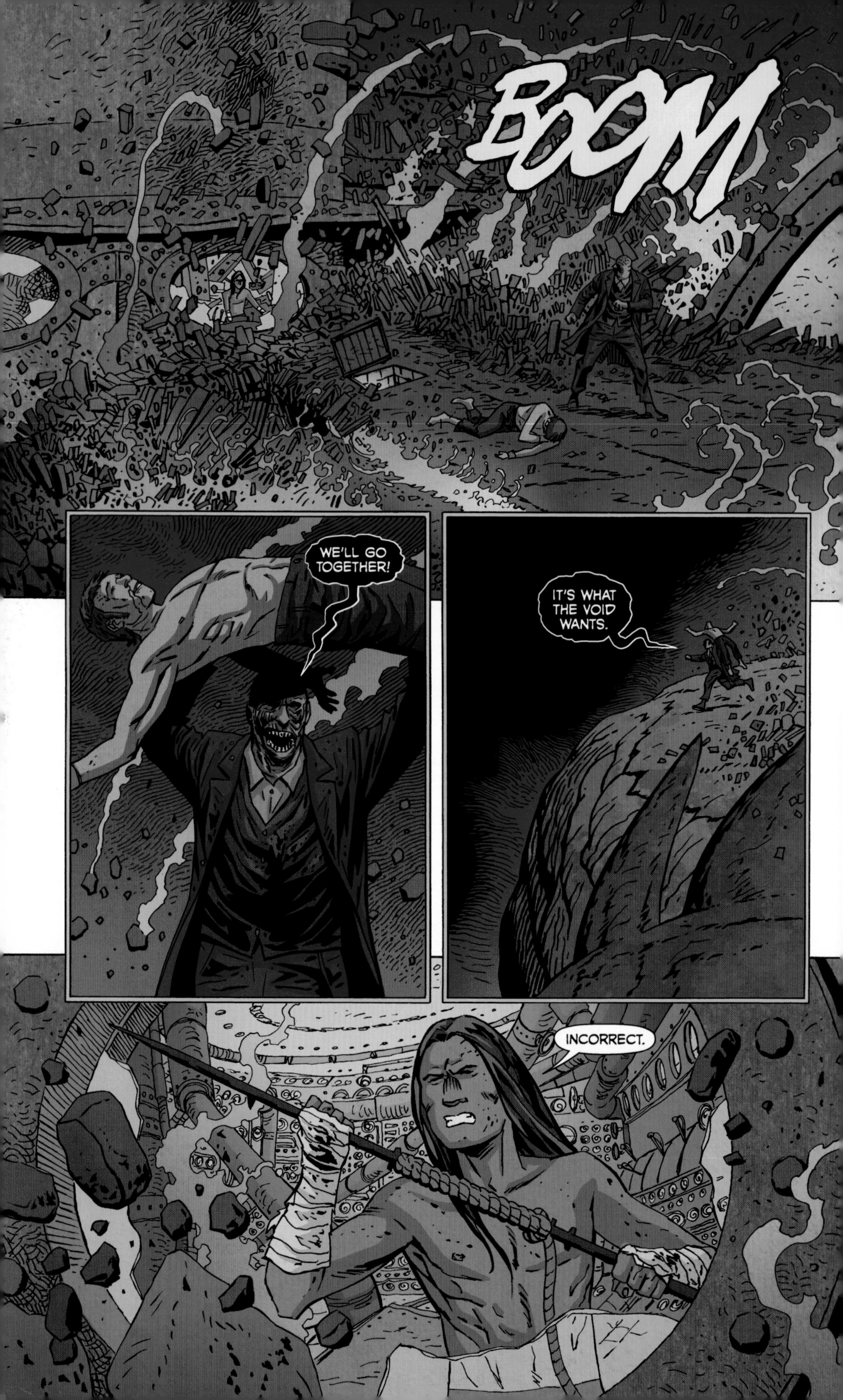
BOOM
WE'LL GO TOGETHER!
IT'S WHAT THE VOID WANTS.
INCORRECT.

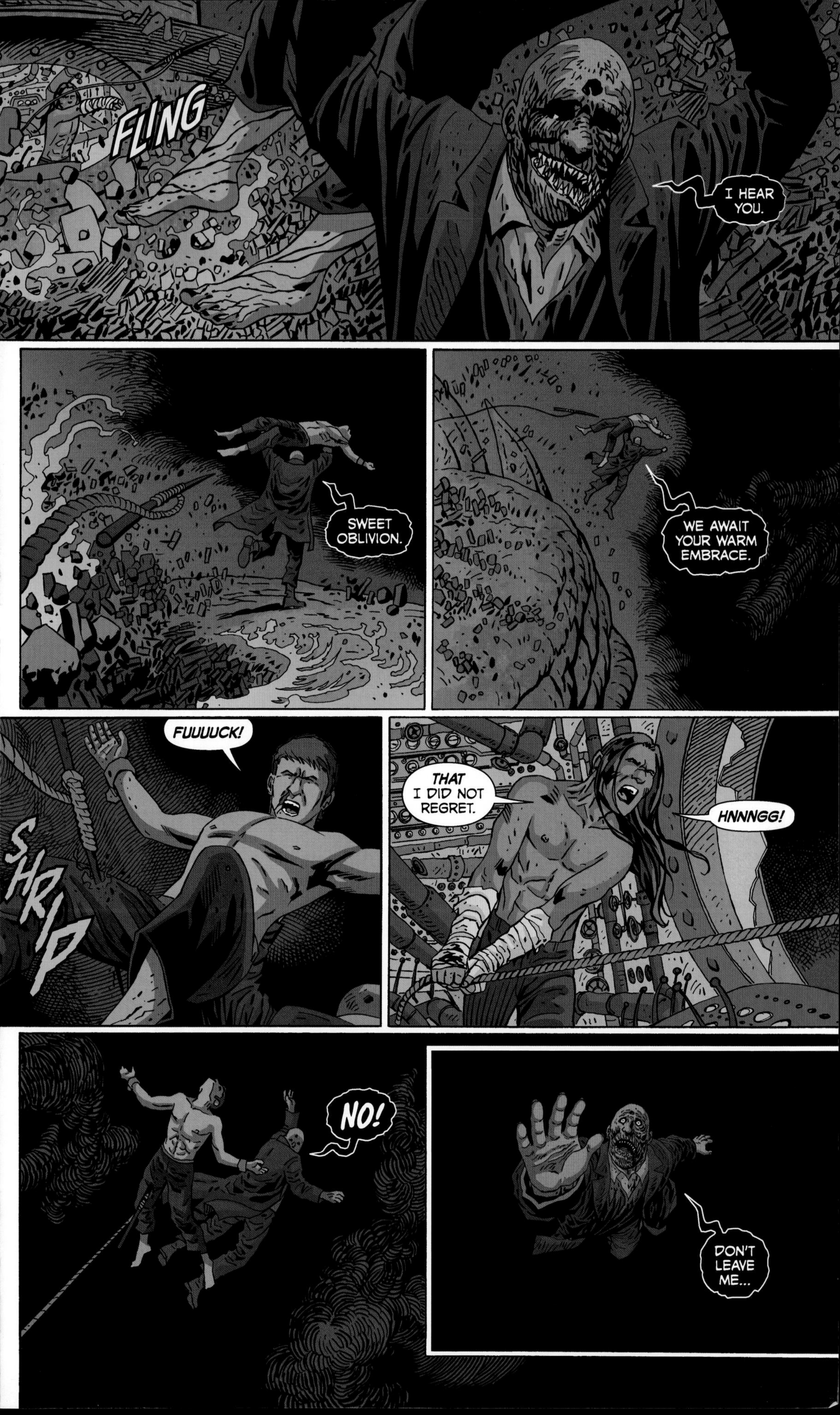
FLING
I HEAR YOU.
SWEET OBLIVION.
WE AWAIT YOUR WARM EMBRACE.
FUUUUCK!
SHRIP
THAT I DID NOT REGRET.
HNNNGG!
NO!
DON'T LEAVE ME...

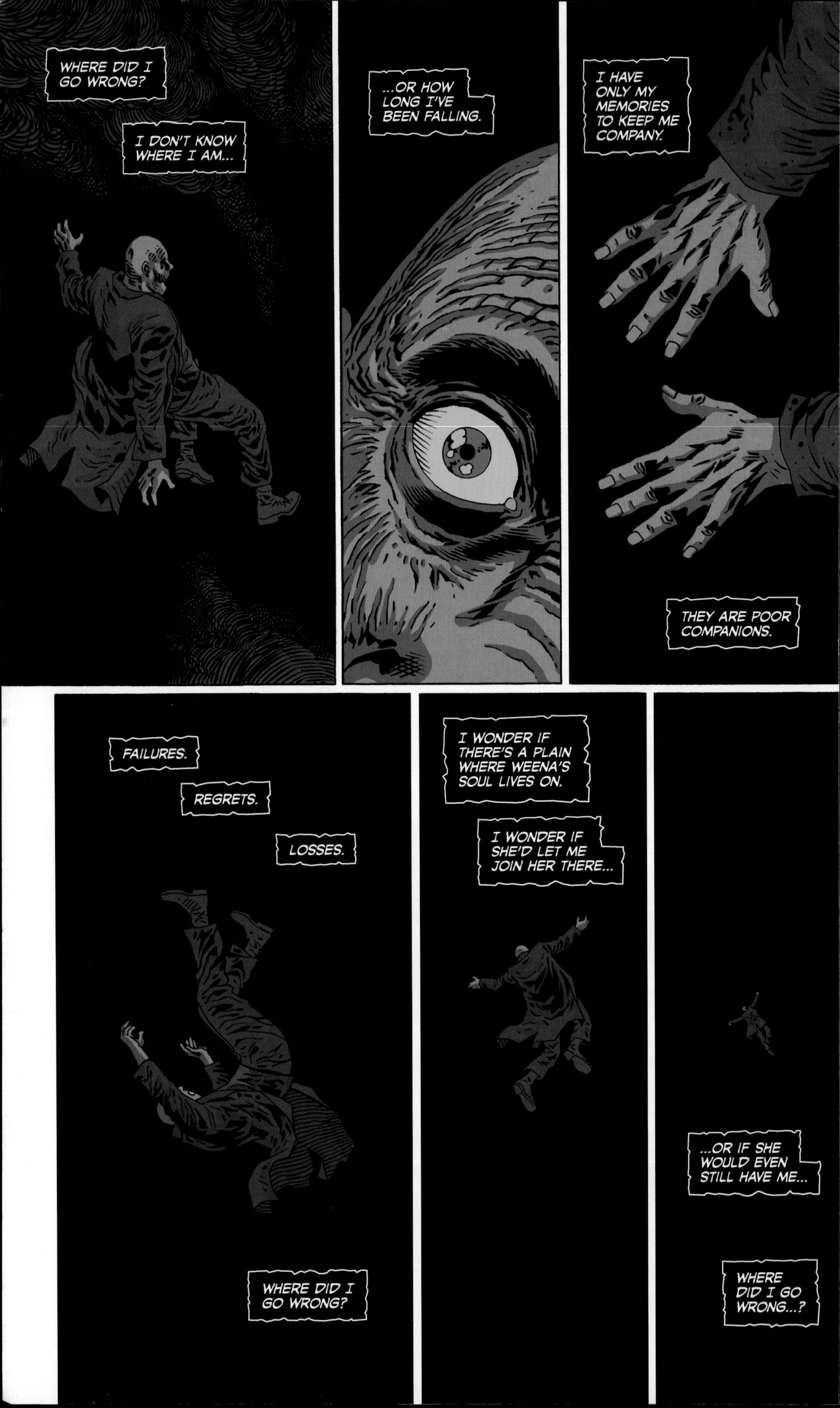
WHERE DID I GO WRONG?
I DON'T KNOW WHERE I AM...
...OR HOW LONG I'VE BEEN FALLING.
I HAVE ONLY MY MEMORIES TO KEEP ME COMPANY.
THEY ARE POOR COMPANIONS.
FAILURES.
REGRETS.
LOSSES.
WHERE DID I GO WRONG?
I WONDER IF THERE'S A PLAIN WHERE WEENA'S SOUL LIVES ON.
I WONDER IF SHE'D LET ME JOIN HER THERE...
...OR IF SHE WOULD EVEN STILL HAVE ME...
WHERE DID I GO WRONG...?

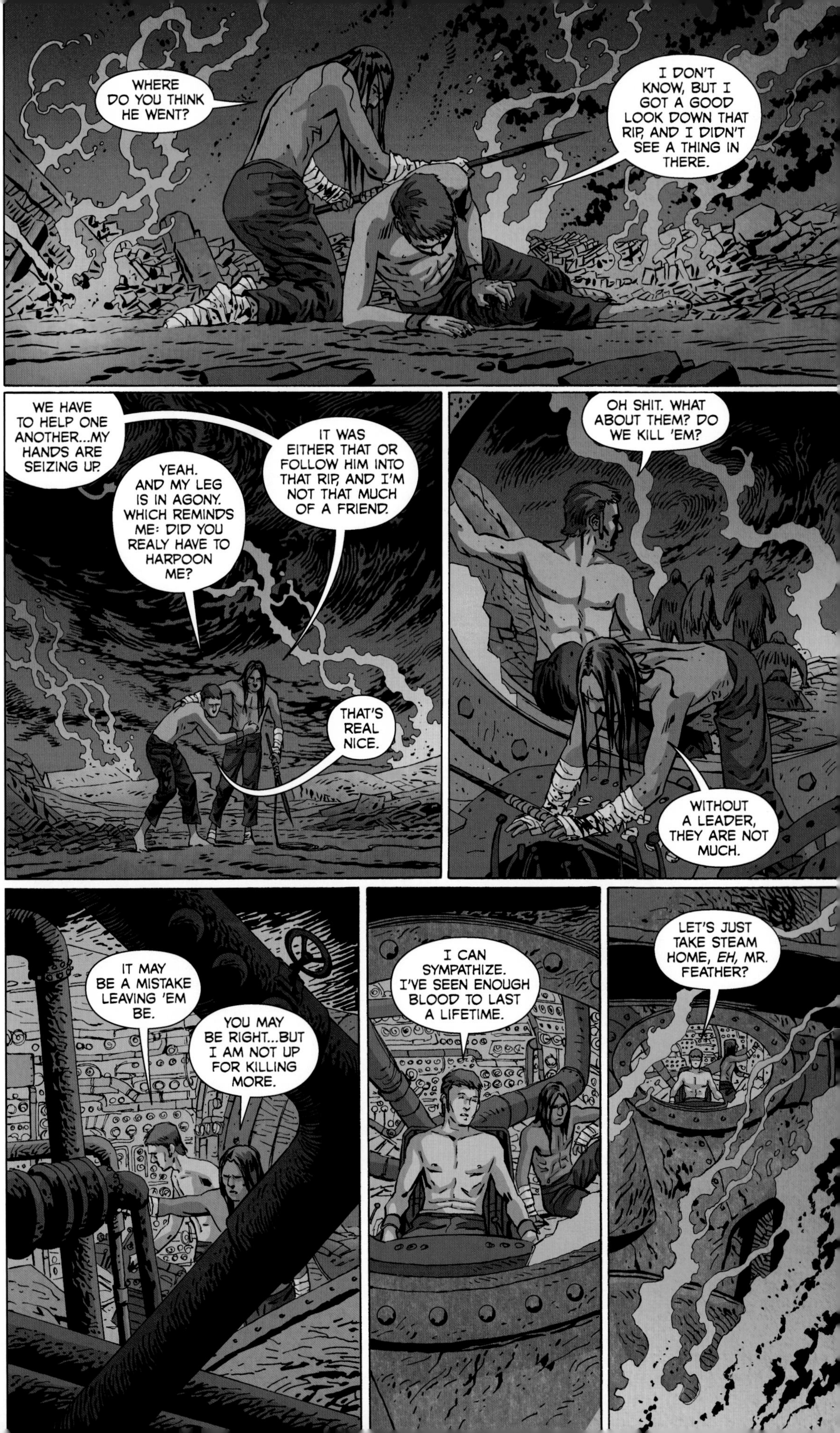
WHERE DO YOU THINK HE WENT?
I DON'T KNOW, BUT I GOT A GOOD LOOK DOWN THAT RIP, AND I DIDN'T SEE A THING IN THERE.
WE HAVE TO HELP ONE ANOTHER...MY HANDS ARE SEIZING UP.
YEAH. AND MY LEG IS IN AGONY. WHICH REMINDS ME: DID YOU REALY HAVE TO HARPOON ME?
IT WAS EITHER THAT OR FOLLOW HIM INTO THAT RIP, AND I'M NOT THAT MUCH OF A FRIEND.
THAT'S REAL NICE.
OH SHIT. WHAT ABOUT THEM? DO WE KILL 'EM?
WITHOUT A LEADER, THEY ARE NOT MUCH.
IT MAY BE A MISTAKE LEAVING 'EM BE.
YOU MAY BE RIGHT...BUT I AM NOT UP FOR KILLING MORE.
I CAN SYMPATHIZE. I'VE SEEN ENOUGH BLOOD TO LAST A LIFETIME.
LET'S JUST TAKE STEAM HOME, *EH*, MR. FEATHER?

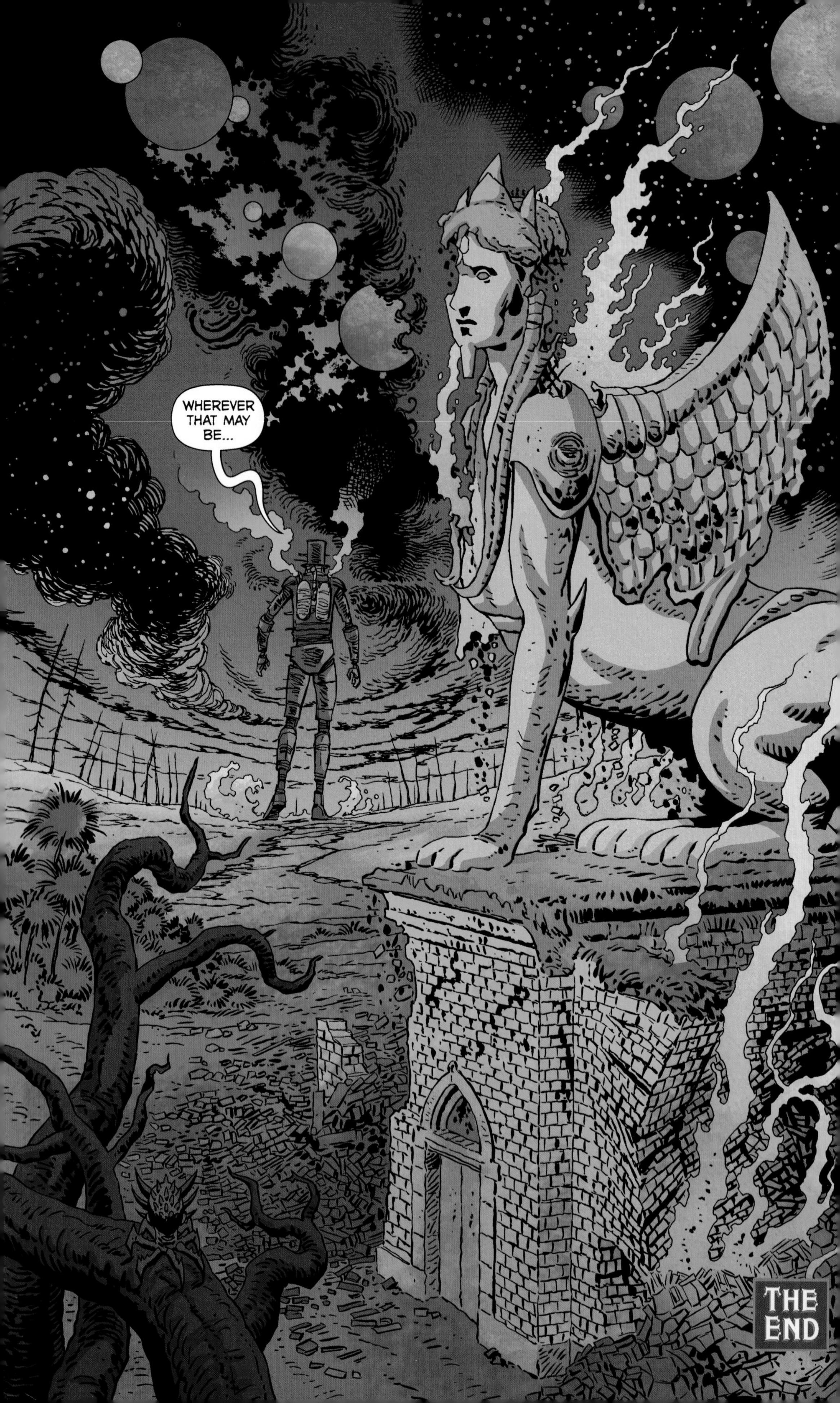
WHEREVER THAT MAY BE...
THE END

The Steam Man

SKETCHBOOK
NOTES BY PIOTR KOWALSKI

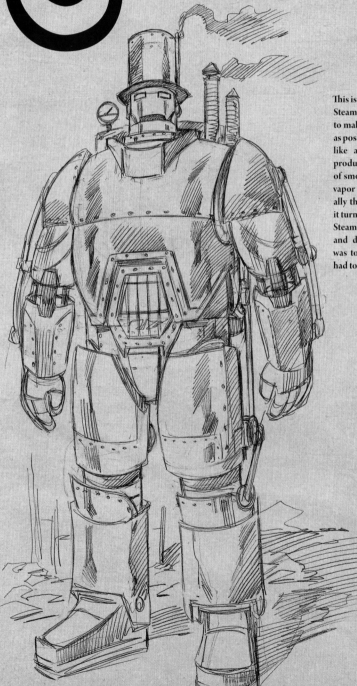

This is the very first sketch of the Steam Man. My initial idea was to make him as bulky and heavy as possible. I wanted him to look like a walking steam factory, producing a lot of gas and a lot of smoke and leaving a massive vapor trail behind him. Eventually this design was rejected, as it turned out that we needed the Steam Man to be much slimmer and definitely more agile. He was to do a lot of fighting and had to move fast.

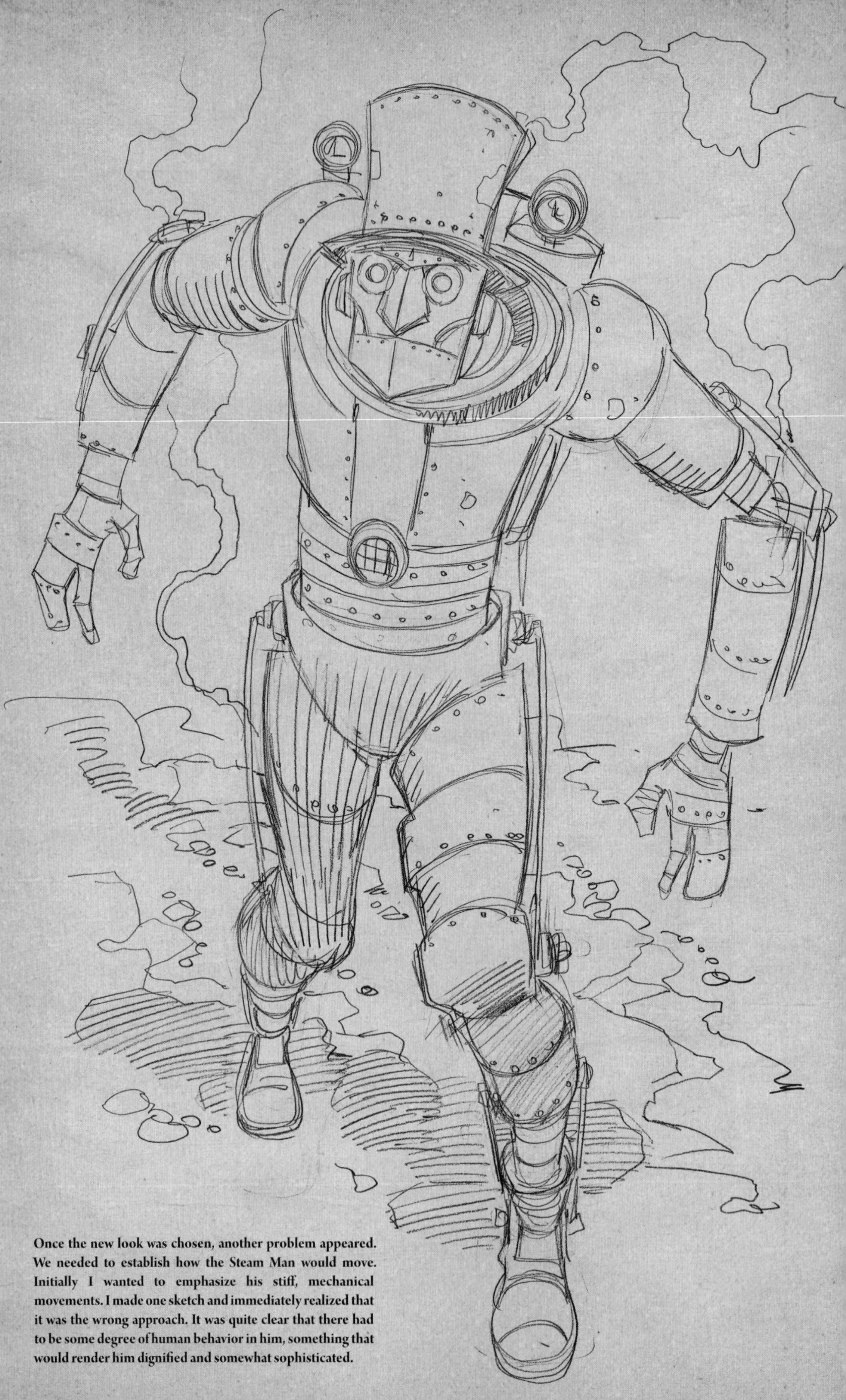

Once the new look was chosen, another problem appeared. We needed to establish how the Steam Man would move. Initially I wanted to emphasize his stiff, mechanical movements. I made one sketch and immediately realized that it was the wrong approach. It was quite clear that there had to be some degree of human behavior in him, something that would render him dignified and somewhat sophisticated.

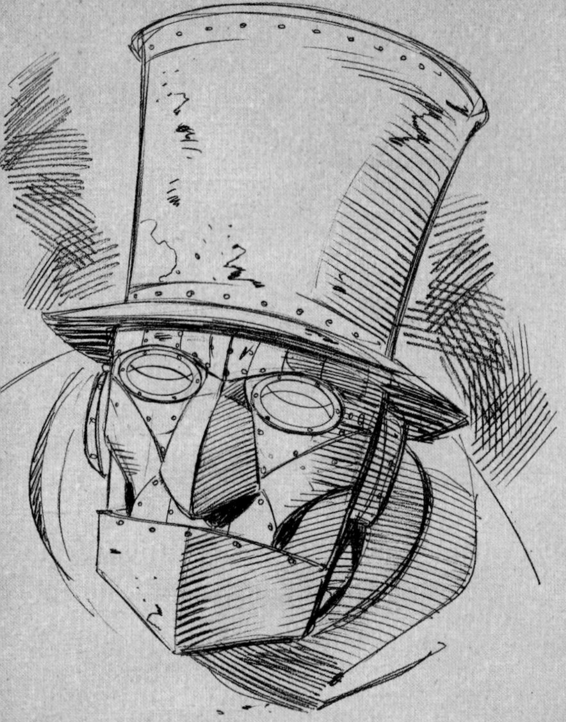

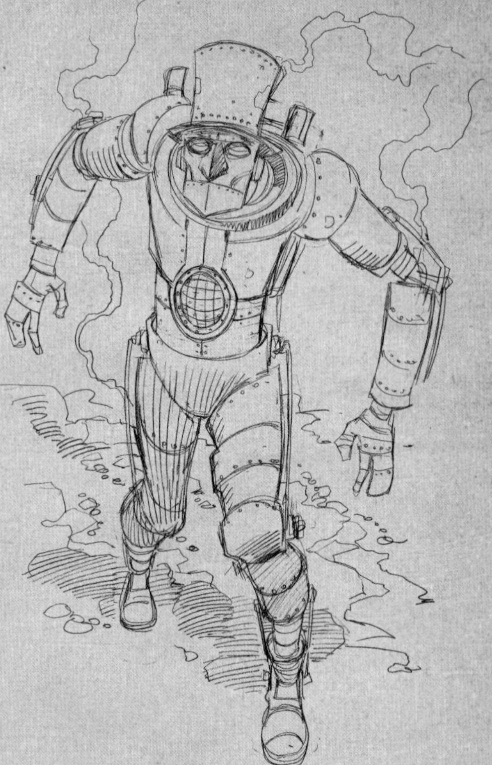

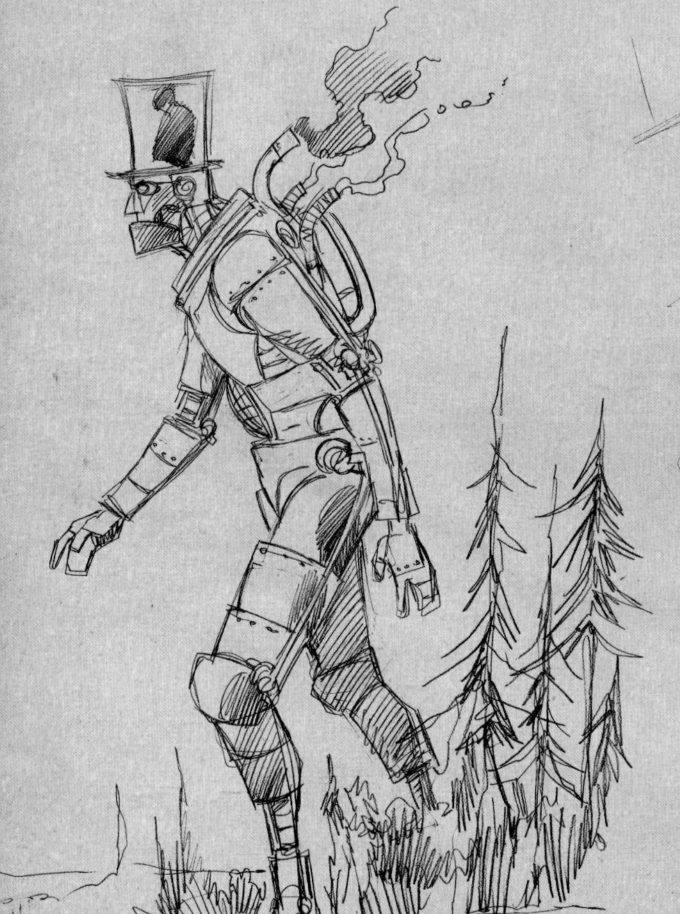

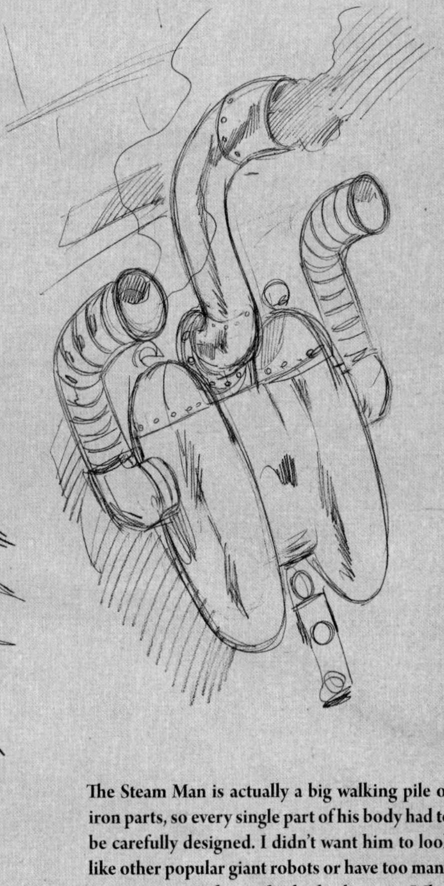

The Steam Man is actually a big walking pile of iron parts, so every single part of his body had to be carefully designed. I didn't want him to look like other popular giant robots or have too many moving parts and complex body elements. What I wanted was a real simplicity. I thought that if I were to construct a huge robot in real life, I would go for a simple, functional shape.

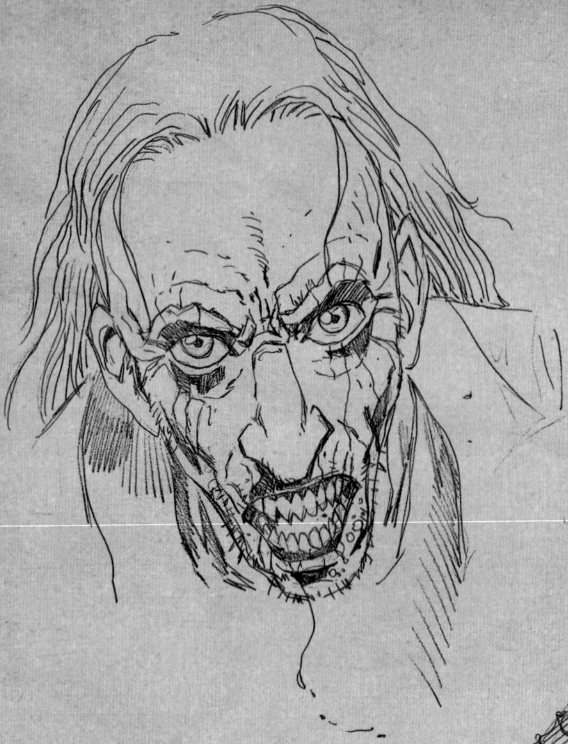

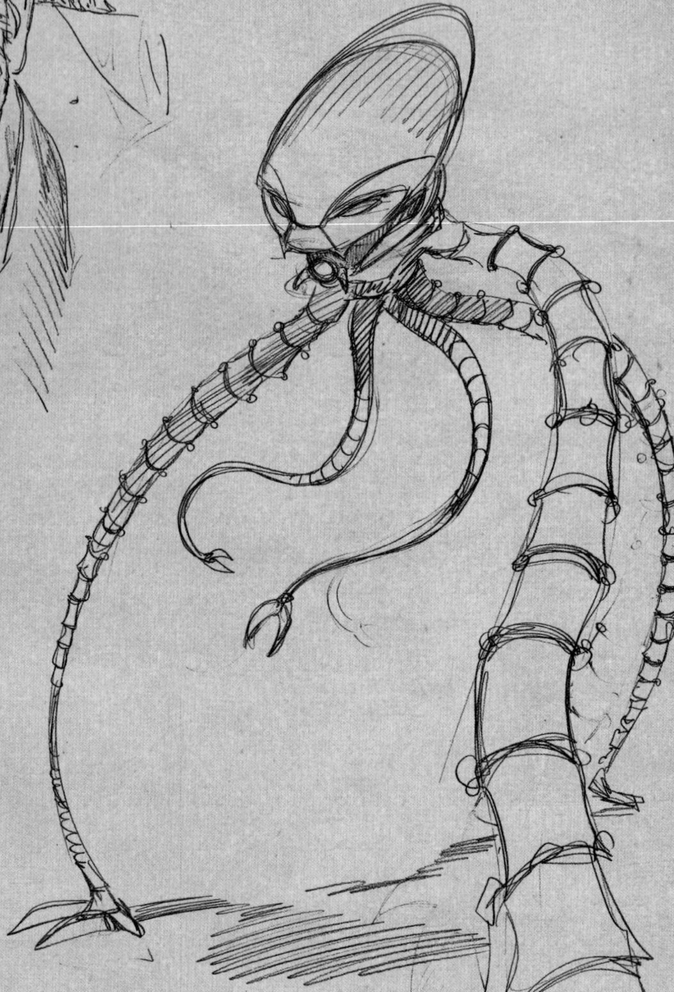

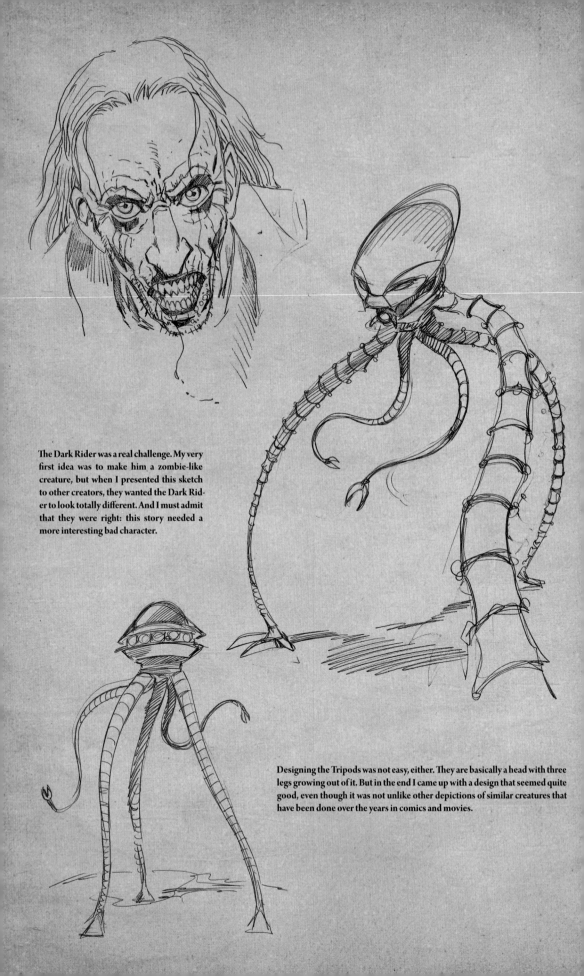

The Dark Rider was a real challenge. My very first idea was to make him a zombie-like creature, but when I presented this sketch to other creators, they wanted the Dark Rider to look totally different. And I must admit that they were right: this story needed a more interesting bad character.

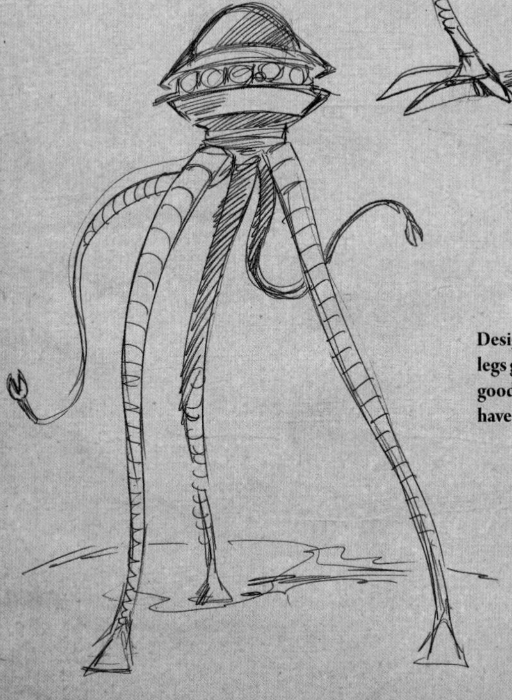

Designing the Tripods was not easy, either. They are basically a head with three legs growing out of it. But in the end I came up with a design that seemed quite good, even though it was not unlike other depictions of similar creatures that have been done over the years in comics and movies.